PLANNING IN SCHOOL ADMINISTRATION

The Greenwood Educators' Reference Collection

School Law for the 1990s: A Handbook
Robert C. O'Reilly and Edward T. Green

PLANNING IN SCHOOL ADMINISTRATION

A HANDBOOK

Ward Sybouts

The Greenwood Educators' Reference Collection

GREENWOOD PRESS
New York · Westport, Connecticut · London

Library of Congress Cataloging-in-Publication Data

Sybouts, Ward.
  Planning in school administration : a handbook / Ward Sybouts.
     p.   cm.—(The Greenwood educators' reference collection, ISSN 1056-2192)
  Includes bibliographical references and index.
  ISBN 0-313-27272-7 (alk. paper)
  1. School management and organization—Planning.   2. Educational
planning.   I. Title.   II. Series.
  LB2805.S94   1992
  371.2′07—dc20   91-18596

British Library Cataloguing in Publication Data is available.

Library of Congress Catalog Card Number: 91-18596
ISBN: 0-313-27272-7
ISSN: 1056-2192

First published in 1992

Greenwood Press, 88 Post Road West, Westport, CT 06881
An imprint of Greenwood Publishing Group, Inc.

Printed in the United States of America

The paper used in this book complies with the
Permanent Paper Standard issued by the National
Information Standards Organization (Z39.48-1984).

10 9 8 7 6 5 4 3 2 1

Copyright Acknowledgment

Examples of Delphi instruments are used courtesy of Kelvin McMillin and Jean R.
Snell.

Contents

Figures and Tables

FIGURES

TABLES

Acknowledgments

A special thanks is extended to my wife, Suzie Sybouts, for the time and effort she gave in editing this work. There were also several individuals who made a very specific contribution: Ken Jensen, Bud McMillin, Randy McClanahan, and Dorothy Jo Stevens. There are school administrators, too many to name, who have contributed to this book in a variety of ways.

Hopefully, this book will be of assistance to future planners so that steps may be taken to achieve excellence in education and every pupil, regardless of age, will have the best possible educational experience.

1

Introduction to Planning

Planning is something that virtually every person has done and will continue to be involved with in various ways. Some individuals seem to have a well-organized approach to life and are orderly in what they do and how they do it. Such individuals seem to know, by some intuitive part of their nature, how to plan. By contrast, we have all known persons who are in a constant state of disarray, arrive at meetings late, are unable to keep track of materials and information, and, when it comes to planning, are random and disorganized in their thinking. Some people are good planners, and some people are—why not admit it—pure dolts at planning. Planning skills can, however, be learned. A "natural" planner can enhance skills with an increased knowledge of planning approaches and techniques. The unorganized person with poor planning skills can also learn to use planning approaches and techniques that will improve results.

APPROACHES TO PLANNING

Intuitive Planning

Intuitive planning may be identified as the first level of planning and is done by all functioning individuals. Intuitive planning "comes naturally" and does not require much time, nor does it involve the use of any resources other than an occasional notepad on which to scribble a list of things to do. When a person needs to stop on the way home from work and pick up the cleaning, dash into the grocery store for milk and microwave popcorn, and put gasoline in the car, such efforts are, as a general rule, planned intuitively. Knowing that the cleaners and the grocery store are in the same little shopping mall enables a person to make one stop. There may be three filling stations where gasoline is purchased by the intuitive planner, and the one most directly on the route home from the office may be near the shopping mall and the person's residence. Intuitively, the three errands on the mental list will be completed quickly, and the planner will be home in nothing flat. If the person is an absent-minded professor, however, the first stop may be at the dry cleaners, where there is something to pick up but he isn't sure just what it is. The next stop would be at the filling station, and the stop would be made with a certain sense of pride that he hasn't run out of gas. The third stop would be in his own driveway as he arrives home without the milk and the microwave popcorn. The intuitive planning skills were insufficient in the latter case to get the job done efficiently.

Intuitive planning has obvious limitations. To rely upon intuitive planning for anything other than simple, short-term, or immediate tasks becomes a process of increasing risk and probable failure. Intuitive planners or, in some cases, "nonplanners," typically overlook planning ahead. Planning skills are often replaced by a heavy reliance upon habit. When habits are established or patterns of operation become set sufficiently, the intuitive planner is free to employ random thought patterns, and little attention is paid to routine matters, once those routine matters have been patterned by habit. Intuitive planners will commonly fail to search out innovative approaches as they follow well-worn paths or stray randomly through each day. Intuitive planning generally does not reach levels of creativity.

Individual, Formal, or Structured Planning

Individual, formal, or structured planning is done by all educators and is a step up the ladder of complexity from intuitive planning. When an individual teacher plans lessons or a field trip, a formal planning process is generally involved, even if that process is at a very elemental level of formality or done within a prescribed framework. When a school administrator prepares for a meeting or pulls together information for a weekly bulletin in which the schedule of events is given, that level of planning, even if considered a simple task, is a form of formal planning. As planning done by individuals progresses from the intuitive level to more formal or structured operations with a greater number of variables involved, such planning may remain at a level of sophistication in which complex processes or expanded resources are not required.

Operational Planning

Operational planning is a higher order or level of planning and may involve more than one person. In fact, operational planning is generally considered a process in which teams of persons may be involved. Operational planning is that level of planning required to make an organization or bureaucracy function by bringing together the prime resources needed to make the system function smoothly. Operational planning can be effective only when it is conducted in such a way that the purpose and goals of the agency involved are addressed in the operational plan. Operational planning involves multiple tasks and processes and may extend throughout an entire school year or budget year.

The management of a budget is an example of operational planning. Budget management includes payroll and staff benefits, the acquisition of instructional materials, and the maintenance of buildings and grounds. Such management extends over an academic year. In each of the examples of budget—payroll, maintenance, and instruction—the operational plan should reflect the goals that have been identified for the agency involved. This need clearly implies the need for goal setting. It also implies that different persons in the agency will have to coordinate their efforts. The number of individuals, the number of tasks and processes, the extent of the resources, and the amount of time involved all suggest the need for a more formal and complex process for operational planning that includes monitoring and procedures for accountability.

If the illustration of managing a budget is viewed in still more depth, one can see that planning a budget, in an educational agency that is tax-supported, involves still more encumbrances or relationships, both internal and external. The laws of the state as well as the requirements of auditors will have to be taken into consideration. The economic conditions and the mind-set of the citizens or patrons of the school district involved must enter into the thinking processes of those persons responsible for planning and managing the budget. Operational planning, as a generalization, involves a number of variables unique to the system that emerges from the setting in which the planning takes place. Some of the variables, such a state regulations governing the budgeting process, will confront the planner without the planner's searching for them. By contrast, other social or culturally based variables may be just as significant or powerful as a law but are less formal; such variables may even require the planner to be sensitive, to search out the dimensions of the influence, and to be politically astute in making the analysis. Operational planning is never done in a vacuum.

Long-Range Planning

Long-range planning is, as the term implies, planning that is done with consideration given to an extended span of time. An example of long-range planning is a maintenance schedule for replacing the roofs on school buildings in a district in which there may be 20 different facilities. Such a plan may reflect consideration of budget issues, insurance policies, an inspection schedule, and procedures for letting bids for reroofing established according to a calendar that may extend for a 7-year period or possibly a period projected for as long as 15 years. Long-range planning is a form of operational planning that encompasses a time frame involving a number of years.

Strategic Planning

Strategic planning has cycled through periods or phases that have run the gamut of early recognition, a bandwagon era, and a period in which suggestions have been made that strategic planning was on the wane.[1] Perhaps strategic planning has now reached a phase of maturity where it is recognized for what it is and is no longer touted as containing capabilities beyond reasonable limitations. Strategic planning is a form of planning that involves a process of looking at the setting, environment, or climate in which an agency functions and determining the mission and goals appropriate for the agency based upon the needs and the setting. Strategic planning is used by leaders to identify or clarify the direction in which an agency is to be taken. Strategic planners use forecasts and attempt to anticipate and project the future as they plan to posture their institution so it will meet the future in a proactive stance.[2]

No shortage of information is contained in the literature regarding strategic planning. As suggested above, strategic planning has been through a wave of popularity not too different from the fads teenagers become involved in with respect to designer labels on their clothes. There has been sufficient time since the introduction of strategic planning concepts to observe the results of strategic planning by military leaders, city planners, state agencies, and school leaders. Some critics have stepped forth and suggested that strategic planning is not all it was acclaimed to be by its high priests. There may be, as a result of the critics and the detractors, the emergence of a more mature and constructive view of strategic planning and what can be achieved through the process.[3]

By definition, long-range planning and strategic planning are sometimes used interchangeably. Some authors state emphatically that long-range and strategic planning are one and the same, while other authorities suggest there is a distinct difference between the two.[4] The distinction that is generally drawn between long-range planning and strategic planning is based on the fact that long-range planning may be much more simply done; such operational planning extends over a period of time that may run for several years, as, for example, in the case of a roof replacement schedule. By contrast, strategic planning is more involved and takes into account the environment and complex social parameters that form the context in which the planning is done and in which an institution is operated. Strategic planning is considered as a means of setting direction or mission for those persons who are responsible for the operation of an institution. While long-range planning may be done by one person or a small group, such as a maintenance staff, strategic planning frequently involves a much wider array of people in the process. Where strategic planning is used to set the direction or mission for an institution, long-range planning should adhere to the mission established in the strategic planning process. Consequently, strategic planning, as a general rule, may have much more far-reaching implications than does long-range planning.

DEGREES OF COMPLEXITY

As planning is viewed on a continuum from intuitive to strategic, the degrees of complexity increase. When one person plans a project, there is little or no negotiation of positions or posturing to gain advantages. When groups of people are involved in planning, the level of complexity increases, roughly with a mathematical exponential factor reflecting the increased numbers. The higher the stakes, the greater the complexity. Individual planning may be viewed as the least complex as contrasted to operational and long-range planning, which become more multifarious as the number of people involved increases, the time frame is extended, and the number of variables are amplified. Strategic planning is often conducted at a level that involves larger numbers of people, deals with future considerations that cannot always be specified with certainty as projections into the future are studied, and embraces strategic issues that impact upon mission, goals, and priority settings. Strategic planning can reach out to all the members of a school district, a community or city, or even a national agency. Consequently, strategic planning has political considerations that can reach the school board, the city government, state governments, or even national legislative bodies. With every added dimension to the planning process, the degree of complexity grows.

Planning for physical, mechanical, or technical devices is less complex than planning for human processes or social structures. A school building can be measured and the materials that go into its construction can be determined with a fairly high degree of precision. As physical, mechanical, or technical devices become more complex in size and function, they require more planning effort and are less predictable. A pair of pliers, for example, can be designed and produced with far fewer potential problems than can a microcomputer; yet both can be produced with a high degree of predictability, although the predictability will decrease as the complexity of physical devices is increased. The school building can be designed and the outcomes much more predictably specified than the educational program that will be housed in the building. It is much easier to control the materials and, ultimately, the outcomes that go into the construction of a building than the "materials" and "outcomes" of an educational program.

The degrees of complexity of planning can be viewed by looking at what has been accomplished in the educational enterprise. Educators have been very proficient, as a general rule, in managing facilities. Even the volatile issues often surrounding the closing of a school building fail to suggest that facilities have not been well planned. As populations move and fluctuate and communities mature and reach climax, the needs for buildings change, and these changes, coupled with the aging of some facilities, can generally be traced to patterns of events that may lead to the necessity of closing selected buildings. The issue of closing the building from a facilities management point of view is not, however, what becomes so volatile. The issue of greatest complexity is how to deal with the public and how to cope with feelings and values or perceptions. The human dimension is much more enigmatic than the brick and mortar. An experienced and somewhat scared superintendent expressed his frustration over the closing of a school by noting, "It has always interested me to view the criticism of education and to hear how poorly we are doing until we get ready to close a school, and then everybody and his cousin arrive at the board meeting to explain how much they love that school and to explain why we simply can't close it."

As planning moves from the simple, predictable levels to the complex levels in which more individuals are involved and, particularly, when planning reaches the political arena, there are, on the part of the planner, less control and more uncertainty. The planner is confronted with the issue of the power base required to accomplish the process and carry out the plan. No great insight is needed to comprehend that an individual teacher planning within a prescribed structure can move directly to the task at hand and accomplish the work of planning lessons with little intrusion from external forces if, of course, the teacher is in tune with the mission, goals, and priorities of the system. By contrast, as educators and their community constituents address issues of local and national concern, which have been debated on the floors of the national Capitol and the halls of the state legislature and which are legally and culturally encumbered— as is the case of drug abuse or the topic of AIDS—it is quite evident the degree of complexity has grown to staggering proportions and the predictability in planning has become less precise. As the political process accelerates and as the political stakeholders become more intense and involved, the level of predictability is lowered. Politically laced planning is much less precise and is subject to slower and more ponderous controls and diminished levels of predictability than is operational planning. Politically based planning is typically less data-based than is operational planning, may have less theory or principles upon which decisions are made, and relies much more heavily on expediencies and compromises than is true of operational planning. Planners need to understand the flow of power in the political arena and relate that knowledge to the level of agency with which they are involved.

In a representative form of government, a flow of power moves from the people to the legislative system and through the judicial system to the major agencies or bureaucracies that are created to serve the needs of society. From the agency level the flow of power moves on to the level of a given institution, to a facility or division of the institution, and ultimately to the individual administrator or staff member within that facility or division.

While it was pointed out earlier that the more political the involvement in the planning process, the more difficult it becomes to manage and to predict,[5] one should also note that once a planning process has moved to or through the political process, there may be more power to support the plan. In past decades when special education provisions were legislated at both the national and state levels, a high level of influence, control, and power was established with that process. The special education legislation was supported by a preponderance of public opinion, as resources, staffing, and programs were marshaled to provide the least restrictive environment for students with special needs. A further confirmation of the establishment of special education was underscored by various court rulings.

Planners need to be fully aware of where they are working within the hierarchy of power. If operational planning is involved, a less complex set of environmental factors may need to be considered in the process than will be the case when strategic planning is under way. If strategic planning is to reach into community levels in which political issues are involved, the planner must be fully cognizant of all possible dimensions of the local political scene. The more politicized the setting, the more political astuteness is required by planners.

WHY PLANNING IS NEEDED

One of the characteristics of human beings that separate them from other forms of life on earth is the power of the mind. Human beings have the ability for rational thought, which can control portions of the environment, as contrasted to other forms of life that are controlled to a much larger degree by instinct. For example, ants build complex communities and dwelling places, as they have for untold centuries. But the communities and dwellings constructed by ants have not changed appreciably over a time span of several million years. The argument can also be made that changes in anthills have come about through various evolutionary developments and not through a planned effort on the part of the ants. Robins build nests in the spring just as they have since Johnny Appleseed planted orchards that bloomed, and there seems to be little improvement in the structure, size, or comfort of a robin's nest. People are different. People, at least some people, constantly strive to build a better mousetrap. The desire to improve, as demonstrated by humankind, is a key factor with numerous implications and makes people unique creatures.

Some people are builders, inventors, and innovators. Some people lead. Some individuals are risk takers, while others are analysts who move more cautiously or judiciously. There are people who are visionary and cannot take their eyes off what they see as possibilities. There are those who, when presented with a set of possibilities, can become one of many who form the great armadas of human resources and contribute to the achievement of a better world. There are investors in the process of making things better; some have great human capabilities, and others have less to offer but nevertheless are contributors. There are those who work and contribute with their hands and those who study and search for knowledge to add to the process of building a better environment. And there are the planners who strive to provide the catalytic ingredient by which the steps leading to the achievement of specific and desired goals are specified.

The history of humankind has, as is well documented, been frequented by individuals and groups of persons who have been unscrupulous and destructive, seeking to destroy other people and institutions or at least take advantage of them for their personal gains. There have been the unscrupulous who have been powerful leaders and those who have occupied the position of a noncontributor at the level of the petty crimes. And there have been the complacent who have displayed neither the insight nor the desire to strive to improve their personal lot or the environment in which they languish.

Society is made up of three kinds of people—those who contribute, those who simply watch the world go by, and those who tear down or destroy. Planners are among those who can make a marked contribution. Planners, however, are also those who, for various reasons and motivations, can use planning to accomplish negative results. People who understand planning can use it as a powerful tool to make improvements, or they can use it equally effectively as a means of detracting, prohibiting, or destroying. Knowledge of the planning process, therefore, becomes a source of power. The ethics of planning lies within the individuals who use the tools of planning and not in the tools or the planning process itself.

THE RATIONALE FOR PLANNING

Critics of the educational enterprise have suggested various degrees of need in planning for a better system. Supporters of what public education has accomplished suggest there are enormous benefits society has derived from its investment in education. By contrast, critics have suggested that only with major surgery will the educational patient survive. Shanker wrote in 1990:

After more than six years of intensive effort, public education in America is still at the edge of disaster. Virtually every state and thousands of school districts have applied their favorite remedies to their schools to little avail. Why are the results in student learning still so disappointing? The first is that public schools haven't really carried out the reforms. . . . The second explanation is that six years is too soon to expect to see much change.[6]

While many educators from within the structure can see excellence in American schools, critics have expressed concern because of a lack of excellence. The tide of criticism sweeps on; Glasser suggested: "In today's world, only organizations whose products and services are of high quality will thrive—and our schools are far from thriving."[7] Part of the relentless wave of criticism comes about as a result of conflicting or unclear expectations held by the various publics regarding education. What one interest group may hold up as excellent, another group will condemn. A lack of clear mission is shrouding the educational enterprise in a veil of confusion and conflicting demands. Consequently, there have been conflicting views regarding educational outcomes as well as disagreement regarding the educational process.

Limited Resources

As educators face the increasing demands for more and better educational programs, there is a constant challenge to meet demands with limited resources. Public education, supported by tax dollars that are made available through the legislative process, is faced with the problems of limited resources. Since public funding for education is subject to the vagaries of changing political winds, gaining support for education has become increasingly politicized.

Bureaucracies

Education is conducted within a bureaucratic structure. There are characteristics in bureaucracies that generate stability and at the same time demonstrate strong resistance to change. Most bureaucratic organizations have well-defined procedures that tend to foster two conditions: (1) there is a tendency to "ratchet up" in terms of expenditures as efforts are made to maintain all segments of a bureaucracy and resist the deletion or removal of outmoded portions of its structure and (2) bureaucracies inherently tend to produce inertia, "both in the definition of problems and in the range of alternative answers" to problems.[8] Observers have noted that bureaucratic growth will take place in which the "ratchet-up" principle is involved during the early history and expansion of the bureaucracy, but seldom will there be a decline in budgets even "when their ostensible purpose has diminished or disappeared."[9] While politicians have chosen a path of legislating changes in education, they have subsequently expressed frequent frustration because their legislative efforts have failed to generate the changes within the bureaucratic structure they had envisioned. While legislating changes for education seems seductive to legislative bodies, the end results have often fallen short of expectations. Test scores, drug abuse, and dropout rates have remained largely untouched by the rash of legislative enactments that followed the publication of *A Nation at Risk* by the National Commission on Excellence (1984).

An obstruction to planned change can be posed by the very nature of bureaucratic structures. Yet bureaucratic organizations, with strong leadership and sound planning procedures, can and do change. Educational bureaucracies, like all bureaucracies, tend to become more conservative with age. The size of a bureaucracy also has an impact on its ability to adjust, as large institutions have more complex communication patterns. In larger institutions there is often a tendency for subordinates to tell the superintendent what they think he or she wants to hear; in so doing, subordinates often strain out reality, which the superintendent should be sensing. When a bureaucratic organization is threatened, that threat causes retrenchment, a loss of vision, an increased emphasis on preservation, and an accompanying reduction in the number of options for consideration. There is also a decline in the amount of risk taking demonstrated by the threatened staff. These are natural responses, since it is only through preservation of the organization that individuals within that organization can maintain their employment or, even more significantly, their sense of identity. The unfortunate aspect of the reaction of self-preservation and territoriality in the face of external threats is that personnel are blinded to internal threats, and this blindness causes them to undertake strategies that may be 180 degrees off-target. All too often there is a tendency to draw in, play cards close to the vest, and go on the defensive at a time when more innovative options are needed to launch an offensive. In the final analysis, planners need to understand how bureaucracies are structured and function so they can work within the structure with a reasonable degree of success.

The Changing Environment

The environment in which the educational enterprise operates has constituted an overwhelming set of circumstances with which the educational planner must contend. Discussions have been generated from the writings of Naisbitt and Toffler regarding the major trends in our society as seen by analysts and futurists. The changes that have been experienced in society and that have, or should have, an impact upon education have been presented, discussed, and reviewed in numerous settings. There is no final listing of topics that go into the cauldron for debate. Although debate can be generated easily at the local level regarding various issues emerging from the culture, arriving at a clear view of the implications and the solutions becomes much more difficult. Some issues seem to have immediate and local impact, while other issues may seem less immediate.

The changes that have occurred in the home and family structure emerge in many discussions regarding cultural changes that impact upon the school. A considerable amount of concern about the changes in the family structure has been evidenced, and a concerted effort to make some meaning out of such changes has taken place.[10] As contrasted to the clientele confronted by educators during the first half of the century, school personnel work with a different clientele as this century draws to a close. Researchers have documented clearly that the amount of disruption in the homes of the United States has increased dramatically in the last half of the century. The disruption in the home is reflected in the behavior of students in school—the greater the amount of disruption in the home, the greater the amount of disruption in the school. School officials have had mixed responses to the changing home structure. Some officials advocate changing the schools programs to be more attractive to all pupils; other propose alternative schools; and others push for more rigorous requirements for graduation. Some school officials, in concert with local judges, are arranging to fine parents when their children do not attend school. To force attendance and acceptable behavior or to attract pupils to school may be a moot point of debate as long as there are major levels of disruption in the home that are carried into the school by the pupils from these damaged environments.

Drugs have received a considerable amount of attention and debate among local and national political figures. While great sums of money have been allocated to combat the use of illicit drugs, sincere concerns have been expressed that the sum of money is not sufficient and is being misdirected. According to the media and discussions with school officials, there is little doubt that there are no schools in which the impact of drugs in one form or another has not been felt. The toll on society is devastating and cannot be overlooked by educational planners as a major factor that influences the students in our schools.

Protecting the environment of a world that is continuing to grow in population is becoming increasingly difficult. Feeding the population of the world emerges as a recurring and highly emotional topic; at the same time discussions of how to dispose of nonbiodegradable diapers and atomic waste are reflected in the media with growing regularity and intensity. While asbestos has been an in-house environmental issue, such an issue has been only one of many that must be dealt with by school officials.

The competition among the nations for the production and marketing of consumer goods looms as an ever-growing concern. Politicians and unemployed assembly line workers address the issue from distinct vantage points. The taxpayers and consumers in the United States continue to look to the political institutions at the national level for some solution to a growing deficit and imbalance of trade that seem to be growing so rapidly that a threat of some undefined proportion lurks just over the horizon of each calendar year. While the debate of how to handle the issues associated with world competition takes place, there are voices pronouncing the need for schools to help prepare workers for the future—whatever the future might bring.

Educators, both classroom teachers and administrators, have become aware of growing technological capabilities in the areas of management and curriculum and instructional processes. Educators' expectations of the future technological developments and their knowledge of how to apply them judiciously to the educational process have not, to date, generated the results anticipated by many advocates of technology.[11] Technology is an area in which careful planning is called for if the benefits of technology are to be realized.

The expanding knowledge base has been discussed and explained in various ways by different scholars. From the time of Christ up to the Renaissance and on to the American Revolution, the growth of knowledge has been depicted as a time of gradual growth. The period from 1800 to 1900 could be called one of accelerated growth in the accumulation of knowledge, or the dawning of the scientific era. The citizens of the twentieth century have witnessed an explosion of the knowledge base in which the accumulation of information more than doubled with each new decade. As persons realized the information age had arrived, scholars began searching for enhanced ways to access and synthesize it more efficiently. The amount of knowledge has become so overwhelming that the task of determining what to teach has become an issue of debate. With technology, how can every student access the vast amount of information, synthesize that information, and know how to manipulate it to solve the problems of the future?

Coping with affluence is another factor that has confronted school officials. While the average cost of building a home in the United States has risen to over $100,000 during the last decade of the twentieth century, the number of homeless who crawl and search for shelter on the streets and back alleys of many cities has risen dramatically. The cost of clothing for a schoolchild has risen to such a point that some public school officials have experimented with the idea of requiring school uniforms to save money for the parents and reduce the distinction between those students who wear designer labels and those who cannot afford to buy the latest styles. The levels of expectations brought about by affluence have not been totally analyzed, and the implications are not clearly defined; however, it becomes obvious that school officials must face the issue. Coping with affluence involves dealing with the issue from various perspectives, which include values, motivations, sensitivity, and insight. To try to ignore the impact of affluence on American schools will lead to expanded problems that will detract from the concept of education for all American youth.

Education continues to be under the influence of politics. Board members working within the local political arena are generally interested in being provided with the information and leadership that will enable them to have a good school system. Moving from the local level, we see that education has been a major item on the agendas of state legislators for a number of decades. As a whole, state legislators have been favorably disposed toward educational issues; however, they are often concerned, even confused, by the contradictory signals they receive from educators. Special interest groups within the educational establishment have sent conflicting messages and demands to legislators in the various state capitals across the nation. Legislators have voiced the opinion that over the years they have tried to respond to the requests of the educational community and yet the desired results have not been forthcoming. In fact, measures such as standard test scores have declined over recent decades. Thus, the frustration level among state legislators has increased.

Part of the problem, which in some degree has entered into the political arena, has been the lack of a clear understanding of what education, as an institution in a complex society, should accomplish. A clearer identification of the mission for education from the national perspective is needed. Once the agenda for education can be agreed upon at the national level, it can be translated for implementation in local districts. As the decade of the 1990s began, there was a call for restructuring schools in order to reach the quality desired by legislative bodies and their constituents. One of the obvious problems with the call for restructuring was the lack of a clear definition of what was to be accomplished through the restructuring process. Yogi Berra was quoted as saying, "You have to be very careful when you don't know where you are going or you might not get there." [12] "The logic of restructuring as a reform strategy appeals to common sense, and its advocates are persuasive. However, there is little agreement regarding what restructuring means or how it should be implemented." [13] Thus, school officials face a wall of confusion and uncertainty with respect to restructuring as long as what is expected of the restructuring process is not known. Planning in the face of such uncertainty calls for strong leadership at the local level, a clear vision of what is needed in a local district, and a confident grasp of the planning process.

THE FOCUS ON PLANNING

Planning for the improvement of education will not be accomplished in a vacuum. There are innumerable factors that influence the plans for education and how they shall be accomplished. Numerous observers have noted that the one assurance upon which educators can bank is the fact that change will occur. Change is a certainty; it is and will continue to occur in the foreseeable future. The discomfort for some comes about in the fact that changes cannot always be predicted. In fact, most changes are not predicted with high levels of accuracy, and uncertainty prevails.

Planning is needed so that the best approaches to the management of an educational agency can be assured. Better management practices can always be defended, and good planning can provide some assurances that the best practice will be employed in managing a school system. "Indeed, one may well wonder why Americans have not demanded more planning, not less from government agencies [and schools] in order to improve public control of them." [14] Good planning at the local level can generate more ambitious and stimulating goals for those who work in the organization, generate a system and climate that foster efficiency, influence morale in a positive manner, visibly impact upon the quality of human relations within an agency, and become a fundamental condition for "staying in the race." Finally, good planning can provide a means of avoiding failure. Ewing stated, "There is a good reason for believing that many of the failures [in public agencies]—two-thirds of them, perhaps—are *not* inevitable." [15]

Planning for new or improved school facilities has been accomplished with a rather high level of proficiency in most school districts. As a general rule, facilities are built with acceptable to good levels of quality control and assurances of functionability. Planning for new facilities is usually considered to go beyond the level of planning for management, and, although it involves a wide range of variables, facilities planners have demonstrated predictable results in a vast majority of building projects.

In addition to keeping the ship on an even keel and well housed, there is a need for the planning and implementation of innovative programs in education. Programs are much more difficult to plan and implement than physical facilities because of the higher level of human factors and the lower degree of involvement of physical materials.

Better planning is called for in short-range projects, in long-range projects, and in strategic dimensions. Educational planners need not fear running out of a job. The demand for quality planning has never been greater than at the current time as educators face the new century in a time when history is literally "overdosed" with change and conflict.

EDUCATIONAL PLANNING HAS FALLEN SHORT OF EXPECTATIONS

Critics of education have voiced their opinions in print, on the radio, and on television and have stated flatly that the American educational system has failed. Such a flat rejection of the educational system is unjustified in the eyes of educators, as well as large numbers of patrons and citizens. A rather high regard for the local school system but a very negative perception of education at the national scene is found in some local districts. As stated previously, part of the question of how good or how poor American education is stems from the failure to understand what education is to accomplish. At times, it seems everyone knows what education should do, yet nobody agrees.

Planning is difficult. As suggested previously, the complexity of the societal setting in which schools are operated and in which educational planners must function places the process in a constant state of flux. Not only is there uncertainty about the environment, but matters are made even more unpredictable by the fact that what people do or how they react cannot be totally predicted. There can be uncertainty about value judgments and how people will act out or react to various situations that are value-laden.[16]

The politics of change is complex, and when it is mixed with the style of management found in educational settings, persons have suggested that coercive management falls short of affecting change. Glasser referred to administrators who have assumed an inappropriate approach to management as "boss-managers." Glasser's contention was that tradition-driven "boss-managers firmly believe people can be motivated from the outside; they fail to understand that all of our motivation comes from within."[17]

END RESULTS

The tides of change swirl around each educational system, and the eddies and currents are indeed treacherous. One reaction to the tumultuous setting is to go with the tide. But there is another option.

Planning is the only way educational leaders will be able to direct the fortunes of their educational institutions. If educators are to have any voice in their own destiny, they have no choice but to plan. Planning must be directed toward change. "To change is to risk something. That makes us insecure. Not to change is a bigger risk, but it seldom feels that way. . . . There is no choice but to change."[18] "Unless an institution has the capacity for change, it will not succeed for long. Dynamic institutions have the capacity for self-renewal. They deal with challenges by changing—by reexamining what they have been doing and by reshaping it to new circumstances."[19]

NOTES

1. Daniel H. Gray, "Uses and Misuses of Strategic Planning," *Harvard Business Review* 64, no. 1 (January–February 1986), 89.

2. L. L. Byars, *Strategic Management: Planning and Implementation* (New York: Harper and Row, 1987).

3. Robert H. Waterman, Jr., *The Renewal Factor* (New York: Bantam Books, 1987), 27.

4. Shirley D. McCune, *Guide to Strategic Planning for Educators* (Alexandria, Virginia: Association for Supervision and Curriculum Development, 1986), 35.

5. Byars, *Strategic Management, Planning and Implementation.*

6. Albert Shanker, "The End of the Traditional Model of Schooling—and a Proposal for Using Incentives to Restructure Our Public Schools," *Kappan* 71 (January 1990), 354.

7. William Glasser, "The Quality School," *Kappan* 71 (February 1990), 426.

8. Peter Hall, *Great Planning Disasters* (London: Weidenfeld and Nicolson, 1980), 242.

9. Ibid., 243.

10. Nick Stinnett and John DeFrain, *Secrets of Strong Families* (Boston: Little, Brown, 1985), 3–12.

11. Ward Sybouts and D. J. Stevens, *Technology in Education: The Past, Present and Future* (Tempe, Arizona: University Council on Educational Administration, 1990), 7.

12. Blount, Roy, Jr. "Yogi," *Sports Illustrated* 60, no. 14 (April 2, 1984), 84.

13. Thomas Timar, "The Politics of School Restructuring," *Kappan* 71 (December 1989), 266.

14. David W. Ewing, *The Human Side of Planning* (London: Macmillan, 1969),11.

15. Ibid., 23.

16. Hall, *Great Planning Disasters,* 5.

17. Glasser, "The Quality School," 432.

18. Waterman, *The Renewal Factor,* 338.

19. Shanker, "The End of the Traditional Model of Schooling," 356.

2

Systems Theory

INTRODUCTION

The concepts encompassed in systems theory are revealed in various ways and through numerous entities, ranging from the universe and its subsystems to simple mechanical devices created by people. Systems are identifiable that are natural phenomena, such as the solar system, biological phenomena, such as a living creature, or those created by the minds and hands of human beings. The most complex systems emerging from the minds of people are social systems that encompass complex subsystems. Advanced technological systems, such as a spacecraft or a computer created by humans, are complex, yet perhaps less complex and certainly more predictable than social systems. Mechanical or physical systems created by people can range from large structures, such as the Empire State Building or a Boeing 747 jumbo jet, to a simple hand tool or a mousetrap. The rudiments and concepts of systems theory emerge from the various observable systems and subsystems.

Information describing systems can be found in documents prepared by engineers, with the obvious emphasis placed on man-made-mechanical and technological devices. People who have written about systems theory have, however, come from various disciplines, including the social sciences. While it would be possible to summarize much of what has been written about systems theory and categorize the concepts in various ways, including mechanical, biological, or social, this chapter has been presented as a short story in which systems theory, from a broad perspective, is introduced.

SYSTEMS THEORY AS TAUGHT BY GRAMMIE HART

Beth was excited because she was going to spend the weekend with Grammie Hart. It was Friday, a beautiful Indian summer day in November 1987. There had been some cool and blustery days, but this day was warm, and the clear sky seemed to give off a soft autumn glow.

The Hart ranch was near the end of the long bus route. Beth, who lived in town, had permission to ride the school bus that went past the Hart ranch. As the school bus pulled up to the mailbox by the driveway, Beth's face was next to the window. The bus came to a stop, and Beth ran to meet Grammie.

Grammie was raking the yellow leaves that had fallen from the ash trees growing along the road in front of the ranch house. Grammie, known to her clients as Dr. Elizabeth Zicek-Hart, had taken the afternoon off work from the veterinary clinic in which she was a partner. Grammie had a radiant smile and a physical bearing that seemed to misstate her years.

The two turned their energy to raking leaves. Grammie let Beth light the fire in a pile of leaves, which burned rather slowly because of their dampness. The smile was never gone from Grammie's face as her eyes followed Beth's lively movements and efforts with the rake.

"How come you can burn leaves out here on the ranch, and we can't in town?"

Grammie started to say there was a city ordinance that prohibited open fires in town, but she knew that reply would simply generate the "why" question, so she explained the what and the why of fire hazards and of air pollution; to her amazement Beth responded, "I see."

Raking and conversation continued until it was time to stop for dinner. When Beth and Grammie emerged from the kitchen after eating their fill of pizza, the sky was growing dark, and the stars were starting to emerge in the east. The chill of the night was pleasant, and the smell of the burning leaves permeated the yard around the ranch house. The pair of pizza eaters raked a fresh pile of leaves on the smoldering fire and watched them flame up and cast their soft orange light on the perimeter around the bonfire.

"That should do it for now," suggested Grammie. "We can check on how the fire is doing before we go to bed."

Beth ran to the back porch and emerged wearing one of Grammie's sweaters and carrying two apples she had grabbed from a basket. As they bit into their apples, Beth said, "Just look at the moon, Grammie. It's so far away, but it looks so bright and close. You know, it isn't quite round tonight, but not too far from it."

"It's a pretty moon, isn't it?" responded Grammie.

"Grammie. See that bright star sort of above the moon?"

"Yes, that's Jupiter," indicated Grammie.

"Jupiter?"

"Yes, Jupiter."

"Do you know the names of all the stars?"

"No, I'm afraid I don't know the names of very many stars," Grammie chuckled. "Actually Jupiter is a planet. One of several in the solar system."

"Jupiter is awfully close to the moon," observed Beth.

"It may not be as close as it looks," suggested Grammie. "It is simply in line with the moon and the Earth so that as we look out past the moon, our line of sight goes on out and picks up Jupiter. Jupiter is way out there some 483 million miles from the sun, while the moon is circling the Earth, which is only 93 million miles away from the sun."

"Earth is a planet," announced Beth. "All the planets rotate around the sun." Beth paused. "Why don't they ever bump into each other, Grammie?"

"Because they each have a separate path or orbit they follow, and each orbit is of a different size. That is, each planet travels in a circle around the sun, or our sun. Each planet takes different amounts of time to make a complete circle around the sun. So some planets are closer to the sun than others. But that is how the solar system is put together."

"But the moon circles the Earth."

"That's right, honey. The moon circles the Earth. But Jupiter, which is way out, has a bunch of moons. When I was in high school, I was told there were nine moons around Jupiter, but now that more information has been gained from space probes, I think the official count is higher. If you were to look at Jupiter tonight with the telescope, you would see at least four moons by Jupiter."

" 'By Jupiter', are you sure of that?" teased Beth.

"Maybe you'd like to look at Jupiter through Uncle Ben's old telescope," Grammie suggested.

"Four moons! Wow! That would be pretty if you were sitting on Jupiter."

(It would be almost two years before Dr. Hart would pick up a copy of *Newsweek* at the office while waiting for a phone call with the needed results of a lab test and read about the flight of the spacecraft Voyager as it reached and fled past the planet Neptune.

The Neptune flyby was the closest Voyager had come to a planet. . . . Steering the craft within 3,000 miles of the globe's cloud tops, at 61,148 miles an hour, required some of the most complicated engineering NASA has ever undertaken. For years flight jockeys . . . had fine-tuned its trajectory. Last week it was just 21 miles wide of where scientists in the 1970's expected it to be—the cosmic equivalent of sinking a 2,260-mile putt.[1]

A space trip that had started on August 10, 1977, had reached a triumphant and climatic point during the fall of 1989 after being guided 4.43 billion miles.)

"Grammie, what keeps planets spinning around the sun and moons spinning around the planets?"

"I'm not an expert on these matters, but there are forces of gravity. These forces are created by one body in space attracting another body; then there are the forces caused by the movement or rotation of bodies in space. These forces tend to set up fields of force that are held together as a solar system. The sun is at the center of our solar system, and the planets, just like spaceships around the Earth, circle the sun. Their speed and the forces of gravity hold them in place.''

"Why is it all called the solar system?"

"The solar system is an entity—a total thing, a system, a cluster of terrestrial bodies locked together in a system. The system functions as one whole thing or unit (or entity) as it is made up of its parts. Each of its parts is also a sort of system, like the Earth and its moon. The two of them form a unit or part of the solar system, and the Earth, for example, functions or works in that context. The Earth seems to do its thing as a part of the total solar system.

"Grammie, can we look at Jupiter and the moon through Uncle Ben's old telescope?''

"Yes." The two walked to the back patio of the ranch house, where Grammie had made advance preparations. The telescope was on its stand and aimed in the direction of the eastern sky. After Grammie made some adjustments, Beth looked through the eyepiece of the little telescope and remarked the moon looked just like its pictures. When Grammie aimed the device at Jupiter, the reaction was what she had hoped for. Beth was fascinated with the view of some of the moons that orbited the distant plant.

"How can the newspaper people tell when there is going to be a full moon? Or how do the people who make calendars know when the moon is going to be full a whole year ahead of time, Grammie?''

"Well, Beth, the planets all follow the path of their own orbit around the sun, and since they stay in their orbit or their path, people who study the movement of planets and stars and galaxies know when objects out in space will complete their orbit. You know, the Earth takes 365 one one-fourth days to go around the sun. The moon goes around the Earth in about 28 days. Since all of these follow what seems almost like a set pattern, their movement and the time it takes them to complete an orbit can be predicted in advance. So it is not only possible to determine ahead of time when the moon will be full, but happenings like Halley's Comet or an eclipse of the moon can also be predicted.''

Grammie continued, "While it may seem like all these orbits and patterns are totally fixed, they are not. Every once in awhile, the official time on Earth has to be adjusted by a second or two. All clocks have to be adjusted. This adjustment is due to the fact that the solar system does not repeat all its cycles in exactly the same time. The system is changing very gradually.''

"You know, Grammie, the solar system must be pretty simple if the Earth and moon are a key part of it.''

"They are just two parts in the total solar system if you look at them as just one moon and one planet. But Beth, think how many parts there are to the Earth itself.''

''I don't understand.''

''The Earth is made up of a lot of different kinds of systems or smaller systems (subsystems) that, when put together, make up the whole Earth.''

''Can you explain more?'' asked Beth.

''Well, suppose you went down to the creek and followed it until it joined Plumb Creek near town. Then you followed Plumb Creek to the Niobrara River. You then got into a canoe and went to the Platte, on to the Missouri River and on to the Mississippi River and clear to the Gulf of Mexico?''

''So what?''

''Well, that trip downstream would be a part of a river system that has been cut by nature over millions of years and is used to drain water off the land; the water goes back to the ocean, where it evaporates and turns into clouds, which are moved by the wind in over the land. When the conditions are just right, the clouds drop their rain on the Earth, and the rain that is not absorbed trickles back into the creeks. These creeks meet up with other creeks and form rivers, which eventually run back to the ocean. That is how a river system becomes a part of a weather pattern or system that cycles water and distributes it over the Earth.''

''Are you saying, Grammie, there are a river system and a weather system and they work together?''

''Yes. The river system is a system all by itself, but it is only a part of the systems (subsystems) that are all tied together to form the weather system. The winds are caused by the fact that the surface of the Earth is at different angles to the sun during the different seasons, so there are warming and cooling effects. Wind is created that moves the clouds around and distributes the moisture. So you have a weather system (as a subsystem) that is related to the sun.''

''You are saying the seasons are caused by the angle of the Earth to the sun so that some parts are in summer and some parts are in winter,'' confirmed Beth. ''And water runs from here to the Gulf of Mexico and comes back as rain. It just goes round and round.''

''Right you are, Beth. That is an example of how one system, which is a part of a larger system, is affected by the larger system and must operate in rhythm or be coordinated with the larger system and at the same time, as part of the larger system, contribute to the way the larger system seems to work.''

''There must be different uses of the word *system* 'cause they use terms like the *city water system* or the *school system*. How come?''

Before Grammie could explain, Beth interrupted, ''Hey, I got it! The water system is made up of parts that are all tied together. . . .''

''And the parts are dependent on each other,'' Grammie interjected.

''And the school system is made up of parts too, only they are not all buildings—there are people parts.''

"That's right! And each system is intended to perform or help people accomplish a different task or job," Grammie added.

"You know, the school has seasons just like the solar system, doesn't it?" suggested Beth.

"Well, sort of. Seasons are cycles; that is, they come and go. So I guess you could say a school has seasons. Everything has a life cycle. We have been raking leaves tonight, and that tells us the growing season is over. In time, those ash trees out front will stop growing and die. Everything has a life cycle. Everything starts out, grows up, and eventually comes to an end."

"Grammie, think of my cat, old Ruffy. He was a tough old cat. Remember when he got in that awful fight and got his ear just about torn off? He got well that time."

"One of the things about a healthy system, like old Ruffy, is that it can get well; it is what we call self-correcting."

"Yes, but when he got to be almost 19 years old, he didn't 'self-correct,' did he?" reflected Beth. "But Grammie, that isn't so with the solar system."

"Oh yes. The solar system has a life cycle. It had a starting point." (It would be over a year before Grammie would get a copy of *A Brief History of Time*,[2] but she had read enough to suggest that there was a beginning of the Earth according to scholars who studied the universe and that there was an alternate definition of the birth of the Earth by those who preferred to consider creationism.) "According to some scientists, it's not a matter if the sun burns out or some other event causes the solar system to come to an end, but it is simply a question of when the solar system comes to an end. However, the "when" time for the solar system's end is probably several millions or billions of years away."

"Grammie, would you call Ruffy a system?" inquired Beth.

"Well, yes. A cat, a cow, or a person is a system made up of a lot of subsystems or parts that all work together. You are a system, Beth. You have a digestive system, a circulatory system, a skeletal system, a nervous system, and several other systems. Other creatures have similar kinds of groupings of parts or subsystems. All your parts (subsystems) must work smoothly together to make your whole system run right."

Grammie continued, "But just as the solar system changes enough so we have to adjust our clocks every few years, our bodies are changing. We think that at one time the appendix served a much more important function for the body than at the present time. Now it is useless; perhaps a few million years down the road, people will not have an appendix. If something like the appendix isn't needed, it gradually disappears. That is part of how our systems adjust or change."

"Daddy says people are getting bigger. He and Grandpa Hart were talking about how tall basketball players are now. Grandpa Hart said when he went to college, the tallest player was six feet five inches. We have two players taller than that in our high school."

"That is right," agreed Grammie. "The trend now is taller basketball players. Beth, do you know what a 'trend' is?"

"Is it when the stock market keeps going up or down? Mom and Dad talk about the trend in the stock market, and Grandpa talks about a trend in cattle prices."

"Yes. Trends happen over long periods of time. For example, over several years, basketball players become taller, which suggests the trend is that people are getting taller."

"Do systems have trends? Is that the way they work?"

"They sure do."

"But Grammie, if there are a solar system, a river system, a weather system, a water system, and someone like me who is a system, how many kinds of systems are there?"

"I don't have the foggiest notion," Grammie responded. "There are systems made by nature and systems made by people. People can make mechanical (or technical) systems like cars or waterworks or even satellites that can orbit the Earth. But people can also make systems that are social systems or people systems. For example, the school has buildings and buses, but the school is really a system in which kids like you can go and learn. But there are lots of other kinds of systems to help people do what they want to do or need, such as banks, economic systems, legal systems, churches, and labor unions."

Grammie continued, "One of the things you can see about these systems that are people-made is that the people in each of them protect them and try to keep them going. In fact, not only do people try constantly to protect and preserve their systems, but they try to expand them and get them to grow."

"Do these people-groups or systems go through cycles and trends?" asked Beth.

"Surely. For example, your grandpa and I used to belong to a farming organization called the Grange. In days past, just about everybody attended Grange meetings. Now the Grange has faded, and people have begun to join other kinds of organizations."

"Can you predict when people-made organizations will die or what their cycles will be like?"

"I'm afraid not. People, as individuals or groups, are less predictable than some physical systems and much less predictable than mechanical systems," explained Grammie.

"But if people make people organizations, why can't they make them work?" Beth was puzzled.

"That's a good question. It is hard to understand and predict what people are going to do."

"Grammie, Mother said she would never have predicted Uncle Ben would have done what he did. Does anybody know why he did what he did?"

"I guess none of us really understood Uncle Ben's thinking." (Grammie often puzzled over the difference in the choice of lifestyles her own children had made. Ben had been an above-average student in high school who played basketball and baseball. He worked side by side with his father and went on to attend the same university as his parents. He had married during his senior year in college; shortly after graduation, he and his wife settled in their new home and had a baby girl. It was shortly after the birth of his daughter that the family learned Ben was homosexual. Six months later Ben moved to San Francisco, and in the next four years there was little contact between Ben and his family. A mutual friend informed the family when Ben died of AIDS.) ''Sometimes we don't know what other people are thinking. I guess we just have a lot to learn about how individual people think.''

The whole family seemed not to have understood Ben and certainly had not predicted his behavior. Grammie pondered how one family could have a daughter who was so predictable and at the same time have a son who heard no harmony in the sounds of life that others found so appealing.

Grammie reflected on things that were simple and predictable, as contrasted to things that were complex and less predictable. She had just acquired a copy of *CHAOS: Making a New Science*.[3] She wondered if the things that seem less predictable are in fact less predictable, or if it is only our view as people, in a given time and place, that makes us perceive less predictability when, in fact, we may be viewing something very predictable but simply on a less familiar cycle. Grammie, as mentioned before, had not seen the *Newsweek* report of early September 1989, in which it was suggested that after 12 years in space, Voyager

has soared through the outer reaches of the solar system, sending back spectacular photos of Jupiter, Saturn, Uranus and . . . Neptune. It has proven to be the most successful space probe ever launched by earthlings. In its wake, astronomers have discovered more about the world beyond Mars than they'd learned since the ancient Chinese first spied the wandering ''stars'' that we now know as planets. In fact, Voyager has found more than science has been able to digest.[4]

The universe is gradually divulging the nature of its system. The unknown has not been hidden as a secret but has been simply undiscovered and unfathomed by humans. Perhaps, Grammie mused, we mortals will find doors to open and ways to uncover more of the inner workings of human beings in order to understand each other better and the social institutions that are created by our own hands. When we develop greater understanding of social systems, we may also enjoy the ability to make more accurate predictions. Perhaps when we earthlings learn more about how all things go together—and we surely will, thought Grammie—we can do a better job of controlling elements of our environment.

PLANNING CONCEPTS DERIVED FROM
SYSTEMS THEORY

As people have searched for greater understanding of the world in which they reside, an expanding knowledge base and improved theoretical framework have emerged, upon which approaches to planning have been built. "Thus, 'understanding planning' as a problem really means that the planner faces the challenge of constructing an image of himself [or herself] . . . as a planner; the agencies in which he [or she] operates; their procedures; the environments it is affected by, and is affecting."[5] A portion of the base of understanding for more sophisticated and productive planning efforts can be provided by systems theory.

There are identifiable concepts derived from systems theory that constitute the basis for planning. The concepts that contribute to an understanding of the planning process may be manifested in the form of a model. Such an approach is in contrast to that which was identified by Faludi, who suggested the construction of a model grew from a rationale, and the construction of "models . . . [is] the next phase in the development of theory. A model . . . if validated, becomes theory."[6] A model may be inadequate, or it may lead to an oversimplified perspective. Models are most appropriate and can be of maximum benefit when the underlying concepts are thoroughly understood. Planners would be well advised to work from a conceptual framework rather than simply following a model or combination of models.

The primary concepts underlying the planning process may be summarized as follows:

- Every system or plan functions as a part of a larger entity or environment with which it must be in tune.
- Every system or plan should be created to accomplish a defined purpose. If a system fails to accomplish its intended purpose, such a system will ultimately disappear. A failing system or subsystem will impact the larger system of which it is a part.
- Every system or plan is composed of parts or subsystems, and each part must be in synchronization with the whole in order to contribute to the total system.
- Systems are dynamic. Complex systems have a life cycle and thus reveal, if understood, demonstrable cycles or trends.
- Systems have inherent dimensions of predictability and at the same time, because of complex interrelations, demonstrate chaos or areas of less predictability.
- Systems tend to be self-preserving and self-perpetuating.
- Since time and systems conceptually progress or move forward, systems planning is a process that is future-oriented.
- Systems are logical or rational.
- Some systems can be devised and controlled by the human mind.

The logic of systems has led to a place in the world of planning for the systems analyst who use conceptualizations and sequential procedures to study complex systems. "Basically, systems analysts are interested in (1) defining systems . . .; (2) defining goals . . .; (3) understanding the processes involved in reaching goals . . .; (4) assessing resources . . .; and (5) choosing preferable ways to use resources to reach desired goals."[7] In some respects, the logic of systems and systems analysis seems deceptively simple. In reality, due largely to unpredictable and uncontrollable human dimensions, the process of planning and systems analysis becomes anything but simple. The demands associated with the human dimension of the planning process are much more complex than the technical or mechanical aspects of the process.

NOTES

1. Sharon Begley and Mary Hager, "A Fantastic Voyage to Neptune," *Newsweek,* September 4, 1989, 52.
2. Stephen W. Hawking, *A Brief History of Time* (New York: Bantam Books, 1988).
3. James Gleick, *CHAOS: Making a New Science* (New York: Penguin Books, 1987).
4. Begley and Hager, "A Fantastic Voyage to Neptune," 52.
5. Andreas Faludi, *Planning Theory* (Oxford: Pergamon Press, 1973), 8–9.
6. Ibid., 25.
7. Guy Benveniste, *The Politics of Expertise,* 2nd ed. (San Francisco: Boyd and Fraser, 1977), 10.

3

Strategic Planning

INTRODUCTION

The motivation and perceived need for planning are not without dissonance among the legions of educators who are charged with the responsibility for the educational enterprise. Frustration grows from the issues surrounding the need for planning and from the process that is involved. Part of the hesitance that has accompanied planning has stemmed from "evidence of the inadequacy of planning theory."[1] Planners are confronted "on the one hand by an acute awareness that their environment is dominated by politics and that rational, comprehensive planning may well be futile, and on the other by a conviction that they should attempt it anyway."[2] Dissonance or confusion about the process cannot be used as an excuse for avoiding the imperative need for planning. Planners must understand the environment in which they work and acknowledge the chaos that is present. The mind of the planner should be motivated to respond to chaos and gain insight into the need for planning. Commitment will emerge from a comprehension of needs and confidence to move forward, bolstered by an understanding of the planning process.

Educators cannot afford the luxury of avoiding planning because of the fear of failure. Planning, like all human endeavors and especially efforts that involve values and social organizations rather than physical or mechanical devices, is not precise, nor can it be totally predetermined. Plans will never work perfectly because they involve people, and people are not entirely predictable, nor are they subject to precise measurements and calibrations.

As plans move from the level of one individual to the political arena involving large numbers of persons, they become less precise and the potential for them to become diverted is expanded; they move from the immediate access for control to levels of control that are remote and difficult or impossible to manage. When the planning stages progress from the confines of one person or a small group of people and are moved to larger, more complex, and often political levels of concern, the self-interests or hidden agendas that have a major influence upon the planning process and the implementation of the plan may become impossible to identify, let alone control. Although planning is an imperfect human process that will not always yield precise results, the existing limitations do not invalidate the need for planning. By contrast, the human vagaries that enter the planning and implementation arena simply build a more demanding and compelling rationale for the need for better planning methods.

From a historical perspective, scholars have looked to the past to identify causes for change and the effects or responses of identifiable influences. The primary events or cultural changes in history have been studied to identify the forces and influences perceived through hindsight. The historical conclusions, valuable as they have been, still carry a considerable degree of "interpretation," or hunches that suggest chance or luck—good or bad—in the shaping of history. The typical actions taken by leaders within each historical time frame have often been in the form of "reactions." As futurists and strategists have entered the arena of contemporary planning, a visionary endeavor designed to shape the future has supplanted waiting for chance and fate to shape the future.

As suggested in Chapter 1, there are various levels of planning; consequently, numerous planning models have been presented in the literature. The various models for planning were developed to help communicate how planning is done. Planning can be undertaken to achieve self-seeking desires, to control and manipulate, or, by contrast, to create a better world in which the education process functions. "The most ambitious view of planning is to look at it as a mode of deliberate intervention with history. As compared with other modes of deliberate intervention with history, such as heroic leadership or purely intuition-based statecraft, planning presumes to be [a] 'rational' and 'professional' " means of improving conditions or making a better world.[3] Consequently, planning may be viewed as a very presumptuous activity when considering that mere humans may undertake to identify what the future should be and go about the process of attempting to create history.

Various levels of planning, with accompanying models or approaches, have been suggested for the educational enterprise. In general, planners have expressed a need for "strategic planning" and "operational planning." Operational planning can apply to curriculum and instruction or to the area of management. There is a natural progression that enters the planning discipline at the level of strategic planning and moves to and through operational planning to levels of implementation.

While planning is generally described as being conducted in a static state in which starting and ending points can be identified, if real life planning is more similar to working with a moving picture rather than dealing with a snapshot.

Starting and ending points become transformed into the need to renew or conclude cycles in a perpetual process.

Concepts derived from theory that serve as a foundation for constructing various models underlie the process for planning. Models contain inherent limitations and as such may become devices, if oversimplified or used with blind adherence, that prove to produce a disservice or net loss when the final balance sheet is reviewed. Mechanical adherence to a model, without understanding the theory or concepts underlying it, can result in the misuse and abuse of the planning process; the only hope of success can emerge from random chance or sheer luck. If chance is the best for which educators can hope, the potential of planning has been negated.

APPROACHES TO PLANNING

A review of various approaches to planning, as presented in the writings and models of experts in the field, reveals several commonalities. While models designed to depict the planning process possess common elements, they also reflect distinct differences or nuances that reveal the conceptual processes of their designer.

Some models, but not all, include a step that takes into account the setting in which the planning is to be done. When the creator of a model has not incorporated a step in which the setting or the environment is taken into account, one presumes or takes for granted that a consideration of the setting has occurred.

The identification of a need to be met is contained in all planning models, although it may be expressed in different ways. The need is translated into a mission, a purpose, or goals. A means of conceptualizing the steps involved in planning models is provided by goals and subgoals.

Identifying options or selecting alternative approaches for achieving desired outcomes is a part of most planning models; however, the way in which proponents depict the listing and selection of options varies considerably.

While implementation, as a step in the planning process, is not presented in the same fashion in all planning models, it does tend to be listed by planning specialists in one form or another.

Of all the elements in planning models, evaluation is least frequently identified, expanded upon, or elaborated. Evaluation is, in some instances, assumed to be present; however, implicit or assumed elements of a planning model may be overlooked and forgotten. Not only is the evaluation component of planning the most frequently overlooked of all elements presented in models, but in actual practice evaluation is the component that is given the least attention in the vast majority of cases.

The concept of "feedback" is now generally incorporated in formal planning approaches, but again when we look at actual practice, feedback may or may

Figure 3.1
The Progression from Strategic Planning Through Operational Planning

not be utilized. The logic of feedback in the planning process seems apparent, but in some models, the inclusion of feedback is only assumed or implied.

There is a natural progression from strategic planning through operational planning and eventually to implementation. Examination of the levels of planning makes the progression become apparent and lets the distinction between strategic and operational planning be discerned (see Figure 3.1). A detailed discussion of strategic planning is continued in this chapter. Operational planning is presented in the following chapter.

STRATEGIC PLANNING

Strategic planning was developed in the military, adapted to the business world, and ultimately expanded into various governmental and municipal agencies before it was, as a formal process, translated for education. The works of writers in the field of educational planning began to be printed one or two decades after the works of the proponents of strategic planning had permeated the industrial world.[4] Even before the concept of strategic planning had made a major appearance in education, there were those in the world of business who were suggesting that the process was flawed and of questionable value. Those who questioned the value of strategic planning based their concerns largely on the fact that the process, as it was being practiced in the 1970s, was not designed to take into consideration political implications or strategic management considerations.[5] As a more advanced or mature view of strategic planning has developed, however, experience has proven to be a competent teacher. Strategic planning has been accomplished, in recent years, with a greater appreciation of its strengths and an understanding of how to avoid its limitations.

The term *strategy* has been employed in the planning literature to mean various things. Some writers use the word synonymously with the word *goal*. Others have suggested a definition that seems to be more in line with the meaning of the word as found in the dictionary; in so doing, they have used the word in a seemingly clearer and more defensible way. A strategy is an "organization's preselected means or approach to achieving its goals and objectives while coping with current and future . . . . conditions."[6] The use of the word *strategy* can be traced from military sources and into the planning literature. A polite debate can be generated about the true meaning of the term with respect to whether it is a statement of goal, a statement of process, or an approach to achieving a goal; however, such an extended discussion is probably a great deal more than most people want to know. As used here, strategies refer to the means or approaches selected to achieve goals.

The term *strategic management* emerged and reflected the concepts that were suggested to strengthen or overcome the key weaknesses of strategic planning. Strategic management was defined as being broader than strategic planning and included the means to move toward implementation.[7] Strategic management has been presented by its proponents as an extension and refinement in the evolution of strategic planning.

The emergence of strategic management as a refinement of strategic planning came about, in large part, because strategic plans in educational institutions failed to generate desired results. The perceived shortfall in strategic planning frequently resulted because the budgetary process and allocation of human resources were not committed to the plan. While some observers suggested strategic planning was failing, other observers argued the actual failure occurred simply because the plan was not implemented. Thus, strategic management was designed to foster strategic planning and to set the stage to implement the plan.

Strategic management has been defined as "the process by which top management determines the long-run direction and performance of the organization by ensuring that careful formulation, proper implementation, and continuous evaluation of strategy take place."[8] Others have stated that strategic management is making and implementing strategic decisions.[9] Planners who have embraced the term *strategic management* and explained the concept have defined it as a broader concept than strategic planning, which is inclusive of strategy formulation, implementation, and strategic control.

While some planners use the terms *long-range planning* and *strategic planning* interchangeably, a distinction should be made between the two terms. Long-range planning has been recognized as involving four basic elements: (1) monitoring, (2) forecasting, (3) goal setting, and (4) implementing. (While implementing should involve evaluation, often evaluation is, in practice, ignored.) Strategic planning has been described as involving: (1) environmental understanding, (2) organizational goal definition, (3) option identification, (4) decision making, (5) implementing, and (6) performance evaluation.[10]

The terms *long-range planning, strategic planning,* and *strategic management* are still used by different persons in different ways to mean the same or different concepts. Confusing? Perhaps assigning more literal meanings to the terms may help clarify and distinguish them (see Figure 3.1). As vision and commitment emerge on the part of the superintendent of schools and members of the board of education, the way is cleared for strategic planning. Once strategic planning is accomplished, the mission statement will provide an expression of why an institution exists. Goals can specify what is to be accomplished.

Strategic management extends the strategic plan by formulating alternatives for implementation and strategic control. Strategic management may be likened to a broad-stroke sketch of the major steps to be considered to reach a goal that was specified in the strategic planning process. Operational planning is used to design the specific tasks to be completed in reaching the goal. A strategic planning team is generally responsible for the strategic planning process. The superintendent and board of education should take the responsibility for strategic management. Specified staff members assigned to accomplish designated goals are charged with the responsibility for developing the operational plan. The superintendent, working in conjunction with the staff, is responsible for directing monitoring and evaluation efforts.

Commitment of Prime Resources

To implement a strategic plan, administrators who are responsible for implementation will be called upon to demonstrate various and numerous skills, one of which is the commitment and allocation of prime resources. Prime resources consist of (1) people, (2) time, (3) information, (4) space, and (5) facilities. In the total planning sequence, strategic management is the stage in which the superintendent and board members must be willing to commit needed resources. The allocation and utilization of prime resources will be required in the operational planning process.

People. People constitute the most important resource in the total planning process. The quality of the staff members and their level of expertise constitute the basic resource with which a leader or an administrator works. Consequently, it is essential for the administrator to develop the human resources with which planning will be accomplished.

Time. Time is one resource that can be allocated with precise equity to all persons involved in the planning process. Inequity occurs when some individuals use the time allotted with less efficiency or effectiveness. In many instances, not enough time has been allocated to carry out a planning effort. A classic illustration of the failure to recognize the importance of time for planning is one in which teachers are expected to serve on the planning committee or task force of a major planning effort while carrying out their normal assignment of meeting classes every day. After classes staff members may attend a weekly scheduled meeting that is designated as the time when the planning committee will ''report.'' Such scheduling of planning efforts is unreasonable, unproductive, and generally frustrating; however, it is not uncommon. Sufficient allocation of time for planning is essential. If teachers are expected to be involved in planning, release time can be allowed, substitutes hired, or extended contracts used to allocate sufficient time for planning.

Information. Information, as a prime resource, is another essential. Planning cannot be fruitful if attempted in a vacuum. In the information age, it is neither necessary nor reasonable to plan without information. Planning in an information void fails to build on the data base that is available to educators. Persons who assume they have a data base in their own idiosyncratic, mental computer that gives them a license to avoid the knowledge base of the profession are taking steps backward at a time when informed planners who can point to ways to improve the educational enterprise are needed. In the information age, there is no one fountain of knowledge. Knowledge or information is to be found throughout the environment and, like gold, must be mined and refined in a never-ending quest.

Space. Space, both physical and psychological, is needed for planning. If appropriate physical space is not available, people generally search for a place that is convenient and structured to facilitate their work. By allocating space that is appropriate, the administrator is indicating to staff members an awareness of the importance of the task being undertaken. Thus, the quality of the space also carries with it a message to the persons charged with the work of planning.

Facilities and support resources. Facilities and support resources, like other prime resources, should be allocated to the staff members responsible for planning. Planning consumes prime resources and transforms them into approaches that are intended to improve the quality of education. Educators who are assigned the task of planning, have scheduled appropriate time, and have been provided with appropriate knowledge or information need resources such as good lighting, software, hardware, and support staff. Such resources help assure staff members that the undertaking to which they have been assigned will be achieved.

The mortar that holds the prime resources together in a productive pattern is provided by the administrator in the form of leadership that exudes high expectations, fosters a positive working climate, and provides an effective reward structure. Leadership, buttressed by organizational ability, good judgment, sensitivity to the needs and wishes of individuals, good communication, decisiveness, and enthusiasm, is the most important ingredient or skill demonstrated by the administrator. Leadership needs to be cast in a vision and belief that things can be improved. Vision is used by true leaders to harness the emotional and psychological resources in an organization. Vision sharpens values, commitment, and aspirations.[11] While reality confronts each member of a planning effort daily, nevertheless, if a staff, as individuals and as a collective body, "is unwilling to entertain at least some dreams or visions for resolving its strategic issues, it probably should not be engaged in strategic planning."[12] The superintendent should assume the responsibility to articulate the broad vision of a district's future position and to manage the organizational forces "to refine and implement the attainment of that vision."[13]

Definitions of Strategic Planning

Growing numbers of educational leaders have looked to strategic planning in an effort to exert greater influence on the educational agencies for which they are responsible. In large part, the growth of strategic planning in education is a reflection of a state of mind, a matter of strategic thinking.

For many superintendents of schools, strategic planning has been seen as a protracted form of long-range planning with the added steps of environmental scanning. Some educational leaders have, however, understood the potential of strategic planning to bring about organizational renewal. "They applied the technique not only to planning, but also to restructuring programs, management styles . . . fiscal arrangements, and relationships with the community." [14]

Various definitions can be reviewed to present a collage of the major elements of agreement about strategic planning:

A strategic plan is a framework for carrying out strategic thinking, direction, and action leading to the achievement of consistent and planned results. [15]

Strategic planning is concerned with the long-term development of an institution, its essential character, its personality, its essence. Therefore, strategic planning is concerned with decisions which have enduring effects that are difficult to reverse. [16]

Strategic planning is a written, comprehensive, long-range plan that gives overall direction to the organization: a plan that is formalized. . . . Strategic planning involves making strategic decisions. . . . It recognizes the outside environment and explicitly incorporates elements of it into the planning process. . . . It has a long-term focus, often 3 to 5 years, but sometimes as many as 10 to 20 years. . . . It is conducted (or at least initiated) at the top of the organization and at the top of the organization's major divisions (although the process requires the involvement of a wide range of participants from the horizontal and vertical dimensions of the agency and its constituents). . . . It involves making decisions that commit large amounts of organization resources. . . . It sets the direction for the organization by focusing on the organization's identity and its place in a changing environment. [17]

Strategic planning is a disciplined effort to produce fundamental decisions shaping the nature and direction of governmental activities within constitutional bounds. [18]

Strategic planning is the means by which an organization constantly recreates itself to achieve extraordinary purposes. . . . Only strategic organizations can do strategic planning. . . . A strategic organization is *autonomous*. Strategic organizations have the prerogative and the responsibility to determine their own *identity* [and] have the prerogative and responsibility for acquisition and allocation of *resources* . . . for providing the *vision, values* and *leadership* that control, guide, and sustain." [19]

As previously mentioned, strategic planning has been perceived by some to have fallen short of its potential to achieve what it was intended to accomplish. Forty-five percent of the *Fortune* 500 firms in the United States were using some form of strategic planning in 1979; however, the leadership of these firms acknowledged that the technique had not lived up to expectations. [20] In fact, it was suggested that U.S. firms had been steadily losing ground to firms in other countries where strategic planning was not pursued to the same degree.[21] A growing awareness emerged that strategic planning had to be extended into the realm of strategic management or into the phases of implementation and control. As greater sophistication developed in the process of strategic planning, observers identified the need to keep the process less rigid and to have more frequent input into the renewal process of the strategic plan. There was the realization that a high level of participation among significant actors or stakeholders was essential, if for no other reason than to ensure communications. The internal structure had to be periodically juxtaposed to the strategic plan to determine if it was congruent and provided incentives for "internal entrepreneurs."[22] While strategic planning is a process that should generate receptivity to change and foster a responsive and proactive posture for the staff in a school system, it has been suggested that when rigidity is found in the process, the benefits and intent of the process have been lost through misuse.

Strategic planning is not and cannot be rigid if it is to help leaders in the field of education direct the educational enterprise. Strategic thinking must be implicitly receptive, even flexible, to change or to new ideas if it is to lead a complex bureaucratic agency into a changing environment with some assurance of success.

Most renewing companies have moved away from rigid planning methods. . . . What has evolved, instead, is planning that better comprehends the realities of change. It is more fluid, more flexible, more realistic than the old ways. . . . Planning sessions bring people . . . closer together. . . . The planning process . . . makes them work together. . . . The importance of planning is the *process* [and] on the surface that seems odd. But thinking of planning as communication resolves the mystery. Of course the process is important. That's the way people all over a company [or school district] confer.[23]

Some assumptions as to what strategic planning is not can be found on the flip side of the coin. It is not simple adherence to a few planning steps or some "academic exercises." It is not, or cannot, be a politically motivated edict or pronouncement that mandates specified actions. It is not a planning activity that can be done in the privacy of one individual's office. It is not the borrowing of a plan from one school system and implementing that plan in another district. It is not a device to implement predetermined or hidden agendas that are the creation of one person or even a special interest group.

Strategic planning can foster a strategic state of mind—strategic thinking. Various observers have suggested the strategic plan in and of itself may be of limited value. The strategic planning process through which a staff progresses may be extremely valuable if the staff is able to confront and clarify its mission, if the awareness for change in a turbulent environment is afforded greater appreciation and acceptance, if greater flexibility can be acquired, if a more enlightened responsiveness to changes in society is developed, and, ultimately, if staff behavior is congruent with the strategic planning process and leads to strategic management, which in turn can move toward operational planning that moves a school system to the accomplishment of its mission. "No one really knows how to do strategic planning (or everyone has a different idea about it, which is the same thing), but it is often thought of as a management technique for increasing rationality. Institutions hungry for solutions may embrace strategic planning even though there are few data suggesting that it works."[24]

A definition or a process on which there is total agreement with respect to strategic planning is hard to find; yet, conventional wisdom keeps reiterating, or at least inferring, there is value to be derived. The claim persists that through strategic planning, leaders in institutions, such as local school districts, will be better postured to control their futures.[25] Observers have also suggested there are benefits in resolving conflict and improving long-range resource allocation decisions.[26] In the private sector, strategic planning has been found to foster strategic thinking; as unexpected events occur, often as a fast-moving and surprising set of circumstances, managers are able to respond constructively and even take advantage of the unexpected.

Political Realities

Strategic planning, much more than operational planning, operates under the influences of political realities. The nature of strategic planning frequently places the persons responsible for such efforts in the political context and thus demands they think and act strategically to be effective.[27] The realization that comes from systems theory applies in a poignant manner as planners need to be acutely aware that what is being planned, or the system being conceptualized, is going to function in an existing environment as a subsystem within a larger system.

An important consideration in strategic planning is the persons who are involved. In the business world, the call is clearly for the chief executive officer (CEO) to take the leadership. The CEO must demonstrate the vision necessary for strategic planning and at the same time encourage the presentation of multiple options that come from bringing together the ideas from diverse points of view through "direct autonomy." "In directed autonomy people in every nook and cranny of the company are empowered—encouraged, in fact—to do things their way. . . . The boss knows that his or her job is to establish . . . boundaries; they truly get out of the way."[28] Just as there is a transition in the total planning process, or the extension of strategic planning into operational planning, there is a transition of human actions and levels of involvement. Strategic planning must have the clear involvement of the person or persons at the top of the bureaucracy—the superintendent and the board of education. The process then must involve opinion leaders and stakeholders from the breadth of the district and from the top to the bottom of the school system. Although large numbers of significant individuals must be involved throughout an agency in the strategic planning process, the effort necessitates strong and informed leadership at the top.

What is the appropriate role for the strategic planner? . . . What is most important about strategic planning is the development of strategic thinking, and, therefore, it may not matter who does it. However, it does seem that the most useful strategic planning influences decision making in desirable directions and that strategic planning done by line managers is most likely to be implemented.[29]

The superintendent of schools and the school board, once they have developed the commitment to strategic planning, must immediately involve other persons. Strategic planning cannot be done in secret. For strategic planning to come to fruition, various significant others must become involved.

Planning facilitator. A planning facilitator, whether that person is a consultant from outside the district or a specialist from within the ranks of the district, is an important, even essential, person in the strategic planning process. The facilitator is able to keep the planners on task, help clarify and resolve differences or conflict, and provide assistance or direction to assure that internal consistency is maintained. The facilitator can prescribe or recommend approaches for involving persons in clarifying and reaching consensus. The facilitator can often nurture and motivate by questioning and providing information. Assistance in helping people stay on task, keeping the process from lagging, or causing persons to pause at essential points for clarification are all part of the facilitator's job. Appointing a facilitator is an important step in the strategic planning effort as that person plays an essential role in the process—a role and function that should not be left to chance or taken for granted.

A facilitator from outside the school system can bring some distinct advantages to the strategic planning process. First, a facilitator should be knowledgeable and skilled in the process and required techniques of strategic planning. In addition to a high level of competence, the carefully selected facilitator from outside the district should maintain a posture of impartiality, be a source of new ideas and information to enrich the process, and possess that undefinable ability to gain the respect required to generate confidence among the staff. Every facilitator should leave his or her personal agenda out of the strategic planning process.

Support staff. Support staff are also important in the strategic planning effort. If planners have needed secretarial assistance, data management systems, and individuals to assist in the various and numerous tasks that must be completed, the process can be enhanced and more efficient than if such support persons are not provided. The superintendent and board of education should provide support staff; the work of the support staff should be directed by the process facilitator.

Specialists. Selected specialists, such as futurists or specialists in a given discipline, may be of invaluable service to the strategic planning process. Such specialists may be called upon to make specific presentations to the persons involved in strategic planning. Two general areas can be supported by calling upon the services of selected specialists: (1) expert advice or information regarding selected topics can be gained, and (2) strategic thinking on the part of the planners can be developed. An option to bringing in specialists to make presentations to the planning team is to provide information in the form of written or mediated materials. There is a voluminous amount of information published dealing with strategic issues such as technology, economics, family structure, ecology, energy, advertising, media, world trade, changing values, world politics, and many other topics that have a bearing on the future of education. Providing the persons who are at the center of the strategic planning effort with such information is key to the development of strategic thinking.

Strategic planning team. The identification and appointment of a strategic planning team or task force are responsibilities that should be given careful thought. Other than the facilitator and the superintendent of schools, the people selected to be on the strategic planning team are the most important persons in the process. They should be drawn from all segments of the personnel roster so a representative group of opinion leaders from the staff is involved. Central office personnel, building administrators, members from the teaching staff, and classified personnel should be enlisted. Strategic planning and information flow from the "top down," and operational functions and information flow from the "bottom up." The strategic planning team should be composed of persons who reflect the "strategic" and "operational" levels of involvement and responsibilities. In the strategic planning process there is also a need to enlist from the community opinion leaders who have an interest in education and community development. When identifying opinion leaders in the community, there is a tendency to draw heavily upon the power brokers. While it is advisable, even essential, to draw upon the power brokers, opinion leaders from the ranks of the community that may not be represented among the power figures should also be enlisted. The school administrator who demonstrates the ability to communicate and deal effectively with all socioeconomic groups in a community is more likely to enlist key figures from all walks of life on the strategic planning team. The selection of the planning team becomes crucial not only during the strategic planning process but also later in the total effort when acceptance and approval of the strategic plan are sought.

The question of how large to make the strategic planning team needs to be addressed. As implied above, full representation on a strategic planning team could result in a rather large number of persons. One solution to the potential problem is to have no more than 12 to 20 persons on the team. Group dynamics researchers have suggested that 12 is a very workable number of persons; if the number exceeds that limit significantly, the ability for all persons to remain involved is noticeably diminished. A strategic planning team should not exceed 24 persons. Another option that can be used to involve all segments of the school and community in the planning process is to establish several teams to work with a planning council. The establishment of teams (or subcommittees) involves more people. Such teams can provide important benefits, but the process should be structured to ensure that it functions smoothly and generates worthwhile results. One model for structuring teams is to have the facilitator, who is responsible to the superintendent, serve as the convener of a council consisting of the chairperson of each task force or subcommittee in the total planning team (see Figure 3.2).

The planning council should meet with the combined subcommittees at prescribed times. After such meetings, each task force or subcommittee should meet separately. Communication between and among all segments of the structure is crucial.

Operational planning teams should be appointed once the goals of the strategic plan have been established. One team may be assigned to each goal to develop a plan for its accomplishment. The superintendent of schools should be responsible for assigning selected staff members to each operational planning team. Since staff members may desire to work on goals that interest them and that are in their area of expertise, volunteers can be invited to help fill the ranks of operational planning teams. Operational planning teams should have a designated chairperson, and team members should be given instruction in the planning process to be used in developing plans.

Each operational planning team should be given a specific charge or set of instructions and a time for submitting plans. The operational planning team is not expected to implement its plans, but the team should develop a plan in which measurable outcomes are specified that are consistent with the mission and the goals of the strategic plan. The specific steps to be completed in the operational plan should be specified, the criteria for assessment indicated, the sequence of activities outlined, and a listing of prime resource needs identified, including a cost-benefit analysis. When all operational plans of the goals established in the strategic planning process have been completed, they are taken to the board of education for approval and final budget allocations.

CONCEPTS INVOLVED IN STRATEGIC PLANNING

The basic concepts involved in strategic planning are simple—at times deceptively simple. Strategic planning may be likened to wine making. Wine makers will acknowledge that the steps involved in the process are few and uncomplicated, but the technique and craft, even artistry, are complex. Strategic planning is fundamentally a discipline that involves stakeholders working collectively to (1) review selected basic considerations or conduct a strategic analysis, (2) clarify mission and goals, (3) select strategies to move toward goals, and (4) operationalize the strategic goals into working plans (see Figure 3.3).

Figure 3.2
Strategic Planning Council and Task Force Composition

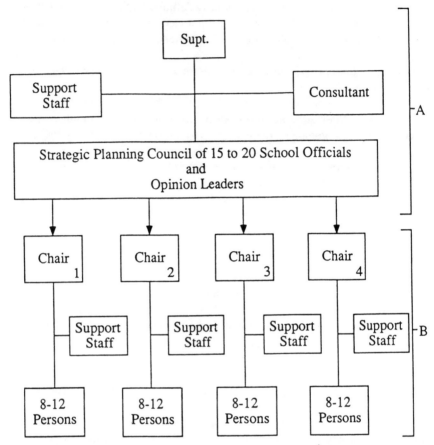

Note: A = strategic planning council of 15 to 20 school officials and opinion leaders who will conduct strategic analysis, clarify mission and goals, and select strategies; B = strategic management planning task forces; each task force is assigned the responisiblity of developing a detailed plan to implement a goal.

Strategic Analysis

Strategic analysis is the entry into the strategic planning processes once a commitment has been made by the superintendent and board of education and a strategic planning team has been formed. The rationale for strategic analysis is straightforward. The rationale is to generate strategic thinking, or a strategic set of mind, among the stakeholders, to provide information or data upon which decisions can be made, and to establish a common base of understanding and agreement and, ultimately, ownership upon which subsequent planning steps

Figure 3.3
Strategic Planning

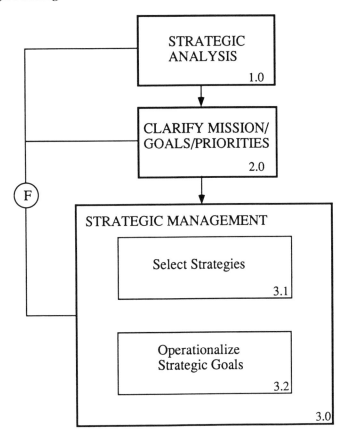

will be built. As suggested by Waterman, the strategic state of mind is far more important than the strategic plan itself.[30] The culminating activity and the end product of strategic analysis will be a set of pronouncements or conclusions upon which the people involved have reached agreement.

Strategic analysis is the data base of the strategic plan . . . the external and internal factors that are likely to have the greatest impact on the future of the organization. This leads to prioritizing critical issues that need to be addressed. . . . Strategic analysis is the most time-consuming element in the process. Because the strategic plan is by nature a conceptual plan, there needs to be a solid data base to support the key concerns.[31]

At the introductory level of strategic analysis there can be a review of any prior mission statements that may have been generated in previous planning efforts or accreditation studies. It would be unreasonable to assume that some form of mission statement was not on file and available for review. In practice, persons have commonly found that while a mission statement may have been on file, it may not have been a "working document" that either was taken seriously or had any influence on the behavior of staff members.

Strategic analysis will engage planners in a futures search, including a probing look into the future. Planners will also consider what people will value and, based on all considerations, including the possible writings of futurists, generate a list of assumptions.[32]

Environmental scanning. Environmental scanning is involved in making a strategic analysis. "The word 'environmental' includes the totality of the natural environment [with which we are not concerned except at those few points where it interacts with matters of structures, design, and material]"[33] affecting the institution involved. "Environmental scanning is the generic term used to describe a series of activities aimed at providing an organization with the information it needs to make decisions about its present and future."[34]

Environmental scanning can be divided into the external environment and the internal environment. If a school system is to function in a complex society or complex environment, it is essential for planners to understand the key influences upon the local school system that are derived from the environment in which the system operates. The areas relating to the external environment that are frequently examined are legal requirements established by law or court rulings, the influence of media, demographics, cultural climate, politics, economics, world conditions, family structure, geography, and the influence of other institutions and agencies. Actually, any factor that may have a significant influence upon a school system should be considered. There is no fixed list of topics to cover in scanning the external environment of a school system, and there is no fixed amount of data that must be considered. In fact, it is possible to create a data overload in an environmental scan. Therefore, a judgment call is required in terms of what factors should be considered from the external environment and how much information is necessary or useful. As a part of the external environment scene, it is generally beneficial to draw upon the thinking of futurists and to study trends. Futurists and prognosticators can perform an important function by assisting persons involved in the strategic planning process, presenting data that may not be available from local data bases, helping to develop an understanding of significant trends, and providing assistance in generating strategic thinking.

An internal environmental scan is used to identify major strengths and weaknesses within an institution. Internal environmental scanning may take into account the nature of the student body, the school climate, financial restraints or resources, staff resources or limitations, facilities, equipment, internal politics, school policies, or other internal factors that may have a significant influence on the system. The student-related information should be analyzed to develop a clear profile of demographics—sex, age, socioeconomic levels—and the identification of trends with regard to grade point averages, test scores, records concerning disruptive behavior and dropouts, and other data sources including the number of students going on to universities and community colleges.

Strategic planners need to have as clear a picture of local needs as possible. Data that record the level of achievement of the students in the district, the breadth and nature of the education program, and the identified strengths and areas of needs should be reviewed. Follow-up studies regarding the mobility and possible out-migration of graduates from the district and school-community characteristics of children and youth should be examined. Needs of the adult population in the school district can add to a profile of the family structure within the district; such information may become indispensable to future steps in the planning process. In general, all salient data that may have a substantial impact upon the future of the district need to be reviewed.

Consensus regarding the philosophy and educational values that will influence what planners do and the direction set for a school should not be overlooked as part of the strategic analysis. There is an inherent danger in assuming that all people are in agreement about such things as values and philosophical positions. If philosophical issues are not reviewed and discussed, such an omission can later come to haunt the process. As hidden agendas stalk the minds of stakeholders and erode the process of planning, finding consensus becomes more elusive.

How much information is needed? How long should the process take? These are questions for which there are no ready answers. There should be general agreement on the part of those persons involved in the strategic planning on basic and underlying considerations. This base of agreement becomes crucial to the future steps in the planning process in order to provide assurance that there is a coordinated effort to generate movement in a given direction. The process should be data-based. Information upon which a base of agreement can be built is generally more defensible and understood by all concerned than a simple reliance on opinions. The strategic analysis may require two to four intensive days to complete the process. All phases of strategic planning may take a semester or even a full year in some cases.

"We agree" statement. The end product of the review of basic assumptions or environmental scanning is a statement of the points on which agreement has been reached. Such a "we agree" document need not be voluminous but should consist of 6 to 12 brief, succinct statements with a rationale of one or two sentences, or possibly one or two paragraphs, to support the assumptions associated with the strategic analysis process. Such a statement of agreed-upon beliefs, recognized needs, and assumptions is used to foster agreement and coordinated action among the planners and can be communicated to the personnel of the district and the patrons of the community at large.

Strategic planners deal with policies that come from various levels. National goals, policies, and laws can never be ignored and actually constitute the first policy level. The mandates and policies of state legislators, frequently projected by officials from within state departments of education, comprise a second policy level. Local district policy, approved by local boards of education and supported by statutes and court decisions, constitutes a third level of policy considerations. A fourth level of policy is actually generated in the strategic planning process and has been identified as "strategic policies."[35] Strategic policies, contained in the "we agree" statement, are acknowledgments of the boundaries within which the strategic planning and the implementation process will be realized. Strategic policies are statements carrying a commitment to perform or not perform certain acts or functions. Strategic policies should reflect the commitment of the leaders in the school and community to such a degree that there is clear support for, and adherence to, a set of values and a code of institutional conduct.

The stochastic world. There is need for an additional comment regarding strategic analysis. The persons involved in the process of strategic analysis must remain receptive to changes. While it is necessary, or at least easier, to describe strategic analysis as if it were being conducted on a stationary platform, the reality is that strategic analysis is being conducted in the midst of a constantly shifting environment. The environment can be changing so rapidly that it is difficult to keep abreast of the currents and eddies, which in turn can have an influence upon the institution. Consequently, incoming data must be monitored and, if judged essential, assimilated into the strategic analysis. Incoming data can come in just about any form and at any time. Such data can be positive and constructive, with a potential for being capitalized upon, or it can pose a threat or obstruction that will have to be contended with in the planning process. Generally, the incoming data will intrude upon the external scanning process. Internal changes in conditions can occur, however, such as the resignation of a key staff member or damage to a building by fire. In short, the unexpected becomes the expected, and planners must retain the resilience to be able to respond to the unexpected.

"It is a stochastic world," in the words of Waterman, who means that there are many unpredictable events driven by random forces that come to bear on a strategic plan. The stochastic nature of the environment adds to the ambiguity faced by strategic planners; forecasting and making predictions become more of a risk than planners would like. There may be few, if any, guarantees. Every applecart has the potential of being upset. The one thing that can seemingly be forecast is continued change, which is often fast and unpredictably driven by sometimes known, sometimes unknown forces. "Most companies try to overlay rational linear, deterministic techniques, which they call strategy, on an underlying process that is random, full of surprises . . . in other words, stochastic. It doesn't work. . . . We must adopt strategic methods that fit the unpredictable forces at work."[36] The stochastic nature of the environment does not preclude arriving at intelligent decisions and projections, but it certainly does create ambiguity and at the same time places a premium on "robust adaptive procedures" that not only foster responsiveness but demonstrate an anticipatory posture that enables planners to capitalize on the unexpected. Being alert to incoming data is essential in order to place a school system in a position to take advantage of unannounced opportunities and to avoid the pitfalls that can accompany the arrival of the unknown (see Figure 3.4).

CLARIFYING THE MISSION, GOALS, AND PRIORITIES OF THE DISTRICT

Mission Statement

Undoubtedly, few school districts can be found in which there is not some form of a mission statement. It is not uncommon, however, for a mission statement to consist of one or two sheets of paper in an obscure document that is filed in a small drawer; such a mission statement might occupy even less cranial space in the thinking of people in a given district. Strategic planning should provide a means to clarify the mission for the personnel and patrons in a local school district, convert it into an empowering document, and generate agreement, support, and commitment to the accomplishment of mission or direction.

The mission statement should provide direction for the staff and community. It should contain the vision of a stronger and improved school system, in which the school enhances the quality of life in the community as defined in the immediate and distant future. The mission statement should be brief and deal in broad definitions, not specifics. Staff members and patrons should be able to gain from the mission statement a clear sense of why a school system exists. Thus, a mission statement should not reinforce the status quo but rather project a commitment and vision and point toward a definition of what the school district will ultimately become.

The mission statement needs to be conceptualized by the strategic planners as an outgrowth of the strategic analysis. There must be a test of internal consistency applied to the mission statement. All items upon which there was agreement and that were ultimately contained in the "we agree" statement, which was the end product of the strategic analysis, need to be held up to the mission statement and checked for consistency.

The mission statement, if it is to be a visionary document, must be aimed high. It should be expressed in terms and contain the necessary substance to provide clear direction for the staff and patrons. If a superintendent of schools is to be a leader in the truest sense of the word, directing the strategic planning process may well be one of the most important leadership functions to be accomplished. Strategic planning can set the stage for one of the "finest hours" of the superintendent of schools. Therefore, the mission statement cannot be anything less than a visionary document to be used to give direction to district personnel and community patrons.

Figure 3.4
Strategic Planning: Strategic Analysis (1.0)

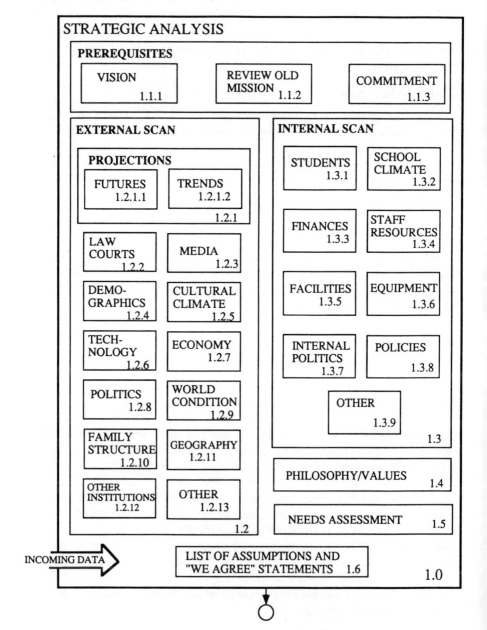

Goals

Once the mission statement has been agreed upon, goals that are deemed necessary to realize the intent of the mission statement can be derived. Goals can be statements that are more specific than the mission statement but that contribute to the accomplishment of the mission of an institution. The goal statements generally focus on major areas of need and are stated in such a way that they convey to all staff and patrons what is to be accomplished in order to realize the mission. While some goal statements may be projected into a time frame of several years, goals are generally focused on a shorter time frame than is a mission statement.

When developing goals, planners need to address the balance between reality and the dream of a better educational system. As indicated previously, a mission statement should be visionary. The mission statement must contain the vision and hopes for a better educational system and community. As such, a mission statement should reflect the vision of the community and school leaders in a district and provide a motivating influence, even inspiration, for personnel and patrons. Excitement should be generated to accompany the commitment to develop and bring to fruition a school capable of helping individuals maximize their potential. The mission and accompanying goals for a school district should motivate people to strive for improvements. Goals must be realistic and achievable; at the same time, they must cause people to look up, look forward, and hold high expectations (see Figure 3.5). (For an example of mission, goals, and strategies, see Appendix A-1.)

STRATEGIC MANAGEMENT

Strategies are approaches to be employed in accomplishing a goal. The term *strategy* has been used in a variety of ways, with various meanings suggested. It has often been associated with the military and used to mean a tactic or maneuver. There has, however, been a fine distinction; strategy has been considered the grand plan or campaign, while the tactics or maneuvers are the techniques or ploys used to accomplish the overall plan. In the athletic world, a strategy is considered a game plan. In the business world, the strategy used by the owners of a given business might be to diversity and go into multiple markets as a means or strategy for expanding profits. The precedent in various fields has been to use the term *strategy* to mean the planned approach or process designed to accomplish the mission and goals of the agency.

A slightly different interpretation of the term has been used by some planners who have suggested that strategy is the goal and approach to be accomplished.

The intended meaning of strategy is extended here to encompass an institution's choice of goals, the plans for achieving these goals, and the deployment of resources to attain these goals. Strategy is the pattern of objectives, purposes, or goals and major policies

Figure 3.5
Strategic Planning: Clarify Mission, Goals, Priorities (2.0)

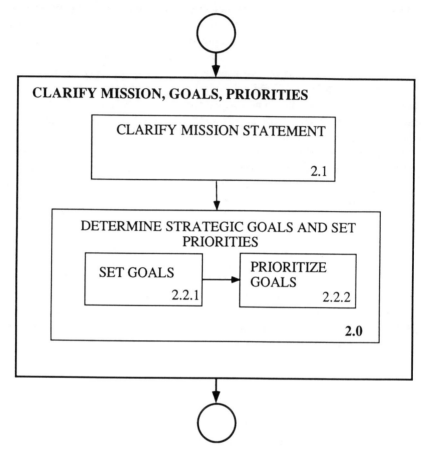

and plans for achieving these goals stated in such a way as to define what the [institution] is or is to become. Strategic policy planning results in (1) the determination of the basic long-range goals of the institution, (2) the adoption of courses of action, and (3) the allocation of resources necessary for reaching these goals—all being integrated and unseparable.[37]

A different emphasis of the term *strategy* is suggested here, with a separation of elements in which (1) goals would be an outgrowth of the mission statement, (2) a strategy would be identified that would be the adoption of a course of action, and (3) the allocation of resources would be a part of the operationalization of the strategic management plan.

The portion of strategic planning that involves the identification and selection of strategies often encompasses (1) the review of strategic alternatives, (2) the selection of strategies from the various options that may be available, (3) the assignment of responsibilities to staff members or units in the agency responsible for carrying out the strategy, and (4) the commitment of resources over the time frame deemed appropriate to accomplish the strategy. The final step in the selection of strategies is to communicate the information to the appropriate persons by the development of an executive summary.

An example of goal statements and strategies is presented below.

Goal No. 1. Develop closer ties to home and community to enhance support for better-quality education in schools.

> *Strategy.* Employ site-based management approach with a strong parent/community component.
>
> *Strategy.* Implement *Renaissance Project.*
>
> *Strategy.* Develop extended day (7:00 A.M. to 7:00 P.M.) with three meals, playground and recreation program, and counseling.

Goal No. 2. Reduce dropout rate.

> *Strategy:* Develop an early intervention program for students at-risk starting in 3d grade, in which parent education and support systems are developed.
>
> *Strategy.* Adopt alternative magnet work-study programs for 9th through 12th graders.
>
> *Strategy.* Implement the *Renaissance Project* to foster reinforcement of pupils and to establish an active reward system for academic achievement for all students.
>
> *Strategy.* Establish an "early warning/early contact" system for and by parents for absentees.
>
> *Strategy.* Develop stronger liaison with police and parents to combat distribution of illegal drugs.
>
> *Strategy.* Make an assessment of school activity participation and, if needed, expand activities to enlist broader participation.

As seen above, goals can be direct extensions of mission statements. They can also be tested for internal consistency with the "we agree" statement that summarized the consensus reached by planning members at the conclusion of the strategic analysis. Goals are outcome-related. Strategies are means of reaching goals (see Figure 3.6).

Executive Summary

The executive summary should be prepared by the superintendent of schools or a designee and contain several key elements. The list of assumptions and the "we agree" statements that grew out of the strategic analysis should be

Figure 3.6
Strategic Planning: Strategic Management (3.0)

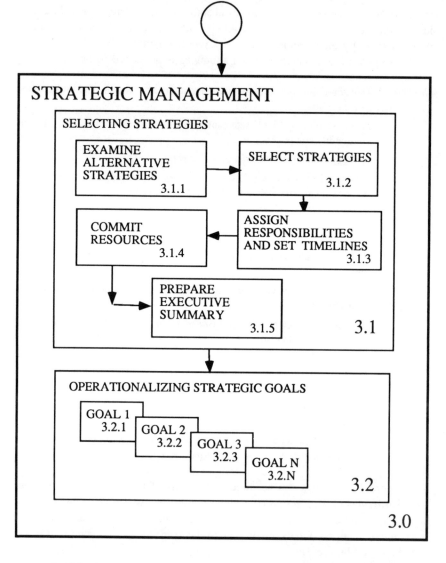

summarized in the executive summary. The superintendent may wish to include summarizing comments emphasizing certain dimensions of the materials and stressing the importance of the process. The mission statement, on which there has been agreement, and the accompanying goal statements should be "quoted" in the executive summary. In other words, the mission statement should be stated exactly as approved, without editorial changes or new or different interpretations. In like manner, the various goals and comments regarding the order of priority need to be specified. The segments of the executive summary are, for the most part, direct quotations from documents generated by the planning team members. The next portion of the executive summary should contain the list of strategies to be used to carry out the plans and achieve the goals set by the planning teams and approved by the board of education. An assignment of strategies to staff members, or groups of staff, is also contained in the executive summary, along with tentative budgets or plans for supporting the work associated with each specific goal. Finally, a time frame for the completion of each goal, or the accomplishment of each strategy, should be established. The superintendent may wish to conclude the executive summary with a statement of the importance of the overall process and a renewal of commitment.

The purpose of developing an executive summary is to provide an official form of communication to staff and patrons that contains a definition of what is to be accomplished, why it is important, and how and by whom it will be accomplished. The executive summary, along with an official commitment, is a step toward making the planning process become a reality. The executive summary announces to all concerned that the strategic planning process is to be taken seriously and that high expectations are supported. Based upon the information contained in the executive summary, the stage is set to move into strategic management and, ultimately, into operational planning.

Organizing the Strategic Plan

Each goal of a strategic plan needs to be translated into operational status. The superintendent is responsible for coordinating the various operational plans that constitute the total planning effort; however, the planning processes employed in operational planning will typically be focused on each goal. The strategies chosen to reach each goal will be embedded in each operational plan. Viewed from a different perspective, operational planning will need to be accomplished to implement each strategy.

Implementation will follow board approval of operational plans. The superintendent of schools is the person who will be held responsible for the outcomes ultimately achieved as a result of the strategic planning process. Perhaps more important than the issue of accountability, however, is the call for leadership on the part of the superintendent. The superintendent should work with the board of education to maintain momentum. At the same time, the superintendent is responsible for coordinating all involved staff and seeing that prime resources are committed and deadlines are met. The superintendent should provide leadership as a manager, supporter, coordinator, and reinforcer of staff. The tone or climate is set by the superintendent. People should know that the plan is being operationalized and that their individual contribution is valued.

Use of Feedback

The general model depicting strategic planning (see Figure 3.3) is an open system, which simply means that in addition to the four components described (1.0, strategic analysis; 2.0, clarifying mission, goals, and priorities; 3.0, selecting strategies; and 4.0, strategic management) there is a feedback loop that brings each of the four mission functions into contact with each other; thus the loop is closed, and information is allowed to flow throughout the system. If the model contained no feedback loop, a closed system would be depicted, with information going from the first segment (1.0), to the second segment (2.0), to the third segment (3.0), and finally ending at the fourth and last segment (4.0). The closed system would provide no opportunity for information to flow back and forth between elements, nor would the planners be given the opportunity and options of taking new data into account. An open system is self-regulating and self-correcting; the closed system is not. The distinction between an open and a closed system should be noted because of the definitions given here as contrasted to the definitions used in some references.[38] One naturally thinks of something that is open as being receptive. The term *open-minded* illustrates one way openness is viewed in a postive light. In like manner, if a person is said to be closed-minded to various options or ideas, he or she is perceived as negative, rigid, or unyielding. An open systems has a feedback loop while a closed system has no feedback loop.

The feedback loop, in the strategic planning process, enables planners to capitalize on a fundamental concept of systems theory as applied to the planning process. In essence, the feedback loop can be likened to a scanner radio in which an electronic device, shown by a running red light through electronic circuits, is actively and constantly flitting from one segment of a system and calling on each other segment in rapid succession. In a closed system, a linear sequence of steps, which goes from 1.0 to 2.0 and on to 3.0, etc., is usually depicted in the model. With the addition of a feedback loop, the linear plan is still viewed as being available, and a sequence is even suggested in a model; however, the feedback loop makes it possible to negotiate within the system in any direction at any time and to ensure that all subsystems remain in tune with the total system. Another analogy can be made; an open system in which a feedback loop is present can be likened to a spreadsheet that makes corrections in the subtotals and total amounts when a change is entered in any cell within the spreadsheet. An effort to conduct strategic planning without a feedback loop would be unrealistic and futile.

SUMMARY

Strategic planning within autonomous educational agencies has matured and been refined; strategic planning holds forth promise as a viable approach to educational renewal. While various approaches to strategic planning have been suggested, the emphasis upon the "discipline" of strategic planning by Cook[39] is an important concept. Models have been developed, and some have depicted simplistic, specific steps to be followed. Other approaches to strategic planning have been predicated upon concepts and contain theoretical constructs that can be used to focus and guide planning efforts. There are dangers in any model when those who would use it perceive there to be a series of prescribed steps to be followed by drawing a picture by connecting lines between a series of numbers scattered on a page. It is most unlikely that any would-be strategic planner can accomplish the development of a meaningful or viable plan in any set of sequential activities when a series of predetermined steps, devoid of any underlying concepts, is followed blindly. To accomplish the renewal of an educational program, strategic planning, as a complex, theory-based, conceptual tool, can result in major advances if placed in the hands of visionary leaders who are committed and willing to stay the course and exert the discipline needed.

NOTES

1. Judith Innes de Neufville, "Usable Planning Theory: An Agenda for Research and Education," in *Strategic Perspectives on Planning Practice,* ed. Barry Checkoway (Lexington, Massachusetts: D. C. Heath, 1986), 41.

2. Ibid.

3. Yehezkel Dror, "Planning as a Mode of Policy-Reasoning," in *Abstract Thoughts: Concrete Solutions Essays in Honor of Peter Nash,* ed. Leonard Guelke (Department of Geography Publications, Series No. 29), (Waterloo: University of Waterloo, 1987), 28.

4. E. E. Chaffee, "The Concept of Strategy: From Business to Higher Education," in *Higher Education: Handbook of Theory and Research,* ed. J. C. Smart (New York: Agathon Press, 1985), 134.

5. H. I. Ansoff, *The New Corporate Strategy* (New York: Wiley) 1988, p. 17; F. W. Gluck, "A Fresh Look at Strategic Management," *Journal of Business Strategy* 6 (Fall 1985), 4–19; R. H. Hayes, "Strategic Planning—Forward in Reverse? *Harvard Business Review* (November/December 1985), 111–119; M. C. Lauenstein, "The Failure of Strategic Planning," *Journal of Business Strategy* 6 (Spring 1986), 75–80; G. Tavernier, "Shortcomings of Strategic Planning," *International Management* 31, no. 9 (September 1976), 45–47.

6. L. A. Digman, *Strategic Management: Concepts, Decisions, Cases* (Plano, Texas: Business Publications, 1986), 5.

7. D. B. Jemison, "The Contributions of Administrative Behavior to Strategic Management," *Academy of Management Review* 6 (1981), 633–642; H. Mintzberg, "Patterns in Strategy Formation," *Management Science* 24 (1978), 934–948.

8. L. W. Rue and P. G. Holland, *Strategic Management: Concepts and Experiences* (New York: McGraw-Hill, 1989), 3.

9. C. Bowman and D. Asch, *Strategic Management* (London: Macmillan, 1987), 4.

10. J. L. Morrison, W. L. Renfro, and W. I. Boucherl, eds, *Applying Methods and Techniques of Futures Research: New Directions for Institutional Research* (San Francisco: Jossey Bass, 1983), 75.

11. W. Bennis and B. Nanus, *Leaders: The Strategies for Taking Charge* (New York: Harper and Row, 1985), 42.

12. J. M. Bryson, *Strategic Planning for Public and Non-Profit Organizations: A Guide to Strengthening and Sustaining Organizational Achievement* (San Francisco: Jossey-Bass, 1988), 59.

13. Digman, *Strategic Management,* 333.

14. Shirley D. McCune, *Guide to Strategic Planning for Educators* (Alexandria, Virginia: Association for Supervision and Curriculum Development, 1986), 31.

15. Patrick J. Below, George L. Morrisey, and Betty L. Acomb, *The Executive Guide to Strategic Planning* (San Francisco: Jossey-Bass, 1988), 2.

16. Robert G. Cope, *Strategic Policy Planning: A Guide for College and University Administrators* (Littleton, Colorado: Ireland Educational Corporation, 1978), 10.

17. William P. Anthony, *Practical Strategic Planning: A Guide and Manual for Line Managers* (Westport, Connecticut: Quorum Books, 1985), 3–8.

18. J. B. Olsen, and D. C. Eadie, *The Game Plan, Governance with Foresight* (Washington, D.C.: Council of State Planning Agencies, 1982), 3.

19. William J. Cook, Jr., *Strategic Planning,* rev. ed. (Arlington, Virginia: American Association of School Administrators, 1990), 74–76.

20. G. E. Yip, "Who Needs Strategic Planning?" *Journal of Business Strategy* 6 (Fall 1985), 30.

21. Hayes, "Strategic Planning," 111.

22. Tavernier, "Shortcomings of Strategic Planning," 47.

23. Robert H. Waterman, Jr., *The Renewal Factor* (New York: Bantam Books, 1987), 56–57.

24. R. Birnbaum, *How Colleges Work: The Cybernetics of Academic Organizations and Leadership* (San Francisco: Jossey-Bass, 1988), 221.

25. J. W. Moore and L. F. Langknecht, "Academic Planning in a Political System," *Planning for Higher Education* 14, no. 1 (1986), 1.

26. N. H. Kelly and R. N. Shaw, "Strategic Planning by Academic Institutions—Following the Corporate Path?" *Higher Education* 16 (1987), 332.

27. Barry Checkoway, *Strategic Perspectives on Planning Practice* (Lexington, Massachusetts: D. C. Heath, 1986), 2.

28. Waterman, *The Renewal Factor,* 82.

29. Checkoway, *Strategic Perspectives on Planning Practice,* 81.

30. Waterman, *The Renewal Factor,* 55.

31. Below, Morrisey, and Acomb, *The Executive Guide to Strategic Planning,* 10.

32. Cope, *Strategic Policy Planning,* 72–73.

33. D.E.C. Eversley and Mary Moody, *The Growth of Planning Research Since the Early 1960s* (London: Social Science Research Council, 1976), 3.

34. McCune, *Guide to Strategic Planning for Educators,* 40.

35. Cook, *Strategic Planning,* 94.

36. Waterman, *The Renewal Factor,* 35.

37. Cope, *Strategic Policy Planning,* 8.

38. Roger A. Kaufman, *Educational System Planning* (Englewood Cliffs, New Jersey: Prentice-Hall, 1972), 26.

39. Cook, *Strategic Planning,* 87, 120.

4

Operational Planning

INTRODUCTION

Operational planning is only one facet or segment of the total, broad planning process. As shown in Figure 4.1, planning starts with a vision and commitment. Planners may, once a vision is acknowledged, move to strategic planning if the situation demands it, or a planner may move directly from a mental view of what is to be accomplished and enter directly into operational planning. Operational planning may or may not grow out of strategic planning.

An operational planning approach may be employed as a means of carrying out a strategy specified in a strategic planning effort. For example, school officials and community representatives may determine, through a strategic planning process, that when they are facing an uncertain future, there may be several goals that are essential to improving the quality of education for the children in their district. For the sake of illustration, assume that school officials have progressed through a strategic planning process. After completing a strategic analysis, they have reached a point where the mission of the district was clarified and goals were specified and put in priority. For the sake of brevity let us further assume that the superintendent of schools in our hypothetical district is quite adept at group processes and internal politics with members of the board of education. After a series of meetings and a planning retreat, the members of the board of education give their approval to the strategies to be employed and are willing to commit resources. Our hypothetical superintendent would have in hand the mandate to write an executive summary that would include (1) a brief review of the key considerations that came from the strategic analysis; (2) a mission statement; (3) goals listed in order of importance; (4) strategies selected to reach each goal; (5) the assignment of responsibilities to specified

Figure 4.1
Systems Planning Model

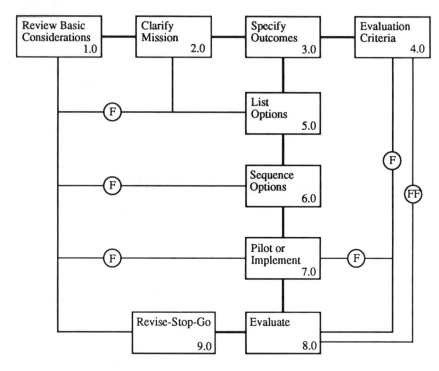

staff (including a target date for completion of plans to operationalize strategies); and (6) the commitment of resources. This executive summary would
provide the marching orders for many a good soldier in the district and would
trigger the next phase of the planning process—the operational planning effort.

To carry the illustration a step further, assume one of the several goals stated
in the executive summary of a strategic plan was to achieve higher levels of
self-direction and improved citizenship among pupils in the district and to reduce the use of illegal drugs and alcohol among pupils. The strategies identified
to achieve the goal could be twofold: one strategy could be to review and
improve the instructional program related to student self-direction as well as
alcohol and drug education, and the second strategy could be to forge a stronger
linkage among the school, the home and community agencies to ensure a positive support system for children and youth. The author of an executive summary could then indicate the person who would be asked to take the responsibility for directing the planning effort to meet each stated goal and specify a
general or suggested time frame in which the goal was to be accomplished and
presented to the board of education for approval. The stage would be set for
operational planning.

Needs may be identified in a district that were not an outgrowth of strategic planning, such as a need to develop a long-range plan for the acquisition, care, and management of athletic supplies in a secondary school. Such a need could be addressed by operational planning. Still another illustration of an area in which operational planning could be employed would be in the development of a plan for evaluating building principals. A perceived need to evaluate principals could come from strategic planning, but it could also come from good personnel development practices in a district in which no strategic planning had transpired. Operational planning can be districtwide; such planning can deal with physical plant planning, program planning that ranges from a total K-12 articulated curriculum or individual lesson plans, human resource planning in the areas of acquisition, induction, supervision, and termination, or planning for routine practices as well as nonrecuring events. Operational planning may be conducted in the central office of a district, at the building level, or by an individual staff member.

Regardless of what is being planned, there are certain concepts that, if followed, can enhance the odds of success. The concepts applicable to operational planning are derived from systems theory and provide planners with a framework and a means of structuring the planning process. Flexibility and responsiveness are provided by such concepts, and at the same time a discipline is posed that can provide a process based on theory and tested procedures to enable planners to avoid the rediscovery of the wheel. The end result of good planning can be a better mousetrap—and more important, a more positive, robust educational experience for pupils.

PLANNING MODELS

A review of various planning models will reflect a number of commonalities. Every planning model has a starting point; however, it is of interest to note that the nature of the starting point varies with different models. In some cases the starting point is "setting goals." There appears to be an assumption that in such models prior considerations were taken into account, needs were defined, resources and limitations were specified, and points of agreement were reached. Goals or objectives, stated in different ways or with different terminology, are always a part of all planning models. Then, just as in decision-making models, various planning models are used to depict the need for listing alternatives or options to be considered in achieving specified goals. A segment that deals with ordering or organizing the steps to be completed is not included in all models. In some models, the assumption has been made that the steps will be sequenced in a way that enables the persons using the plan to achieve the desired outcomes. In one form or another, implementation is contained in most models. Interestingly, the implementation portion of some models is also the concluding step in the proposed planning sequence, while other designers have suggested that there be evaluation and a decision point regarding the future disposition of the plan.

THE SYSTEMS PLANNING APPROACH

A set of concepts can be derived from systems theory that are used to suggest elements to be contained in a planning process. When the various concepts related to planning, as derived from systems theory, are put together into an entity, they emerge as a process model in which the various segments involved and their relationship to each other in the planning process are displayed. There is a danger in presenting a model for planning. If the observer of the model fails to see the underlying concepts, a shallow or faulty level of comprehension could result, which would lead to a mechanistic or even dogmatic adherence to the model, based on a lack of understanding. On the one hand, a model can be presented that appears and is, in fact, quite simple. When one moves on from the mechanistic use of a model to a more sophisticated application and adaptation of the concepts embedded within the model, there can be a level of use that requires deeper insights and even an artistry that rises well above the mechanical use of a model. A model may be an appropriate means of presenting a complex process and breaking it down into its basic components; however, no model can be all or tell all even if its name is changed from "model" to "paradigm." A full understanding of the planning process comes with a conceptual framework that transcends any single model.

With each conceptual component that can be sequenced into a planning process or discipline, elements of systems theory can be identified as supporting the concept and its inclusion in the planning process.

Steps in an Operational Planning Process	Concepts from Systems Theory
1. Review basic assumptions.	Every entity functions within an environment, with which it must relate.
2. Specify purpose or goals.	Every entity serves a purpose, or it atrophies or is discarded.
3. Specify measurable outcomes.	Every entity is made up of related parts that enable it to reach identifiable outcomes. Parts or subsystems, as well as expected outcomes, must be identifiable and measurable in order to know if the process and the intended product are achieved.

4. Specify criteria for measuring outcomes.

The effectiveness of an entity can be determined when criteria consistent with the purpose for the entity's existence are applied to measures of effectiveness. To determine if a system is functioning, definable criteria are needed that are internally consistent with the intended outcomes.

5. List and consider alternatives or options.

Complex systems may have multiple options for reaching desired results. The "best match" between options and intended outcomes yields the best results in most cases.

6. Sequence the alternatives chosen.

Systems are logical and orderly.

7. Implement (pilot, field-test, simulate, or implement).

Complex systems develop perfection and stability over time through self-correcting and preservation of subsystems.

8. Evaluate.

Systems exist to accomplish a defined purpose. Evaluation is one means of determining if a system is functioning properly. If a systems fails to function in a manner that achieves intended outcomes, it will be discarded.

9. Determine the future of a planned program or project.

Every entity has a life span, a period of growth, a time of maturity or climax, a period of decline, and, finally, a point of termination.

10. Feedback.

Every entity, and especially complex systems, must demonstrate internal consistency. The feedback process can provide the mechanism, or subsystem, to enable a system to respond to either internal forces or external influences and thus survive in a changing environment. If systems do not adjust to environmental changes, they are terminated.

If the concepts listed above are put in a systematic mode, they can be viewed as a framework or model that can serve as a conceptual process to guide planners. Persons who comprehend the systematic nature of the process are keenly alert to the need to encompass all the needed concepts or components in the process. Planners who demonstrate the knowledge and insight of the conceptual framework for planning also perceive the significance of the interrelatedness within a system or plan, as well as the importance of external influences on a system or subsystem. A generic conceptual framework for planning, in which systems theory forms the underlying foundation upon which the planning process is predicated, is depicted in Figure 4.1.

A review of basic considerations may be viewed as the first step in the planning process. Such a review is based on the concept derived from systems theory that any entity or project being planned will exist within the context of an environment, in which it must function. The review of basic considerations should be undertaken so the planners are aware of the setting or context that influences their efforts. In many respects, the review of basic considerations is similar to the strategic analysis that is a part of the strategic planning process. The difference is that a review of basic considerations in operational planning is less global and more focused. Such a review takes into account more immediate considerations; however, the review of basic considerations is an important facet of the total operational planning process.

The focus or general purpose to be accomplished in the operational planning effort will suggest the topics to be considered when reviewing basic considerations. For example, if an instructional program were being planned, the topics that might be given consideration could include past achievement scores; state curricular requirements; board policy; staff, budget, and facility resources and/ or limitations; community expectations; needs assessment data; and various areas of staff concern or interest relative to the planned instructional program. By contrast, if a planning effort were undertaken to develop a new transportation system for a newly reorganized school district, the list of basic considerations would obviously be different from the ones considered by the planners of an instructional program. The rule of thumb, with respect to basic considerations, is to explore all areas that could have an impact on the planning process and the ultimate outcomes. The selection of those topics that have the greatest impact on what is being planned is key to the review of basic considerations. Possibly, planners can become so engrossed with a world of considerations they do not have the needed focus on the immediate planning effort. A judgment call is required to ensure that important considerations are not overlooked; at the same time, the essence of the environmental considerations must be refined so that a workable yet clear base of operation is achieved.

If a review of basic considerations is not undertaken and assumptions are made that all parties involved have an understanding of the needs and the setting in which the planning is to take place, a rather high probability exists that the planning effort will fail to reach fruition, or at least the process will be complicated and prolonged by the failure to reach consensus regarding the important factors that set the stage for the planning process. Systems theory can be utilized to demonstrate that every entity is made up of parts and at the same time is related to some bigger entity. If the planning effort does relate to some bigger entity, the planner must understand enough about that bigger entity to assure that the plan can function properly and effectively within its setting.

At the conclusion of the review of the basic considerations there should be a summary document in which the essence of the topics reviewed and their relationship to what is planned are acknowledged. Group process techniques are frequently employed to work with staff or committee members to assist them in arriving at a consensus. In some approaches to planning, especially planning in program areas, a document referred to as a "we agree" statement has been used. The key items that affect the planning effort upon which the planners have agreed are summarized in the "we agree" statement. For major program planning efforts, the "we agree" statement in operational planning serves the same basic purpose that the "we agree" statement does in strategic planning. If the operational planning is done without a prior strategic planning process, the "we agree" statement becomes an important step to complete. If strategic planning is done, the bulk of the thought process and consensus building has been completed and documented. The practice of developing a "we agree" statement can be a valuable step, and the documentation can be used throughout the entire planning process as guiding principles or basic assumptions upon which subsequent planning steps can take place.

The "we agree" statement prepared at the conclusion of a review of basic considerations, which may impact upon what is being planned, should be expressed in sufficiently broad terms so minutia do not become the molehill that obstructs the view of the mountain. Consensus needs to be reached by employing group process techniques on the major items to be included in a "we agree" statement.

As the subsequent steps in the operational planning process unfold, the person in charge or responsible for facilitating the process must use the "we agree" statement as a working document. Discipline is required by the planning team members, who must adhere to the basic considerations upon which consensus has been reached. The leader of the planning process should be accountable for promoting group adherence to the "we agree" statement. If, as the planning process unfolds, it becomes evident that a plank in the "we agree" statement is missing or incorrectly stated, the planning team must review the materials covered in the consideration of basic principles and environmental issues and revise the "we agree" statement so that internal consistency can be maintained. If staff members involved in the process ignore or behave in a manner that contradicts "we agree" statements, the leader of the process must exact the discipline of adherence.

Internal consistency is achieved when each step in the operational planning process is kept in harmony with all other segments in the process. In other words, if it is specified by state law that the secondary school curriculum should include a course dealing with the history of the state and if we assume that legal requirements were acknowledged in the "we agree" statement, it would be incumbent upon the planners of a total secondary school curriculum to include the state history course. Internal consistency assures that each part of a plan is kept in tune with all other parts of the system. Maintaining internal consistency is a part of the discipline required for good operational planning.

Internal consistency is based on a concept from systems theory; when incongruence or a contradiction is found in a system, it must be corrected, or the system may become dysfunctional.

If internal consistency is not understood or is not maintained in an operational planning effort, the likelihood of a successful outcome is diminished to roughly zero. The need for internal consistency seems to be so obvious that a person may wonder why such a topic even needs to be mentioned; however, since there have been such frequent illustrations in which the discipline of maintaining internal consistency was overlooked, one may safely conclude it is not as obvious as one might think. A common example of failing to maintain internal consistency can be found in the number of innovative programs that have been introduced in school systems. In such innovative programs, one set of outcomes was listed; when it came time for evaluation, no evaluation was conducted or an inappropriate measure was applied that did not measure specified outcomes. When such inconsistencies have occurred, the end results have generally been less than enlightening.

The discipline of planning is an essential ingredient in the planning process. Planners are more successful when they first understand the concepts embodied in the operational planning process and are capable of adhering to those concepts. Planners need to understand that the theory underlying planning has generated concepts that can serve as a guide. Second, planners must demonstrate they have the discipline to apply what is known about planning to the process rather than forging ahead blindly. Third, planners need to understand the value of data-based decision making so that plans are constructed on sound knowledge and not whimsical preferences, wishful thinking, or political expediencies. Fourth, in the discipline of planning, the planner must understand the human factor. Planning is not mechanistic; planning frequently requires the input of people. Consequently, those persons responsible for planning must utilize effective ways to capitalize on human potential. As suggested above, the discipline of planning demands internal consistency in the planning process. While the list of dos and don'ts could be expanded regarding the discipline required for effective planning, many planning efforts fail because the planners do not demonstrate the will and the discipline required to develop a sound plan. Idiosyncratic impressionism may suffice as a substitute for good planning in some isolated instances, but over the long term if planning is to be successfully concluded and generate desired results, the planners will have to understand and adhere to the discipline required in the planning process.

Clarify Goals

Clarifying goals is another part of the planning process that is so abundantly obvious it seems it can be taken for granted. Experience, like a mirror, can reflect or reveal some flaws that exist in the reality of practice. It is not unheard of for goals to be ambiguous or for staff members to lack agreement on what they wish to accomplish. There are instances when "everyone jumps on a horse and rides off in a different direction." According to one concept from systems theory, everything must serve a purpose, and once an entity ceases to serve a purpose, it will be set aside for something of value. If a planning project is to reach fruition and serve a productive purpose, those persons who are involved in the planning process must have a clear definition of what they wish to accomplish.

Just as the second step in strategic planning is the clarification of mission, the second step in operational planning is the clarification of goals. In some operational planning efforts that are related directly to strategic planning, the goal or goals may be predetermined. In such cases, the planner is given the mandate to develop an operational plan that will implement one or more of the goals generated in the strategic planning process. But even in situations where a goal of a strategic plan is being operationalized, all persons involved must understand the goal as well as the basic considerations of the platform on which the operational planning is to take place. If people do not see the goal clearly and with understanding, it is unlikely they will make great strides toward achieving the goal.

Many goals to be achieved through operational planning are not created at the strategic planning level, just as many operational plans are not an outgrowth of a strategic plan. The innumerable kinds of planning efforts undertaken all require goal setting. A needs assessment may be done in the first step of goal setting when basic considerations are reviewed. In some instances, a goal may be totally clear; in other situations goals have to be stated, revised, and brought into focus.

Goals should be stated or specified in terms that make them achievable. Goals should not be confused with process. For example, in more than a few schools, concerned educators have wanted to enhance the computer curriculum so that pupils could be more knowledgeable about technology or understand the application of computers. In the educators' quest for achievement in the realm of computer competence on the part of their pupils, they boldly announced their goal was to have a computer laboratory in place and operating by a specified date. To suggest the establishment of a computer lab as a goal is indeed questionable. To propose the establishment of a computer lab as a strategy to achieve a goal of improving the knowledge and skill of students in the area of computers might be defensible or appropriate. The establishment of a computer lab would, however, be appropriate only if the educators determined how the lab would contribute to the goal and the specified outcomes in the area of computers in the educational setting.

Goals need to be congruent with the mission of the institution. When goals have been set in an operational planning effort, a review of those goals as they are juxtaposed to the mission statement is needed. There is also the need to consider goals against the "we agree" statement so that internal consistency is maintained. Goals, whether derived from a strategic planning process or generated as a direct response to a felt need, are broad statements reflecting the purpose that is to be accomplished. A goal constitutes a general target to be reached. By specifying a goal, all persons involved are told where to go.

Specify Measurable Outcomes and Priorities

Goals, once stated, can be applied as outcome statements. A major industry moved into a community; an expansion of the population and an increased enrollment in the school system of approximately 20 percent were anticipated. Board of education members set a goal to provide the best quality educational program they could with the available resources so current students and those coming into the district would experience a quality education. Board members stated they did not want to experience a downswing in the educational program because of an expanded enrollment. Four strategies were identified to reach their goal. One strategy was to implement a more vigorous and focused plan to recruit and develop quality staff to meet future needs. A second strategy was to review program needs and make revisions to assure the curricular needs of pupils were being met. A third strategy was to involve parents in the schooling process in an effort to foster better attendance, higher levels of achievement, and more positive attitudes among pupils. A final strategy was to expand and improve the facilities in the district to ensure that all pupils and staff were appropriately housed.

If the strategy of expanding and improving facilities is used as an illustration, the plan could be extended so that measurable outcomes would be stated. For example, through enrollment projections, a need for a specified number of additional classrooms could be specified, to be used by elementary school, middle school, or high school pupils. Through the enrollment projections, the need for a new elementary school or the addition of rooms in old elementary schools could be determined. A determination could also be made that additions to the existing middle schools were warranted and that an addition to the senior high school facilities would be required. Such needs could be stated as measurable outcomes. Measurable outcomes would specify what was to be accomplished.

When one moves from one planning team to another, the content of what is to be accomplished may differ significantly, while a strong similarity may be demonstrated in the approach. If one moves from the facilities planning team to observe those who were planning for ways to involve the parents in the educational process, which was the third outcome in the above illustration, some interesting differences would be observed; at the same time, some similarities in the process would be perceived. Recall that the third strategy was to develop a plan to involve parents in new dimensions to foster improved attendance, achievement and attitudes of pupils. Conceivably, outcomes could be identified that would point to the establishment of parenting clinics, an increase in the degree of participation of parents in the schooling process, an enhancement in the level of expectations for student outcomes, the establishment of a balance between cocurricular activities and academic work, the improvement of school attendance and pupil achievement, and ultimately an increase in the success of students in postsecondary educational and work endeavors. In each case, the outcomes would specify what was to be accomplished.

Outcomes should not only specify what is to be accomplished but also define the conditions or standards to be met in the accomplishment of specified outcomes. The preparation of instructional outcomes, as specified by Mager[1] some years ago, gained popularity for curriculum developers. The concept of specifying standards to be achieved in various forms of planning has applicability. In the area of noninstructional planning, those who have developed management by objectives (MBO) have provided a structure for stating outcomes in such a way that they are measurable.

Determine Criteria for Evaluation

Once what is to be accomplished or what measurable outcomes are to be achieved has been determined, the establishment of criteria for evaluation should be easy. Shouldn't it? Oh, if it were so! The establishment of criteria for evaluation of outcomes is a complex task, and when the actual process of assessing the results is undertaken, it becomes even more difficult. (In fact, this is such a complex area that in many instances there has been no evaluation of selected programs or planning efforts in school systems.)

Systems theory has been drawn upon to suggest that as one entity is related to another, all parts within the system must function effectively if the system is to survive. Any subsystem must function in harmony with the larger system of which it is a part. Evaluation and feedback subsystems are required to provide assurances that a system and all its parts are functioning.

The idea of considering criteria for evaluation at an early stage in the planning process was suggested by Banathy in his book entitled *Instructional Systems.*[2] Banathy presented concepts for planning instructional programs and emphasized the validity and applicability of proposing evaluation criteria immediately following the determination of measurable outcomes for almost all operational planning efforts.

There seems to be a natural inclination on the part of some planners not to develop evaluation criteria. The omission of evaluation criteria can be disastrous to a planning project. While succumbing to natural inclinations to avoid establishing criteria for evaluation may not be immediately fatal to the planner, it can bring about an untimely and premature end to a project. Even two or three planning failures may not be fatal to a school administrator, but sooner or later the embarrassment of collapsing projects will result in a sense of urgency to contact a placement office. The first of several hazardous inclinations is not to identify planning criteria until after the implementation stage of a project. Another inclination, once the project has reached the implementation stage, is to say, ''Oh, to hell with it. We are very busy doing a lot of important things, and so the evaluation can wait." Another frequently employed avoidance technique is to say, "Well, you know, you can't really tell, er, ah, well, no evaluation is perfect." And, of course, there are situations where no evaluation of a project has taken place, no data have been gathered, and no analysis has been made to determine if outcomes were reached; yet, the results are reported as "very satisfactory." Evaluation is difficult and expensive and takes know-how; however, it is essential if educators are to be able to improve programs and demonstrate accountability.

The question may logically be asked, "Why take time right after determining outcomes to set evaluation criteria when the project has not even been implemented?" This is a good question, and it was thoughtful of someone to ask it so that an answer can be provided.

The first reason for considering evaluation early in the planning effort is to develop a mental set—to think evaluation. Educational results have been perceived as lacking in the eyes of the public and the media. Educators often exchange views of the good qualities of educational programs and are very convincing with one another. What leaders in education have to do is convince the public about the quality of education—not themselves. One way to convince, inform, or educate the public is to present solid evaluation results so all can see the quality of the educational effort and product. Evaluation is one strategy that can be used in the effort to inform the public. To gather the needed evaluation to present the full picture to the public requires forethought, not afterthought—thus the need to think evaluation in a proactive stance.

Educators are continually confronted with the problem of limited resources. On the one hand, there are restrictions or limits placed on the total budget amount that is raised each year for financing a local school district. At the same time, there are practices, at least in most bureaucracies, that are carried on year after year simply because they have been done year after year. It is very difficult to terminate or cut back a program that is embedded in a bureaucracy. Suggestions have been made that it is more difficult to cut back on some phase of a bureaucracy than it is to close a neighborhood school. Be that as it may, when there are limited resources and at the same time departments or programs within the organization (bureaucracy) that could be cut, the chief executive officer should have appropriate data for decision making. For effective allocation or reallocation of resources and the demonstration of accountability, information is needed. Information may be gathered in terms of many program and budget decisions by appropriate evaluation efforts. Thus, again, we have the need to think evaluation.

For various types of assessment there is a need for predata and postdata to be gathered and analyzed. By formulating the criteria for evaluation early in the process, educational leaders are given time to start the predata collection phase of evaluation. Only a real magician can come up with pretest or preproject assessments if no consideration is given to the question of evaluation until after the project has been implemented. While it may be possible to go back into past records and develop a posthoc research design, the potential of an adequate assessment is greatly reduced or potentially lost if no attention is given to the criteria for evaluation at the appropriate time. For projects that will benefit from pretest types of assessment, someone should think evaluation early in the process.

Not all evaluation comes in the form of a standardized achievement test. Projects that are planned for constructing facilities certainly do not yield to an assessment by the use of an achievement test. Every planning effort will have unique assessment requirements that need to be tailored so as to provide information to those responsible for planning and implementation. Consequently, every major project needs to have planners who think evaluation, who determine criteria for evaluation, and who develop the evaluation strategies that will provide information about the process and the product.

Evaluation needs to be perceived as an ongoing effort. The development of evaluation criteria should begin just as soon as the measurable outcomes are established in a planning project.

Once a planning team is brought into the domain of the evaluator and efforts are made to arrive at criteria for evaluation, two points should be considered. First, it is helpful to have a person(s) who knows assessment techniques. Volumes have been written regarding the evaluation of instructional programs. There are computer programs to manage integrated data bases and to assist in analyzing data, formulas, and sophisticated data collection procedures. To utilize the considerable array of techniques and assessment tools available, one needs the guidance of a knowledgeable person. The second consideration may sound something like a gross contradiction of everything that has been said regarding evaluation up to this point; however, it is often a reality. The point is that judgments will be called upon to limit the possible approaches to evaluation. Once a team starts to develop criteria for evaluation, the members can easily become so enthusiastic that they want to evaluate everything. Well, everything cannot be evaluated even if there were time and resources. Consequently, planners will be faced with the necessity of determining, on a selective basis, what will be evaluated, by what criteria, and by what method.

List Options

Options need to be identified, sorted, and organized that will enable a planning team to achieve the desired outcomes that have been established for a given project. Clearly, options will be chosen that are considered appropriate for the accomplishment of specified outcomes. That procedure is only common sense, isn't it? Well, as common as it may seem and as sensible as it obviously is, such is not always the case. A brief account of a planning effort that took place in an elementary school can illustrate the fact that inappropriate options are sometimes proposed. A building principal and her staff were, in the early 1980s, undertaking a planning effort to improve the computer education curriculum in their building. When they first met, they had not considered all factors that could influence or shape what they would be doing with computers in their school. They had not yet determined, as they did later, that what they sought in the way of outcomes was a pupil population that could demonstrate "a greater awareness of what computers are and how they work, a familiarity with the major components of a microcomputer, entry-level skill in operating microcomputers, and an awareness of what place computers play in the workplace and in entertainment in our society." (Please remember that the time was in the early 1980s and that the school from which this illustration was taken had one microcomputer, no staff members who had more than one introductory workshop in the use of microcomputers, and only a few items of computer software available in the school.) As the staff members gathered to discuss the development of a computer curriculum for their school, one teacher immediately held up Bank Street Writer, a software package designed specifically for elementary school children as an entry-level word processing package. The teacher explained enthusiastically what a wonderful software package Bank Street Writer was and decreed it was just the thing they needed for every pupil in the school. Upon careful examination of needs, the constraints that were present at the time (one computer, no staff with more than limited exposure to micros, and virtually no software), and the fact that there were no specified outcomes and certainly no criteria for assessment, the introduction of Bank Street Writer was premature. It may have been an excellent program, but it did not meet the needs of the staff and students and was an inappropriate option in that particular planning effort. Perhaps in another planning effort and another setting, with different constraints, Bank Street Writer could have been a very appropriate option. When one is planning, there is often a compulsion to select an option that is appealing for one reason or another but for which there is not a good fit between needs or desired outcomes and the option in question. In like manner, there is often a temptation to list and ultimately select one option. To list and choose only one option are sometimes essential and appropriate, but more often than not listing only one option is a needless restriction. As a generalization, planners should list as many reasonable options as possible and examine each option to measure its fit in terms of desired outcomes.

Sequence Options (Tasks)

When a planning team has determined what options are to be employed in carrying out the project undertaken, the next task is to list the options (tasks) in the most judicious or appropriate sequence. The sequencing of options will be different for every project, as can be seen in the sequence of options and activities in a building project as contrasted to planning and conducting a basketball tournament. Virtually every planning effort is intended to have a starting and an ending point, and a list of things has to be accomplished in some sequence to achieve desired or specified outcomes.

Various techniques have been developed to enable planners to depict and communicate the specifics of a plan to people who will have to review and approve the plan and to those who have to carry out various portions of the plan. Diagrams of assorted types have been used to enable the planner and those with whom the planner wishes to communicate to conceptualize the total concepts, its parts, and the interrelationships of the different parts of the plan. Selected diagramming techniques are presented in Chapter 10.

The sequencing of tasks, particularly on large projects, can become very complex. The manner in which the plan is presented becomes of major importance to the planner and those with whom the planner is trying to communicate and translates into a major management tool for the orchestration of resources of various kinds. The management of prime resources, which include time, people, space, information, and materials, can be a monumental undertaking in major planning efforts. The managment of resources and the coordination of all facets of a planning project are demanding. When good managers can manipulate a host of resources and coordinate a complex effort, the result can be magnificent. By contrast, when inadequate planning takes place—well, let us simply afford the reader the opportunity to use his or her imagination or draw upon past experience to tell that sad story.

Pilot, Field-Test, Simulate, Implement

There are various ways to begin a project. The choice among the options of piloting, field-testing, simulating, or going immediately to full implementation is determined by a number of factors, including the best judgment of the planners. If a new reading program is being introduced in a school, there may be considerable value in piloting the program before full implementation. By contrast, if new construction is being contemplated, a pilot program should probably not be considered. While the nature of the project may have a major influence on how it is started, there is also considerable latitude for discretion on the part of the planner.

A *pilot project* is often recommended for programs in which there may be perceived risks or major costs. At other times, when planned programs contain a high level of emotionalism, there could be some definite benefits to a pilot project in preference to a full-blown implementation effort. In some instances, particularly when staff training or renewal may be involved, a pilot project can be used to demonstrate the strengths and weaknesses of a newly proposed program.

A pilot project can be used effectively to reduce the risk and cost factors in a project. Since a pilot project is generally limited in scope, patrons can often be more easily involved and their understanding and ultimately their support can be enlisted by giving them opportunities to be observers of a pilot effort. Pilot efforts that incorporate instructional programs also afford the planners an opportunity to select staff members, rather than using staff members who are not prepared or have no interest. Pilot efforts are often employed when implementing a research design in which there are a control group and an experimental group. When a sophisticated research design is warranted, the pilot effort can enable the planners and evaluators to control several variables present in the pilot process.

A *field test* is a common way to try out a new idea that is being planned. A field test can be used to determine the effectiveness of a wide range of "things" and "processes." If a new computerized program was being made available for each building in a district, the program could be field-tested in selected schools and, if results are satisfactory, the planning and the use of the software and procedure could be extended to the entire district or region involved in considering the new product. While a field test is similar to a pilot test in some respects, a field test commonly includes a wider number of persons or processes. A field test may also be less structured and formalized for research purposes than a pilot study. Like a pilot study, a field test should include a means of collecting information and feedback so that when the test is completed, the interested parties will know if they wish to continue testing or want to implement or terminate the project.

Simulations are used to test a process or a product in a setting that is not real but that simulates reality. Simulation, as a means of testing, has been employed by industry, the military, and various social agencies in very effective ways. A simulation may often be a scaled-down version or a prototype. Shipbuilders have for centuries used models of ships to test their designs and to determine the best way to construct a hull or to install rigging. Planners, through the use of computers, can simulate various procedures and test various inputs. The question, What if? has been moved from the realm of speculation to a condition in which people can see the results on a computer when new input is introduced. Perhaps one of the most common forms of simulation is found in the negotiation process when the questions are asked, What if the salary schedule were increased by 5 percent? or What if the benefits package were increased by .05 percent? Computer programs have for some time been employed to provide the immediate answers to the "what if" questions regarding salary schedules in local school districts. Computer programs can be used to analyze bus routes in a school district, and the program can be manipulated to answer the "what if" questions about forming different routes, changing routes, or the timing of bus runs. Computer spreadsheets have become a tool for budget projections and planning; through their use, flexibility and the ability to provide almost instant answers to the "what if" question in budget planning have resulted. Enrollment projections can be manipulated to provide information to planners as they work with changing population patterns. Planners can determine projected enrollments if a factory employing a given number of persons is brought into the district. The "what if" questions could be processed to give various options for consideration, and planners could develop various scenarios to accompany the patterns of enrollment projections generated with the assistance of a computer. The computer has expanded the possibilities in the realm of simulations in numerous ways.

Implementation is called for in numerous planning efforts. In cases in which there is actually little or no opportunity to run a pilot study, to field-test a product or function, the planner is faced with the prospects of a full-blown implementation.

Implementation involves doing and moving on from the planning activities to the realm of reality. As suggested earlier, if a building program is involved, the facility is planned, constructed, officially accepted from the contractor, and occupied. Planning a building is in obvious contrast to planning and testing efforts to begin a new payroll deduction system, which could be field-tested, modified, and tested again before full implementation is considered. In a building program, if the school district officials accept a new facility and occupy it, they are, as the saying goes, "stuck with it"—they have to live with it, like it or not. A person does not have to visit with a great number of school superintendents at a national conference to discover there are some who, when discussing a facility that is relatively new, will comment, "If I had it to do over again, I'd do things differently. I'd . . ." Full implementation does not afford the luxury of test-driving every project like a new car. Consequently, planning projects for which there is no opportunity to pilot, field-test, or simulate outcomes may involves a higher degree of risk. As a general observation, there may be a tendency to move to full implementation too readily when it would have been preferable to pilot, field-test, or simulate a project.

Evaluate

The evaluation process is initiated, or should be initiated, in the mind of the planner early in the planning process. Actually, the criteria for evaluation should be recommended for consideration immediately following the determination of measurable outcomes. Once the criteria for evaluation and preliminary considerations for assessment are given early in the planning process, the stage is set for the evaluation process. The planner who gives the necessary consideration to the evaluation criteria at the appropriate time in the planning process has made certain that an adequate design for assessing the process and the outcomes can be achieved.

Much has been written about how to conduct an evaluation of a program or a process. The concepts, the procedures, and the instruments for conducting evaluations become the tools of the planner. Most assessment efforts can be straightforward and uncomplicated. There are, of course, instances when highly sophisticated and complex data collection and analysis procedures are required to determine the success or failure of a given project. As a general rule, however, assessment can be conducted with straightforward and direct kinds of questions and with data that are understandable and can be analyzed with clear and uncomplicated procedures.

Evaluation should, in most situations, involve the collection of information about how the process worked. There have, from time to time, been debates over the importance of collecting information about how a process worked. Suggestions have been made that it does not matter whether people like the way something works or not; what matters is the outcome or the product. The debate has also splintered off and resulted in the question of whether there should be goal-related assessment or goal-free assessment. When all the sides of the debate about assessment are listed and the question is asked, Which of these forms of assessment is important? the answer may be yes.

Process feedback is important simply because valuable information can be provided about whether something is working or why something may not be working. When it is known why a process or project is not working, attention can be directed to making adjustments or fixing what is not working.

Product, or outcomes, is important. The only way one can determine if a specified outcome is reached is to collect data regarding the proposed outcome and how well it was achieved. Outcomes can involve much more than achievement scores. As an illustration, in an office in which there was a sizable staff responsible for the development of instructional materials, a need to improve quality, to increase productivity, and provide improved services to instructional personnel was determined. At the same time there was a desire to keep costs at or below the level at which they had been operating. As the plan was developed to meet the specified outcomes, a commitment was made to use an office computer network to best serve the needs of the staff of the production department. The staff was trained to use the newly acquired software and hardware, the office network was installed, staff members were given support, and new routines developed. The end result was that productivity actually increased as professional personnel developed and revised instructional materials with the newly acquired software and hardware. The laser printers and reproduction equipment produced instructional materials that were clearly of a superior and more professional quality. The turnaround time for production of instructional materials was reduced. Because of the manner in which the professional staff responsible for the development of instructional materials could work with their new equipment, there was a reduction of clerical staff that more than offset the costs associated with the newly planned and implemented approach.

The above illustration can be used to suggest that for one to assess the outcomes of a major change in an educational institution, it would not take a wizard or a sophisticated evaluator to determine that such a program was achieving its specified outcomes. Obviously, if some doctoral candidates chose to make an in-depth study of the attitudes or perceptions of involved personnel, such an analysis could be done. It is not necessary, however, to spend copious amounts of money and employ the most complex statistical processes ever devised to accomplish many assessments.

Revise, Stop, Go

When the evaluation process of a project has been completed, persons who are responsible for the effort should be provided the information needed to make decisions regarding the future of the project. Planners need to be persons who are capable of using data in the decision-making process. The time of the benevolent autocrat has been demonstrated as inadequate—even dysfunctional and counterproductive. No longer can one person, relying upon a personal perception against a backdrop of an idiosyncratic values base, make all the decisions for an organization. The tools are available to pull together vast amounts of information. The expectations of staff members have changed, and many significant individuals are recognized as having a stake in decision making. The evaluation process, in which the processes are explored and the product is measured, is one approach for providing information upon which decisions can be made regarding the future of a project. Based on the data gathered from the evaluation, decisions can be made regarding the need to terminate a project, modify it, or continue it.

For evaluations to furnish data that are useful and are seen by staff as providing important information, those responsible for implementing a project need to demonstrate that the results of the evaluation effort are taken seriously. In a major school district in which there have been numerous efforts to improve and change the curriculum and extensive planning involving a considerable investment of time and resources, the staff may have learned that "pilot programs" and "field-testing" were in fact not that at all. The staff members may have learned that it doesn't matter one whit what the results of a field test are because once the boss field-tests something, it will be implemented across the board the following year, regardless of the field test. The cynicism contained in the comments of frustrated staff members may reflect the practice of disregarding feedback and evaluation results: "The boss had his mind made up the minute it was agreed upon to field-test the new curriculum." The effect of such decisions, which are not based on data, can be negative in two dimensions. First, there is the possibility that a poor decision is going to be made. Second, staff soon learn that their efforts and investment of their professional expertise were not regarded as important; consequently, they do not feel valued and their dedication and future investment are diminished.

Naturally, persons who have planned a major project, whether it be a building, an administration process, or a new curriculum, want the project to be a success. The Hawthorne effect is alive and well in most projects. (In fact, planners need to capitalize on the power that can be generated through the Hawthorne effect. Good planners will catch the crest of the Hawthorne wave and ride it to their desired outcomes like a surfer on the crest of a breaker at the beach.) By nature, persons who have planned a project want their investment to come to fruition. There are expectations that all planners have for their projects. Consequently, planners want to look for the good and explain away the limitations that emerge in a project. To avoid the natural inclination to perceive only the good in one's project, one needs to rely upon data for decisions about the future of any project. The need for objectivity is why it is often recommended that a project be evaluated by a third, disinterested party.

The highest level of objectivity, supported by the best possible database, is essential at the point in a project where the decision is made to terminate the project, to revise it, or to continue it. A data-based, objective decision should never be avoided, just as there should be no preconceived notions that a project should or should not continue. The decision point that is reached when the future of a project is to be determined calls for tough-minded decision makers who can withstand political pressures, bandwagons, or emotional calls to preserve tradition.

Feedback

The feedback loop is the most pervasive segment of a planning process. The instant there are two or more components to a planning process, a demand is generated for the flow of information from one segment of the process to the other segment(s). The concept of interrelatedness is reiterated through systems theory. When planners conceptualize the components of a plan, they go through a process that identifies the mission and related goals in strategic planning or the purpose and goals in operational planning. The process then breaks the total purpose for conducting the planning project into its major parts. The breaking of a project into its major parts, or the mission analysis, allows the planner to subdivide the planning process even further into the functions and tasks that are to be accomplished in order to carry out the planned project. The feedback loop is the means of keeping all segments of a planning effort in synchronization and the communication system that keeps the left hand informed of what the right hand is doing.

A feedback loop performs several essential functions in the planning process. Feedback is the channel of communication that makes it possible for planners to maintain internal consistency in a planning effort. Major projects, especially those extending over a considerable period of time, may be impacted by a changing environment, such as a new state law pertaining to education. The feedback loop is the channel through which outside information can be brought to the planning process and adjustments made to accommodate the newfound information. In most major planning efforts, miscalculations or wrong perceptions can occur. The feedback loop is the device that can be used to make the needed adjustments to correct errors or miscalculations. In general, the feedback loop connects all segments of a planning effort and is the catalyst that makes the gestalt emerge. The feedback loop generates the dynamics of the system and is the nervous system of the plan. All the subtleties of a feedback loop and how it can be called upon by the planner are hard to comprehend, but good planners are automatically adept at calling upon and capitalizing on the benefits of a feedback loop.

SUMMARY

Many planning models have been presented in the literature and employed with varying degrees of sophistication in practice. Concepts derived from systems theory carry with them some planning "truisms" that, if followed, can be of benefit to planners. Strategic planning is not totally unique and different from operational planning. Clear similarities in strategic planning models and approaches to operational planning can be found. Within operational planning, the concepts that will provide direction for planning a building are similar to the concepts used in planning a curriculum. Various planning models have been conceptualized as an outgrowth of systems theory. Planning models, like virtually all models, are only crude and simplified representations of reality and therefore cannot be taken and used by planners as absolutes in a literal sense. Any planning model must be understood for what it is and what value it can serve to planners. Planners, like good musicians, must be able to deal with fundamentals. But planners must be able to add the artistry, the understanding, and even the skill to improvise when appropriate without destroying the integrity of the process.

NOTES

1. Robert F. Mager, *Preparing Instructional Objectives,* 2nd ed. (Belmont, California: Fearon, 1975).
2. Bela H. Banathy, *Instructional Systems* (Belmont, California: Fearon, 1968).

5

The Mind

INTRODUCTION

As planners approach the complex set of tasks involved in the planning process, there are various skills and tools they need in their work. Some of the planning skills involve the use of mechanistic or technological devices and mathematical formulas, while others require an understanding of people and group processes. Some tasks are highly demanding of a person's conceptual skills; in other instances routine tasks are included in the process. In some facets of planning, there is a need to be able to access large sources of data or to tap major data banks to gain sufficient information to make decisions, while in other situations a call for judgment emerges—a solitary decision made by an individual planner. Planning can involve one person who conceptualizes an entity that is soundly based on data, and at other times planning can encompass large numbers of people in a highly politicized setting. Planning can be very direct and involve one person preparing a single lesson plan, or it can encompass multiple, districtwide needs and complex demands in a strategic setting.

The planner, wielding the available tools, must of necessity be able to span a wide range of functions and be capable of performing a multitude of very different tasks. In the next few chapters, some of the more common tools with which planners work will be presented. The list of tools is not an exhaustive compilation. The list includes those tools that have been identified as most frequently used by planners and those individuals who have studied various aspects of the planning process. While the tools are presented with obvious focus and limitations, planners must select and adapt the tools to meet the needs in any given situation. Planning tools, like any set of tools, can be misused if placed in the hands of an uninformed or unskilled individual. Knowing how to pick up a hammer or how to turn on a computer and call up a software package is not sufficient to demonstrate expertness in the application of the hammer or the computer. Whether the tool is a very simple tool or a complex tool, the planner has to be able to demonstrate appropriate skills in its application if positive results are to be achieved.

THE MOST POWERFUL TOOL

Of all the tools at the disposal of the planner, the mind is the most significant. All theory, concepts, planning models, computers, and formulas are for naught without the mind of the planner. The mind is something over which individuals can, if they choose, exert a degree of influence or control. Individuals have a choice in terms of what they choose to do with their intellects. Those persons who choose to take destiny in their own hands and to plan and shape the future can be the planners and the builders. Those persons who see no further than tending to the immediate needs that come to them day by day and who have no vision of what could be will undoubtedly never experience the world of the planner or the meaning of what it is to be a planner. While a person can plan to manage or to maintain the status quo and daily routine, the essence of planning transcends the limits of control and management. The concept of building is implicit in planning. What is planned and built may be a physical structure, a process or procedure, a curriculum or instructional process, or even an entire social institution. A parallel, implicit corollary is implied in the nature of planning—the entity being planned will be better than what was available before the planning effort. Being a planner means numerous things; one who is the planner must take command of his or her mental capability and demonstrate the will to accomplish and build.

The most outstanding examples of planning have been accomplished by people of vision. Planners are people who are also willing to invest of themselves and take a risk. Two great cities in North America stand out as examples of what can be done by people of vision who are not only visionaries but builders. The cities of Pittsburgh, Pennsylvania, and Portland, Oregon, are living examples of what can be accomplished, on a grand scale, when there are people who can see beyond the cracked pavement of a city on any given day and envision and conceptualize something better. One of the things that made the rebuilding of Pittsburgh and Portland even more fascinating is the fact that both cities were in the depths of a severe economic depression at the time the planning and rebuilding took place. While politicians throughout the nation were campaigning on state and national platforms that encouraged cuts and reductions and appealed to voters for their support at the polls by presenting proposals calling for retreat and budget decreases, leaders in Pittsburgh and Portland were doing the seemingly impossible—they were rebuilding their cities.

Great planners have also demonstrated they have the will, the strength, and the dedication to move forward to accomplish their goals. Characteristics present in the composition of a successful planner are the will to see a job to completion, to work and invest in what is to be done, to stay the course, to show patience, and not to retreat. The terms *planner* and *builder* are, in this context, used synonymously. The plan is essential, but the plan has to be seen through to fruition; thus the planner also becomes the builder, just as it can be said great architects are, in a sense, builders. Builders must have the will to move ahead in spite of adversities in order to see a plan emerge as a product.

Many builders face cultural and bureaucratic obstructions that are supported by special interest groups or individuals who are steeped in tradition and appear to be intractable. Plans are no more than changing symbols unless they can be implemented. There is a growing knowledge base regarding change and how leaders can direct or manage change. Planners, to be successful, must be change agents; they must be students of human behavior and knowledgeable about how change takes place.

Change, especially change in highly bureaucratized agencies, is not only difficult to accomplish but risk-laden. Planners are forced into taking risks. Risk taking does not mean the planner becomes a wild-eyed, nonestablishment radical who charges forward with reckless abandon. It is counterproductive for a builder to be sacrificed in an initial high-risk effort that has been undertaken with little or no regard to present hazards. A deposed leader seldom can give leadership and direction—even if martyred. Stated another way, risks are essential; however, with sound planning in which the environment or setting is known and on which data are available, the planner can reduce risks and improve the footing upon which an effort is made. Administrators or planners must be able to keep their job to do their job. Sacrificing one's body on the first assault is not likely to achieve desired or needed results.

To cope judiciously with risks, planners are regularly called upon, especially in comprehensive or strategic planning efforts, to display political sensitivity. Being politically astute does not mean compromising one's principles. Politics, it has been suggested, is the art of compromise. The planner who is a person of conviction can distinguish between compromises that prostitute the process and compromises that can gain leverage through a principled effort. The planners with the political acumen to achieve constructive, win-win compromises based on principles and avoid political expediencies are the ones who have demonstrated the ability, when handed a lemon, to make lemonade.

Planning calls for discipline on the part of the planner. Those who would be planners must, like great musicians, know the fundamentals before they can achieve full mastery of their artistic talents. Planning is not an easy or frivolous activity; planning is a demanding process that requires those who are responsible to know the fundamentals and to adhere to the discipline required in that procedure. If planners become students of the planning process, there is no need for them to rediscover the wheel. Much information is available about the planning process, the tools, and the techniques required to plan successfully. Consequently, planners who are students of the discipline of planning can move further and faster than planners of previous generations, when much of the planning process had to be done by an intuitive or judgmental process.

Good planning requires sound judgment. Whether the definition of judgment is used that suggests it is the act of judging or the mental operation of comparing and discriminating and thus formulating knowledge of values and relations through mental formulation or whether judgment is defined as "common sense" or "horse sense," good planners have it.

Good planners work from a data base. In some instances, what took place in past decades in the educational establishment was based on opinion rather than upon a sound data base. As more data are available and as technology enables decision makers to collect and sort information at high speed, there is less need to plan based on opinion. In the future, as more data are stored in technologically accessed data banks and as artificial intelligence becomes a tool that has advanced to the application stage, planners will have even greater information resources upon which they can draw. Present and future planners who will be acknowledged for their success will be those who have the mentality to rely upon data in preference to grasping exclusively at their personal experience with its one degree of freedom.

There is a logic to the systems planning approach. The concepts present in systems planning suggest a logical and orderly process. The process of logic contains a flexibility that allows the planner to adjust the planning effort at any point in the entire effort. Dogmatism is not logical; thus, it does not have a place in the logic of systems planning.

Finally, a planner must know both the planning process and the area or topic—content—that is being planned. Generic planners can serve as facilitators for those planning in a given area, but specialists in the given area must ultimately consort with the generic planner if the planning is to be successful.

Planning calls for people working together who can capitalize on the combined mental capacity of those involved. The mind becomes the basic planning tool. Those who demonstrate the vision, who will take the needed risks, who possess the will, discipline, judgment, and the inclination to use data, who demonstrate the logic, and who know the planning process and the subject or area being planned are the planners most likely to succeed.

6

Futures and Trend Analysis

Planners cannot escape looking into the future. Various approaches are used to determine what lies ahead. In fact, there has been a strange fascination throughout recorded history in predicting what the future will bring. In the Old Testament of the Bible accounts of the prophets have been recorded, and the work of the prophets has also been referenced in the New Testament. The future has been told with crystal balls, playing cards, chicken bones, tea leaves—you name it. People not only have been fascinated with the future but have been willing to pay good money to be able to relax with some sense of security in the relative uncertainty that soothsayers have presented. The attraction with looking into the future has enabled astrologers to predict what a president should or should not do—for a sizable sum of money, of course! Readers of archaic documents have, with the passing of virtually every major historical event, been able to delve into ancient scripts and find obscure pronouncements that came from prophets who had predicted what happened. Some early prophets have actually enjoyed a rather high level of acceptance and recognition for their predictions. Nostradamus exemplifies the early prognosticators of renown. Nostradamus was born in France in 1503 in a Jewish family; he has been acclaimed as "the greatest of all prophets of the era of the Renaissance," as he wrote over 1,000 predictions in quatrains. People have endeavored to understand the quatrains of Nostradamus, and only after events that he had predicted have happened can his prowess as a prognosticator be appreciated.[1]

There is, however, more to looking into the future than idle, or even compulsive, curiosity. When planning for the future or, as some would suggest, when planning *the* future, one must know as much as possible about what that future holds in order to confront what is forthcoming in the most judicious way. There are all sorts of poems and catchy sayings about looking to the future; a great deal of the verbal glibness in such sayings may have value. Planners are, by their very nature as planners, future-oriented unless they are consciously "planning" to maintain the status quo and avoid the future. But even in the case of those who would plan to maintain the status quo, there is an awareness, or at least a concern, of the future that is translated into conscious efforts to avoid that future. Thus, with the obvious exception of those who plan to retreat to the past, planners and builders are future-oriented.

FUTURES STUDIES

Futures studies come under various labels. According to some specialists, the term *futurism* is most appropriate.[2] Simply stated, futurism is an effort to be as rational and insightful as possible regarding societal developments and trends that have the potential of affecting the planning process. The purpose for conducting futures research has been indicated as an effort to "cause change and to manage the future."[3] Enzer stated that the purpose for conducting futures research is to provide "greater insights into prospective developments and their interaction in a dynamic society."[4] Futurism is a means of gathering information to investigate trends, anticipate, and help leaders in a school system maintain a stance that will equip them with the readiness and ability to respond to the oncoming events of major importance, even if the arrival of those events cannot be precisely predicted or timed. Futurism should generate a range of alternatives for planners to consider. Through futures studies, educational leaders gain the edge needed to become proactive in selected areas rather than responding after the fact. Futurism is not, as used in this context, predicting what popular entertainer will have a baby in the coming year or identifying which political figure will become ill and leave office. Through futurism, one is given the ability to make predictions on a broad scope and to identify the potential impact on any given agency or the educational enterprise as a whole.

An illustration of a point made by some futurists can be drawn from the discussions regarding the world oil supply. For several decades, futurists have generally agreed there will be intensifying problems growing from the increasing world demand for fossil fuel and the limited, long-range supply available. Various predictions have been made about how long the fuel supply will last. At this point, there are two scenarios that emerge, each presenting a different set of alternatives. One set of futurists points to the dark side and indicates there will be a high probability of world conflict as nations vie for the precious black gold. Cold cities, massive unemployment, and widespread famine are predicted as hordes flee urban centers and "return to the land" to grow their food and carve out a new way of life—a life of basic survival. This theme has been reflected in novels as well as some documents generated by the people who study the issue of a limited supply of fossil fuel.

There are, however, writers who predict a very different set of circumstances growing out of the dwindling supply of fossil fuels. Some futurists suggest that more efficient and economical substitute fuels will be produced. The environment may be cleaner, and, with modifications in the economic and social structure, the world can be made to be a much more livable place.

A third scenario that has been posed points to nuclear devastation, as the globe is ravaged by wars in a death struggle over energy supplies. Greed has been predicted as the force that will ignite the fire of open battle. The battle will erupt at the site of an oil-producing area and explode like an unchecked brushfire on a hot summer's day, perhaps compounded by the unleashing of a nuclear confrontation.

Which view of the future is most accurate? In one sense, the gloom and doom version, as contrasted to the view of a new and more glorious world, may be set aside as being inappropriate. The important point that can be drawn from the futurists is that there will be an end to the fossil fuel supply and that humankind then has a choice: there can be war and destruction or a planned effort to build a new and better world without the massive consumption of fossil fuels. School personnel could choose to accept the gloom and doom side of the futurists' page and teach survival and war games. On the other hand, school leaders could structure the curriculum and the learning experiences to prepare the leaders of tomorrow to plan for and become constructive contributors to a future predicated on a shortage of fossil fuel but with an abundance of new and better ways of supporting an economy and social system. One stance will build hope; the other option would be to accept despair.

School leaders need to be alert to future studies. There is, quite obviously, some wisdom in building school facilities that are energy-efficient. If a newly constructed school facility is expected to last for 70 to 100 years, and it is known there will be a limited supply of fuel oil in a few decades, builders of facilities must look to a future in which there will be a limited fuel supply. There are numerous other views provided by futurists, who have pointed to a changing world that will have major and multiple influences upon schools. *Megatrends* (Naisbitt and Aburdene) was only one of many documents in which the authors pointed to movements or trends in our culture that should be considered major influences when planning for the education of infants, children, youth, and adults of all ages in our culture. Educational leaders need to keep an eye on the works of futurists. As the three major works of Toffler are considered, it is possible to track his view of the future in *Future Shock* (1970), *The Third Wave* (1980), and *Powershift* (1990). As Toffler noted in *Powershift*, various predictions he made in 1970 have come into being.[5] The writings of futurists cannot be dismissed with the rationalization, It never works out exactly like they say, so what difference does it make? Strategic planners in a local school district need to examine what is written by futurists and determine what direction they should face as they develop their mission and goals for building a better educational system.

The history of futures studies conducted in recent decades dates back to efforts by military leaders following World War II,[6] although there have been some writers who have traced futurism back to a period following the French Revolution.[7] It has been primarily since the 1960s, however, that futurism has experienced its main surge of popularity and the entry into the field of education. The Rand Corporation was a pioneer in futures and interdisciplinary policy studies. The Stanford Research Institute (SRI) was soon to follow with its future-oriented Educational Policy Research Center. By the end of the 1960s, futures studies were accepted by leaders in educational circles and applied to strategic planning.

The acceptance of futurism by educators, as well as by political and civic leaders (not to mention military, commerce, and industry personnel who drew upon futurists prior to educators' awakening to the value of future studies), has been predicated upon an awareness of several broad considerations. In fact, the awareness of selected conditions can be transformed into several imperatives, which include such topics as

1. the need to capitalize on the revolution in science and technology and to address the accompanying implications;
2. the need to acknowledge the enhanced power of humans over nature and the positive or negative consequences, depending upon how that power is used;
3. the need to acknowledge the definition of values that take into account the importance of a balance between rights and responsibilities and the ability to distinguish the difference between wants and needs;
4. the need to understand and capitalize on the emergence of a greater awareness of the significance of the human potential and the demand for freedom for people in all areas of the world, which grows smaller each day;
5. the need to comprehend the greater poignancy and awareness of the interrelatedness and interdependency of all people throughout the world;
6. the need to recognize that space and resources are limited and must be shared by the rapidly growing population of the world so every human being is afforded an opportunity to reach maturity and self-actualization and be a healthy, constructive person; and
7. the need to capitalize on the rapid expansion of the knowledge base, in both social and technical sciences, and our ability to access and analyze that knowledge as it becomes applicable to planning the future.

There has been, in addition to the imperatives listed above, a growing awareness of the passing of time as citizens of the world are carried forward to the threshhold of the third millennium. A surge of interest in the future has been detected that in turn has tended to create a greater degree of awareness and acceptance of the fact that the future is moving inexorably toward us minute by minute, day by day, and even century by century.[8] The speed with which changes are taking place is another factor creating a greater awareness on the part of vast numbers of persons. In past centuries, changes were slow, and people saw the world as being primarily stable. While there were some who "saw" changes and pointed to their implications, most of the time one generation was much the same as another generation in terms of day-to-day lifestyles and values. In the twentieth century, people have witnessed such rapid and far-reaching changes that a person who was born during the horse and buggy era lived and saw a man walk on the Earth's moon. Humankind has grown accustomed and indifferent to change. To be able to make predictions about what the future holds is to achieve a measure of control over that future.

In a nutshell, futurists rely upon historical perspectives and current data to analyze trends and arrive at a prediction of what is likely to transpire in the future and to approximate when events will take place. Being able to predict what may happen and when it is likely to take place places planners in a better position to create history, to control change, to build an environment as it can be, and not to accept things as they are. Consequently, the futurist can make a major contribution to the work of strategic planners.

There are three rather common and practical approaches to futures studies that are employed by planners. One is reading and studying the works of futurists; the second is employing the Delphi procedure; and the third is the use of scenarios.

PLANNERS AS STUDENTS OF THE FUTURE

Implicit in what has been stated previously is the fact that strategic planners in a school setting can clearly derive value from being students of futurists. In fact, all school planners, to a certain degree, need to be futurists by their own right. Educators need to keep abreast of the trends in a shrinking world and endeavor to understand the influence trends will have on society as a whole and upon the educational establishment. The fact that the future cannot be predicted with precision is actually all the more reason to study and keep in tune with what analysts and futurists are predicting. Being a student of future trends allows one's thoughts to prepare him or her for the future. If a person is constantly looking down at the feet of the present, it is unlikely that person will be able to take advantage of new and emerging opportunities that appear on the horizon. Educational leaders can keep tuned to the future by studying current events and the writings of futurists.

THE DELPHI TECHNIQUE

The Delphi technique was originally developed by personnel at the Rand Corporation in the 1960s. The Delphi process was designed to arrive at a consensus regarding the probable occurrence of a future event and the predicted timing of such an event, through a series of opinionnaires sent in fairly rapid succession to a panel of experts. The first opinionnaire is used to solicit predictions of future events. The second opinionnaire contains a composite list of the probable "future events" proposed by the experts and a summary of the topics and the time distributions; the median and the interquartile range, or the interval range containing 50 percent of the responses, are given. As experts respond to the second opinionnaire, they are asked to reconsider their original judgments regarding if and when the events are likely to occur and to revise their responses and give reactions if they wish to do so. If a given expert gives a response outside the quartile range, that person is asked to write a justification for the deviation. In the third opinionnaire, the same predicted future events are presented. The respondents are asked to examine the pattern of responses and the revised consensus of the experts. Based on that review, respondents are given the opportunity to revise their previous opinions.[9] The process is to foster communication, although not face-to-face, among the experts.

In its original form, the Delphi technique was designed to collect information from experts regarding a given topic, provide a means of pooling the collective judgment of the experts, avoid the influence of personalities or political influences within the group of experts, and gather information without the necessity of bringing all the experts together in one location. Developers of the Delphi intended it to be used as a scientific tool "to achieve a better understanding of the world and, thus, to develop valid theories concerning observable phenomena . . . to make conditional predictions of the consequences of alternative courses of action."[10] Developers of the Delphi technique saw social technology as an intellectual discipline that would move planning forward; expert judgments would be systematically elicited, and haphazard speculations regarding the future would be replaced. Rand personnel were convinced that an enormous amount of expertise existed in the social sciences, which could be systematically accessed, translated into valuable predictions, and applied to the urgent needs of society.[11] Personnel also perceived that a better and broader array of alternatives could emerge from the suggestions.

While the Delphi was originally designed to provide the predictions of a group of experts, it has since been modified and adapted to gather information from designated experts or opinion leaders in order to determine needs or present expectations. Thus, the Delphi is now used to gather information about what people think are desirable options or goals to be pursued.

In step one of the Delphi, the experts to be involved are selected. Two determinations need to be made: first, what is the area of expertise to be explored, and second, who are the experts in the discipline? Helmer suggested that the selection of "experts" was "usually made on the basis of what may vaguely be called their reputations."[12] A list of prospective expert participants may be obtained by asking leaders in a discipline to name the experts and to arrive at a pooled judgment regarding prospective participants. Typically, if leaders in a field are asked to name experts, a list of those persons most frequently acknowledged to have the reputation or expertise in the field will result. Persons most frequently named on the list can be invited or enlisted to participate.

Early in the history of the Delphi use, acceptance of unsuspecting experts was quite easily obtained. That situation has changed somewhat. Involvement in the Delphi process is time-consuming; as a consequence, some individuals have become reluctant to participate. The acceptance of experts and their full understanding of the time commitment are important; otherwise, as the process unfolds and the full impact of the time requirements for participation is felt by those involved, some of the participants may possible decline to continue to the conclusion of the study. The loss of participants can have a serious consequence on the study, and sometimes there is no full recovery or compensation. The amount of time required of a participant will naturally vary with the number of times to be considered. As a rule of thumb, experts can expect to invest an hour on each round.

In step two of the Delphi, the topics or issues from the panel of experts are solicited. Once an expert or opinion leader has accepted the invitation to be involved in a Delphi survey, that person is asked to provide a list of topics or issues related to the subject at hand. The person is also asked to provide a time frame as to when each topic, in his or her best judgment, may be expected to occur. An example that could be drawn from the general area of technology in education might be found in a response in which the issue or topic of artificial intelligence, with the capability of providing a synthesis or review of the literature on any topic related to education, is identified. The projected time frame for such a development might be specified as a period of time ranging from the year 2000 to 2010. When predictions are gathered from all participants, a composite listing of issues or predictions and of projected time frames is prepared. The composite listing will be used to construct an opinionnaire to collect the second round of information from the experts.

The process of asking experts to develop the list of key issues or predictions has been modified by developing topics or issues from a review of the literature. The basic results are similar; however, if the literature is thoroughly reviewed, it is possible to gain a wider scope of issues or topics than from the panel of experts or opinion leaders. As a generalization, if a Delphi study is being conducted with persons who are clearly recognized as experts in their field, it may be best to solicit first-round topics from such experts rather than from the literature. By contrast, if opinion leaders in a school district or a region are to be involved in a Delphi, it may be most appropriate to draw the initial list of issues or topics from the literature.

In step three of the Delphi, the instrument containing the original topics for consideration and the time predictions is sent to the participants. Respondents are asked to examine each item and give their judgments regarding the prediction on a seven-point scale. The items may be structured in such a way as to elicit various kinds of responses. For example, proposed measures may be presented, and respondents may be asked to indicate the "overall desirability" of each measure, the "effectiveness" of each measure if implemented, and the "probability" of each measure's being implemented. In another example, which could come from a Delphi survey to determine how opinion leaders view the topic of year-round school, participants could be asked for their judgments about the "desirability" of selected aspects of year-round school and what they perceived as the "impact" of the selected aspects of year-round school.

Respondents are asked to check their responses on a seven-point scale and to give comments justifying the reasons for their responses. The written comments become crucial; through this information, participants are able to communicate thoughts as well as simple reactions or responses to other participating experts. If some respondents fail to send back their marked opinionnaire, a follow-up will be necessary.

Experts may also be asked to indicate when they think certain events will occur. When such responses are solicited in a Delphi, a seven-point scale may not be appropriate. For example, a question may be asked experts about a topic that deals with the implementation of the voucher system and the closing of public schools. Estimates of public acceptance or the desirability of such a plan could be solicited by one scale. The judgment of experts concerning the implementation of such a plan could be elicited by another scale. A scale could also be constructed to obtain time estimates, such as 5- or 10-year intervals, and less specific and ordinal categories, such as "later than 50 years from now" and "never." The number of options on such a scale would differ from the suggested seven categories on other items.

In step four of the Delphi process, the responses to the first opinionnaire are compiled, and the median and the first and third quartiles for each response are determined. In some instances, means and standard deviations are also computed. In addition, the medians and quartiles of responses should be computed and plotted, and the comments should be summarized and synthesized so they can be included in the next opinionnaire as feedback information to respondents. In addition to the pattern of responses from all respondents, the response of a given respondent is marked on the second opinionnaire so the expert can see how his or her response compared with the responses of other respondents. The third opinionnaire is thus derived from the responses to the previous round of feedback.

In the fifth step of the Delphi, the third opinionnaire is sent to all participants with instructions for them to study each item and the pattern of responses given by peer experts as well as their previous individual answer. After reconsidering their answer and the comments given by other participants, they are asked again to mark their response. If a given respondent marks a response that is above or below the two middle quartiles shown in the pattern of responses, that person is asked to give a reason for his or her variance from the middle 50 percent of all other respondents.

The nature of the Delphi process starts to take effect following the answers given by the respondents at this juncture of the survey. Each respondent can see the total pattern of scores. Individual scores can be seen in comparison to the norms of the group, and the comments of the other participants can be studied so respondents can gain a clearer perception of other participants' thinking. This interaction of concepts and information, without the influence of any personality or authority figure, begins to reshape the pattern of responses, and a movement toward consensus can be detected in the total pattern of responses.

In summary, the first questionnaire is sent to experts, and they are asked for topics or issues to be considered, along with their predicted time frame of the occurrence of topics. In the second round of data collection, experts are requested to react to the collective list of topics, to make judgments about when they thought the item would occur, and to give a written rationale for their position. In the third instrument, the experts are asked to review their position along with the norm of the group of experts, to read the comments of other experts, and to reevaluate their own position.

In step six of the Delphi, the responses of all experts or opinion leaders received on the third opinionnaire are tabulated, the median and first and third quartiles are calculated, and a summary of all written comments is developed. The information collected in the third opinionnaire thus becomes the source of information for constructing the final opinionnaire.

In the seventh step of the Delphi, the final opinionnaire is sent to respondents, their responses are collected, and the results are analyzed. In the final opinionnaire, respondents are again instructed to consider each item, the pattern of responses from all other respondents, and the summary of comments as contrasted to their previous response. The respondents may leave their response the same on the final opinionnaire if they elect to do so, or they may modify their positions if they wish. As in the previous opinionnaire, each respondent is instructed to state briefly the reasons for his or her variation in the comments space of the opinionnaire.

Upon completing the opinionnaire, each respondent is instructed to return it, generally in a self-addressed envelope. In the last round of feedback, as in the previous rounds, a follow-up phone call or letter should be used to encourage respondents to complete and return opinionnaires. Obviously, a 100 percent response is ideal. Since the number of experts used in a Delphi generally is not large, a high rate of response becomes quite important.

In the eighth and final step of a Delphi, the results are analyzed, and the final report is prepared. There is no fixed format for presenting final results from a Delphi. Some requirements may be imposed on the analysis of data by the nature of the topic being explored and the number of different groups of respondents. (See Appendices B-1 and B-2 for examples of Delphi instruments.)

Quite commonly, when users of the Delphi technique report their findings, they may indicate that a "modified Delphi approach" was used. In many instances, the modifications are justified, and the adaptations are done in such a way that the integrity of the Delphi process is maintained. The originators of the process must, however, wince on occasions when reports are received in which various "modifications" are made that do not protect the integrity of the basic concepts of the Delphi process. There are obvious refinements that have been made in the discipline of futures research and social technology as reflected by Helmer as his work progressed from his book entitled *Social Technology*, published in 1966, to his book on the subject of studying the future, *Looking Forward: A Guide to Futures Research*, published in 1983.[13] Planners who determine that needed information could best be collected by the use of a Delphi approach would be well advised to review a number of the documents from the Rand Corporation and to examine various studies in which the Delphi technique has been used.

QUALITATIVE CONTROLLED FEEDBACK (QCF)

Suggestions have been made to improve the Delphi technique or to modify and adapt the concepts of the Delphi into different settings. The same purpose for which the original Delphi approach was used could be achieved, while refinements to the process would be accomplished.[14] One of the modified approaches is the Qualitative Controlled Feedback (QCF) method, which has been used in Russia and the United States as a means of determining futures based on expert opinion.

Both positive and negative features have been perceived to accompany such techniques as the Delphi process, as well as other approaches such as brainstorming techniques.[15] The Qualitative Controlled Feedback approach was developed in an effort to minimize negative and accentuate positive traits. Thus, the QCF incorporates the following features:

1. Members involved in the group interactions are not required to reach consensus or a group decision.
2. Group members are not allowed to have face-to-face interaction when they are making judgments (as is also the case in the Delphi).
3. Group members are not permitted to know the identities of fellow participants or the individual judgments of any participants regarding any issue or question revealed.[16]

The QCF method has been used in a few scattered sites in the educational setting in the United States and has been demonstrated to hold promise for helping educational planners. McClanahan surveyed opinion leaders in a school district to seek information that would help school officials plan for future facility needs.[17] In her study, McClanahan provided data to be used by school officials on the thinking of opinion leaders from the staff and the community regarding educational needs and how those needs were reflected in needed facilities.

The QCF method, as employed by McClanahan, followed steps that paralleled, or were similar to, many of the steps in the classical Delphi approach.

In step one of the QCF, relevant issues are identified that are to be considered by participants involved in the study. In the study conducted by Mc-

Clanahan, the issues were derived from the literature. Other approaches to the identification of issues could be employed, such as soliciting issues from experts or employing a group process to generate a list of key issues for consideration. The issues to be employed in the process are chosen based on judgments, in which a high level of relevance is the norm.

In the second step to the QCF, as employed by McClanahan, the issues derived from the literature are translated into an instrument, and the instrument is submitted to a jury of experts for validation of the content and for review of the instrument's structure. Feedback from the jury of experts was used to make revisions and refinements in the instrument.

In step three in the QCF, the participants are selected. Like the traditional Delphi method, the participants may come from any location since there is no need for face-to-face meetings. Experts in a given discipline can be called upon, or opinion leaders in a region can be enlisted as participants. In general, it is recommended that the process of choosing "experts" or "opinion leaders" to be involved in a QCF study be done by pooling the perceptions of a team of persons. In addition to choosing people with the competence or expertise needed for collecting valid results, persons should be selected who will be available and willing to commit sufficient time to complete the three rounds of the QCF process. Prospective participants need to have a complete preview of why the study is being conducted, what they are expected to do, and what time commitment will be involved.

In step four of the QCF, the participants are provided with some baseline information by providing selected readings or a review of pertinent literature. In other instances, a fact sheet containing pertinent statistics can be prepared. Still another way of providing information to participants is to present them with various scenarios that have been prepared by futurists regarding the issue being considered. The purpose of providing baseline information for participants is twofold: first, the participants are assured of having some common information and are aware of selected key facts or concepts; second, baseline information can set the stage so that all participants are aware of the arena in which they will be asked to make deliberations.

In step five of the QCF, the first round of Qualitative Controlled Feedback is distributed and collected. An instrument, with instructions, is mailed to each participant. The items that have been included in the instrument are structured in such a way as to elicit one of three responses: no, undecided, or yes. If the respondent's answer is no, that person is asked to give a reason for the answer. If the respondent answers undecided, he or she is instructed to move on to the next question. A respondent who answers yes is asked to indicate his or her perception of when the event is most likely to take place and to give a brief statement of rationale. In the instance of surveying opinion leaders about educational needs and how those needs were expected to impact upon facilities, the respondent was asked to indicate when the need would be experienced and to provide an opinion of what he or she perceived was needed.

In step six of the QCF, the first-round responses are tabulated. The number of respondents who indicated no, undecided, or yes is tabulated to determine frequency and percentage. The rationale, suggestions, or information statements written on the first-round instrument are recorded and condensed into composite statements. Care should be taken to ensure that all statements are reflected in the composite statements and that there have been no omissions or distortions.

The second-round instrument is prepared from the tabulations and composite statements. The corroborative responses are presented on the second-round instrument as "what" and "why" statements that accompany the appropriate item.

In step seven of the QCF, the second-round instrument is distributed to the participants for their completion. Participants are instructed to read the corroborating statements accompanying each item, carefully consider their previous judgment, and indicate their position by answering each item no, undecided, or yes. Respondents are asked to write any additional corroborative responses that were not shown on the second-round instrument but that they feel warrant consideration. Participants are then instructed to mail their second-round instrument to the person responsible for conducting the survey.

In step eight of the QCF, the results obtained on the second round of responses are tabulated. If some respondents are tardy in their return of the second-round materials, a follow-up note or phone call will be needed to spur them along. Obviously, if too many respondents fail to continue with the study, the results at the end of the effort will be questionable.

The number and percentage of each category of no, undecided, and yes responses are again tabulated. New corroborative comments of each respondent are recorded, condensed, and merged into the corroborative statements of the first-round data. The revised corroborative responses are used to replace those used in the second-round instrument and will appear on the third-round instrument.

In the ninth step of the QCF, the third-round instrument is mailed to the participants for their final set of responses. As in previous rounds of data collection, instructions are provided to each respondent. Again, in the event of tardy or delinquent respondents, a follow-up will be required.

In step ten of the QCF, the third-round instruments are tabulated. Frequencies are obtained, and the final draft of corroborative statements, in which the comments written by third-round respondents are included, is developed. In the final report, each item contained in the survey instrument is presented, and the frequency and percentage of responses to undecided, yes, and no are given. Accompanying each undecided, yes, or no response, the corroborative statements generated by respondents are listed as a composite of the three rounds of the survey.

SIMULATIONS AND SCENARIOS

Simulations have been used in a number of ways by planners. When the Australians build a new sailing boat to enter the Americas Cup Race and challenge the best in the world, naval architects have at their disposal various ways to build models and test them in tanks. When an airplane manufacturer builds a new plane, a model can be put in a wind tunnel and tested before a full-scale production model is built. Pilots are trained and retrained in a simulator. School administrators can be trained in certain processes and procedures with the assistance of the in-basket technique, which enables them to go through a simulated experience. Salary schedule negotiators can ask the question, What if? and go to a computer program to see what would happen if a change were to be made in the salary schedule. In so doing, negotiators can test the consequences of a change in the salary schedule through a form of simulation. A secondary school principal can ask the "What if?" question when building a master class schedule and propose a change in offerings or move classes in the master schedule. The principal can then use a computer program to see how many conflicts result from the proposed change. Administrators use models and simulations to "test" plans or ideas in many ways.

The rationale for using simulations is quite simple. A simulation (1) can reduce risks; (2) is economical; (3) may be accomplished in a brief time period; (4) is realistic if properly designed; (5) allows a greater number of options for consideration; (6) is highly adaptable; and (7) is, or at least can be, effective. Simulations may be very complex or relatively simple. On the one hand, a simulation can involve complex computer programming and include numerous variables. By contrast, if a group of planners has been planning a debate contest, they might simply say, "Let's walk through the steps and see if we have not overlooked anything." The mental process of "walking through the steps" is a form of simulation. Obviously, to be most effective, simulations must be well designed, and the key variables that will have an impact upon the planning issue involved must be taken into consideration. A simulation may be applied to immediate planning efforts, or a simulation may become a part of a strategic planning effort.

The *scenario* is a means of communicating potential options for planners and decision makers to consider. Futurists use scenarios to depict their perceptions of what the future will look like. Some scenarios have been written as short, almost abbreviated statements; in other instances, they have been published as novels. As suggested previously, a futurist who perceives grave problems and turmoil growing out of future fossil fuel shortages can prepare a scenario in which war devastates humankind, economies are destroyed, the well-being of masses of people is demolished, and the world is left in waste. Some novelists have worn out typewriters converting such scenarios into novels or television and movie scripts. A different scenario can be depicted in which the logic of survival and the ability of world leaders circumvent the devastation of fuel shortages by planning for the development of alternatives, not only to sustain civilization but to enhance the quality of life.

The value of any scenario is dependent upon the accuracy of its content. Scenarios can be used to pose options. For example, planners can ask: "If strategy A is used, what results can be expected? By contrast, if strategy B is employed, what will happen?" While a scenario seldom or never happens precisely as it is proposed, planners can gain valuable indications if the content of the scenario is realistic. When preparing a scenario for a strategic plan, the questions and the answers become more speculative. In operational planning, scenarios may be more specific and, primarily because of their immediacy, reflect a higher level of accuracy. For example, if a school board is considering moving into a building program and at the same time contemplating changing from a junior high school to a middle school configuration, various scenarios may be presented that give rather specific kinds of information. For example, the information could include the number of square feet that would have to be built in new or renovated facilities if a junior high configuration were kept, or other, similar data could be presented to the board in the event a middle school configuration were to be pursued. Several variables could also be taken into account in each scenario. If the junior high school structure were maintained, transportation routes might remain approximately the same. If the middle school plan were to be adopted, such a plan might cause a major change in transportation routes. The public might be perceived to respond to one proposal with differing degrees of favor or disfavor, and that too can be taken into account in a scenario. Ultimately, the scenario as a planning tool can provide the decision makers with a rough idea of how things would look if one option were taken as contrasted to a second or third option.

SUMMARY

When techniques are used to look to the future, planners and constituents should understand the meaning and value of views of the future. Some individuals become disenchanted when futures are not realized in precise detail. There is a need on the part of some planners to sense absolutes and avoid ambiguity. If such needs are present in those who view futures, these persons will almost certainly experience frustration and disappointments with predictions or scenarios.

Futurists who study predictions can provide a valuable function by helping planners become aware of variables and trends that will influence future events. In addition, the work of futurists can be invaluable in creating awareness and readiness to face the future, to anticipate change, and to posture persons within an organization to respond to any eventuality.

Futures studies and the use of tools such as the Delphi technique or scenarios are important and particularly applicable in strategic planning. Strategic plans do not emerge from a vacuum. Nor does a strategic planner wear a blindfold and get spun around until dizzy, when he or she is then asked to point in a precise direction in choosing a mission for an institution. With all the accompanying uncertainties in a dynamic world, the study of futures remains a significant and integral part of strategic planning.

NOTES

1. *The Prophesies of Nostradamus* (New York: Avenue Books, 1980), 1.

2. Thomas E. Jones, *Options for the Future* (New York: Praeger, 1980), xi.

3. E. C. Joseph, "An Introduction to Studying the Future," in *Futurism in Education: Methodologies,* ed. P. Hencley and J. R. Yates (Berkeley, California: ETC, 1974), 4.

4. Selwin Enzer, "New Directions in Futures Methodology," in *Applying Methods and Techniques of Futures Research,* ed. James L. Morrison, William L. Renfro, and Wayne I. Boucher (San Francisco: Jossey-Bass, 1983), 49.

5. Alvin Toffler, *Future Shock* (New York: Random House, 1970); Alvin Toffler, *The Third Wave* (New York: Morrow, 1980); Alvin Toffler, *Powershift: Knowledge, Wealth and Violence at the Edge of the 21st Century* (New York: Bantam Books, 1990), 54.

6. Ian Miles, "The Development of Forecasting: Towards a History of the Future," in *The Uses and Abuses of Forecasting,* ed. Tom Whiston (New York: Holmes and Meier, 1979), 24.

7. Jones, *Options for the Future,* 3.

8. Barry B. Hughes, *World Futures: A Critical Analysis of Alternatives* (Baltimore, Maryland: Johns Hopkins University Press, 1985), 3.

9. Olaf Helmer, *Social Technology* (New York: Basic Books, 1966).

10. Ibid., 4.

11. Ibid., 12.

12. Ibid., 13.

13. Olaf Helmer, *Looking Forward: A Guide to Futures Research* (Beverly Hills, California: Sage, 1983).

14. S. J. Press, "Qualitative Controlled Feedback for Forming Group Judgments and Making Decisions," *Journal of the American Statistical Association* 73, no. 363 (1978), 526–535; S. J. Press, *Bayesian Inference in Group Judgments and Decision-Making Using Qualitative Controlled Feedback* (Technical Report #47) (Riverside, California: University of California, 1979).

15. Harold Sackman, *Delphi Critique: Expert Opinion, Forecasting, and Group Process* (Lexington, Massachusetts: D. C. Heath, 1975).

16. Press, *Bayesian Inference in Group Judgments,* 1.

17. Randy R. McClanahan, "The Development, Utilization, and Analysis of a Normative Futures Research Method in a K-12 Educational Facilities Survey," Ph.D. diss., University of Nebraska-Lincoln, 1988.

7

Making Projections

Futures studies have become a significant part of strategic planning as educational leaders strive to look ahead in an effort to clarify the mission and plot the course or direction for an institution. Strategic planning has become a tool used by planners to face what comes and to take control, to the greatest extent possible, of the future. Operational planners must also look ahead. Techniques are available to the operational and strategic planners that will enable them to determine what is most likely to take place in the year ahead, or even as far in advance as ten years. The techniques for making projections, like any means of looking into the future, lack total precision; however, they are essential in spite of their imperfection. In light of the fact that procedures are lacking in perfection, the planner must do two things: (1) know how to make projections while understanding the limitations of various projection techniques and (2) learn to examine projections in combination—that is, look at more than one source of information regarding projections.

PROJECTIONS BASED ON EXTENDED FIGURES

The simplest and crudest form of making projections can be found in some approaches to budgeting. An example concerns the given number of dollars spent on telephone expenses in the current year in a given school system. The expenditures for a given year may become the basis for the amount to be budgeted for the coming year. Such a simple extension of a budget figure may be adequate if all variables stay relatively constant. If, however, the phone company plans to raise long-distance rates, the figure extended to the budget for the new year may be inadequate. Another method used to determine budget extensions has been based on per-pupil figures. An example may be found in the way library budgets have, in some districts, been figured on a per-pupil basis. If enrollments change, either up or down, the amount of money budgeted for library materials may be changed in compliance with enrollments.

The process of developing budgets based on extensions of budget lines from one year to the next has been challenged by the advocates of zero-based budgeting. In many bureaucracies, personnel have stubbornly resisted zero-based budgeting and have continued to use the process of extending budget lines from one year to the next. Although there are numerous instances where the process of making direct extensions from one year to the next is highly effective and an appropriate means of planning, there are projection-making approaches that are more sophisticated and more reliable than simply extending a current figure. Trend analysis and cohort group projection techniques are two methods presented below.

TREND ANALYSIS

Before the steps involved in making a trend analysis are delineated, some definitions are presented. The word *trend* has been used rather loosely from time to time. At one time, when a person in a high official capacity was making broad generalizations about educational reform and chastising the alleged failures of education, the decline in achievement scores was pointed out to the American public. There was a "trend" of declining test results that had been tracked for approximately two decades—a time period of sufficient length to establish a trend. After a year of much fuss and several belligerent speeches, the national achievement scores took an upturn—to the delight of many individuals. With the heartening news of higher test scores, a press conference was held. Officials stated that the trend had been reversed! One more year went by. Test results languished. Still another pronouncement about the disheartening news that the trend was again pointing downward was made on national television.

A number of lessons could be drawn from the historical incident described above. Only one point germane to the topic of trend analysis will be made, however; a shift in scores either up or down in a given year does not make a trend. It may be nothing more than a fluctuation.

A *trend*, which may be referred to as a secular trend, is a direction that can be tracked—a prevailing tendency that has been established—over an extended period of time. Trends are generally not determined in less than ten years. There may be fluctuations, seasonal variations, or cycles that can be detected within a trend pattern, but a trend can be established only over an extended time period.

Cycles are intervals or spaces of time in which a completed round of events or phenomena that recur regularly and in the same sequence can be observed. If a school district were located in an agricultural area in which transient labor was a significant part of the economy, an in-migration of students associated with the harvest demands for labor and an out-migration of students when the harvest was terminated could be observed each year. Fluctuations in enrollment associated with farm labor demands are seasonal variations. A drought could, however, be the cause of a significant curtailment of row crops and the need for farm laborers. If such a drought were to take place approximately every four to five years, such weather conditions could be reflected in a *cyclical fluctuation* in school enrollment patterns. Cyclical fluctuations are reflected in periods that are above or below the trend line and extend over significant time periods along a trend. Cycles have a bearing upon trends over an extended period of time.

Seasonal variations are changes of a short duration, usually within a calendar year, that can be observed as high points or troughs that follow the general pattern found in cycles and trends. Like cyclical fluctuations, seasonal variations have an impact on the overall trend of which they are a part. Seasonal variations are shorter in duration than cycles or cyclical fluctuations.

An irregularity is a brief change of direction, up or down, along a seasonal variation. An irregularity may be a sharp drop or rise or a very modest change. In general, irregularities are of little consequence in and of themselves. Not until irregularities become a part of a larger shift can any significance be made of them. If persons place great importance on every irregularity, they will soon find themselves failing to grasp the implications of any trend they might be studying. There is an old saying that some people cannot see the forest for the trees, which would be applicable for persons who try to chase irregularities and fail to see the trend that is operative.

As shown in Figure 7.1, the *secular trend* (T) is depicted by the straight line, which, in the illustration, is a positive slope depicting growth. A decline, if depicted, would be referred to as a negative slope. A wavelike, cyclical fluctuation, occurring over periods of approximately two to six years, can also be seen. The wavy line superimposed on the time series represents the *cyclical component* (C). The cyclical component, over an extended period of time, follows the secular trend. *Seasonal variations* (S) typically take place within each year. As the school year gets under way in the fall, there are often seasonal highs in the attendance figures. Finally, there are *irregular components* (I), which are not depicted in Figure 7.1, that reflect enrollment figures that move up and down due to various unpredicted or uncontrolled events, such as an influenza epidemic or good fishing weather.

An appropriate way to illustrate trends, cycles, seasonal variations, and irregularities can be provided by the weather. Persons have noted that with the destruction of the ozone layer in the earth's atmosphere, a "warming trend" has been predicted, with possible far-reaching consequences. An average temperature for each day of the year has been established for virtually every weather station around the globe. That average temperature for any day of the year has been established over many years of recorded temperatures. Television weather forecasters, when giving the evening weather report, tell their viewers what the

Figure 7.1
The Components of Monthly Time Series for a 12-Year Period

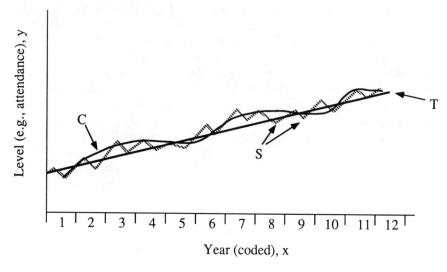

T = Trend, or secular trend
C = Cyclical fluctuations
S = Seasonal variations
I = Irregularities

Note: Irregularities (I) are not shown in Figure 7.1. Irregularities would follow along as fluctuations
    above or below seasonal variations (S).

highs and lows were for the day; they continue by pointing out when the highest recorded temperature was established for the current calendar date and what year had the record low. The "average temperature" for a given day follows the trend line that was established over a period of 100 years or more of recorded temperatures. When the television weather forecaster reports, "For this time of year the temperatures are running well below normal," such information is based on data that reflect cyclical fluctuations. The fluctuations from one date to the next, or even the irregularities between the daily high temperature and the recorded low temperature for the day, can be viewed as a part of the weather pattern or trend. The daily irregularities, the seasonal variations, and the cyclical fluctuations involved in a period of several years all constitute the bits and pieces that ultimately go into developing a trend. Data from a number of years are required before observers can determine if the change in the ozone layer is related to a changing temperature pattern on Earth or before a change can be detected in the trend. Daily fluctuations do not tell the story; they do not, when taken in isolation, depict a trend.

Valuable insights can be developed from the study of trends. When educational issues are considered, valuable information can be provided for planners through the study of demographic patterns and trends. Information about fertility rates, childbearing years of women, or the population tree in general can point to shifts in society that have important implications for the educational enterprise. Planners should understand the difference among trends, cycles, variations, and irregularities in order to derive meanings that are clear and not simply misunderstood portions of a major trend. For example, an annual shift or fluctuation, up or down, in national test scores does not change a trend; such a shift simply reflects an irregularity that typically occurs along a trend line.

Economists, business analysts, demographers, sociologists, and educators have used some standard approaches to determine trends. The following ways to determine trends will be examined. Each approach has its advantages and its limitations.

1. Time-series or linear trends are used to make straight-line projections. In time-series analysis, the analyst takes a set of observed values in a school district (such as enrollment figures, annual test scores, or population data) for an ordered, consecutive set of sequential periods and, based on a mathematical process, determines the trend and possibly a projection extended into the future. There are generally two common means of making straight-time projections. One is referred to as the selected points method and the second is the least squares method.

2. The cohort group survival method is used to study enrollment histories and base enrollment projections on historical information with the use of a mathematical computation.

3. Growth curves are projections that depict a curved line. Two approaches are also commonly involved in making growth curves. One method of studying growth curves is known as the S Curve, and the second is a logarithmic curve in which a growth pattern based on the exponential factor is depicted. Both the S Curve and the exponential trend curve are nonlinear.

TIME-SERIES ANALYSIS

A time series is a set of observed values, such as attendance, achievement scores, or operational expenses for an ordered set of sequential time periods of equal duration. The information used to develop a time-series analysis can be depicted in a table for the sake of organization and display. The same information that goes into a time-series analysis is often depicted in the form of a line or bar graph.

Persons reviewing enrollment figures in Table 7.1 or in Figure 7.2 will find the material presented in such a manner that it is easy to determine peaks and troughs. As depicted in Figure 7.2, the peak years are 1970, 1976, 1979, and 1984. By contrast, the down years or troughs can be found in 1978, 1981, and 1986. More precise information is given to most observers by the numbers in

Table 7.1
Population Figures for Middleton Public School District, 1968–1989

Year	Population (in hundreds)	Year	Population (in hundreds)
1968	4.13	1979	8.40
1969	5.47	1980	7.80
1970	6.53	1981	6.18
1971	5.40	1982	8.12
1972	6.75	1983	8.35
1973	7.44	1984	9.07
1974	7.46	1985	6.72
1975	7.55	1986	6.07
1976	9.10	1987	7.83
1977	8.33	1988	7.52
1978	7.07	1989	7.55

a table than by the line or bar on a graph. A quick glance at a graph will tell
the observer if the trend is up or down. The numbers in a table usually require
more careful examination before they reveal patterns. Numbers in a table, more
than lines or bars on a graph, can be mathematically computed. When consid-

Figure 7.2
Attendance Figures for Middleton Public Schools, 1965–1990

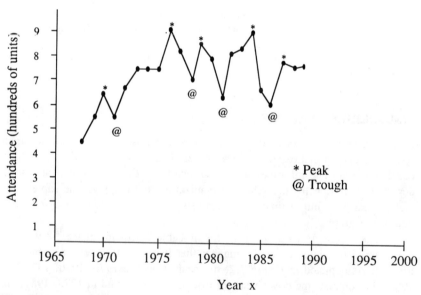

Note: Data from Table 7.1.

ering the use of figures or tables to depict information, one can see clear advantages and limitations to each approach. If a trend line is included in a graph, such as Figure 7.2, the observer can make a crude projection of what to expect in future years. Tables can also be constructed that have similar, but more precise, projection information.

The basic idea underlying time-series analysis is that systematic influences are associated with time and effect values. The analysis is performed to identify and measure the influences of the different time-related factors. Once the separate factors or components have been identified, an analysis can be used to make historical interpretations and forecasts or projections.

The factors that go into a time-series have been identified as (1) secular trend (T), (2) cyclical fluctuations (C), (3) seasonal variations (S), and (4) irregular components (I).

The model used is based on the assumption that the time-series value for any designated period is determined by the joint influences of the factors listed above (i.e., T, C, S, and I). The components of the model are assumed to have a multiplicative relationship. Where Y represents the series value (or trend line), the equation most generally accepted for the time-series model is

$$Y = T \times C \times S \times I$$

Since it is very difficult to separate the cyclical and irregular movements and the effects of each on the value of Y are similar, the model may be rewritten to represent cyclical and irregular components as a single component:

$$Y = T \times S \times CI$$

The analysis of a specific time series can be generally approached by decomposing it into representatives of trend (T), seasonal (S), and cycle-irregular (CI) components in order to study and understand better the related factors for use in decision making.

The trend (T) is represented by a line, computed directly from the data by methods similar to those used in fitting a regression line. The seasonal variation (S) is represented in the form of an index and can be computed directly from the data by the elimination of other components. The cycle-irregular component (CI) is studied as a remainder or residual and is calculated by dividing the original data by the measures of trend and seasonal, thereby eliminating them and leaving only the cycle-irregular:

$$\frac{Y}{T \times S} = \frac{T \times S \times CI}{T \times S} + CI$$

Table 7.2
Population Figures for Middleton Public School District, 1968–1989, with Projections Through 1999

Year	Population (in hundreds)	Code	Year	Population (in hundreds)	Code
1968	4.13	1	1984	9.07	17 (17,7.60)
1969	5.47	2	1985	6.72	18
1970	6.53	3	1986	6.07	19
1971	5.40	4	1987	7.83	20
1972	6.75	5	1988	7.52	21
1973	7.44	6 (6.84)	1989	7.55	22
1974	7.46	7	1990		23
1975	7.55	8	1991		24
1976	9.10	9	1992		25
1977	8.33	10	1993		26
1978	7.07	11	1994		27
1979	8.40	12	1995	8.36	28
1980	7.80	13	1996		29
1981	6.18	14	1997		30
1982	8.12	15	1998		31
1983	8.35	16	1999	8.64	32

Annual data are generally used in the identification of the trend component of a time series, because the influence of a secular trend concerns the long-term direction of movement of a time series.

The choice of mathematical methods for determining trend lines depends in part on the purpose for fitting the trend line and in part on the nature of the data. Trend lines are determined to (1) aid in studying cycles, (2) provide a historical description, and (3) make projections. At least 10 years of data are needed to establish any sort of trend, and it can be argued that no less than 15 years are required to make a time-series analysis of any value. As a generalization, the fewer the number of years of data involved, the shorter the number of years for which a projection can be made.

In the *selected points* method of determining a trend line and making a projection, at least two points must be computed from the time-series data. In one basic computational method, the semiaverages are found, or the mean of the first half of the data and a mean representing the data from the second half of the time series. Selected points are calculated for the data in Table 7.2 by the steps listed below.

All data are divided into two halves. Population figures are presented in Table 7.2 for a 22-year period extending from 1968 through 1989. The first half of these data covers the years 1968 through 1978, while the second half covers years 1979 through 1989. The sum of the population figures for the first 11 years is 75.23. The mean for the same time period is 6.84. For the period extending from 1979 through 1989 the total of all population figures is 83.61, and the mean is 7.60.

Semi $M1$ = (P1968 + P1969 . . . P1978) / number of years

$$75.23/11 = 6.84$$

Semi $M2$ = (P1979 + P1980 . . . P1989) / number of years

$$83.61/11 = 7.60$$

The next step is to identify the midpoint of the first and second half of the data. The year 1973 is the midpoint of the first half of the data, and 1984 is the midpoint of the second half of the data. By plotting the value of 6.84 at the year 1973 and the value of 7.60 at the year 1984 and extending a line through those two points, we find a secular trend (T) displayed. If the secular trend line is projected to future years as a straight line, a crude determination may be made of future enrollments (see Figure 7.3).

The difference between $M1$ (1973) and $M2$ (1984) is + .76. The difference of + .76 is divided by the number of years between 1973 and 1984, which in this instance is 11, to get the average difference per year, which is + .069, or approximately + .07.

To compute projections, we frequently depict the equation of a line in mathematics texts as

$$Y = mx + b$$

m = slope

b = where it crosses Y axis

a = a point or a variable

The equation has been revised to appear as follows:

$$Y = a + bx$$

In the above equation, x is the designated year of the time series.

To find the equation of the trend line, it is necessary to determine what the constant a is and to compute the value of b (the coefficient of x).

In the example two points were established: (1973, 6.84) and (1984, 7.60) or, if shown by code years, (6,6.84) and (17,7.60).

Using the code for the year and also rounding off the mean scores to the nearest tenth, we transform the ordered pairs (points) to (6, 6.8) and (17, 7.6).

$$b = \frac{7.6 - 6.8}{17 - 6} = \frac{0.8}{11} = .073, \text{ or if rounded off, } .07.$$

Therefore, the formula can now be written as $Y = a + .07x$.

To find the value of a, either one of the points can be substituted into the equation. For this example, the (6, 6.8) point will be used for the obvious

Figure 7.3
Trend Line and Projections Plotted via Selected Points Method

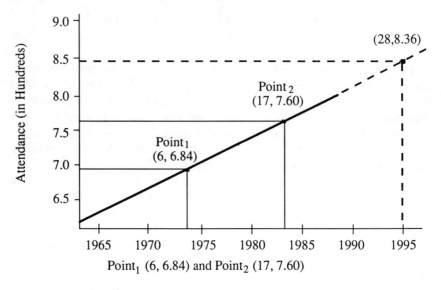

Point₁ (6, 6.84) and Point₂ (17, 7.60)

reason that 6 is simpler to use for computations than 17. Thus by substituting 6.8 for the Y, 6 for x, and .07 for b, the equation becomes:

$$6.8 = a + .07(6)$$

$$6.8 = a + .42$$

$$6.8 - .42 = a$$

a = 6.38 or 6.4 when rounded off to the nearest tenth.

The equation for this trend line using the data in Table 7.2 is

$$Y = 6.4 + .07x$$

While the equation in the example is unique to this trend line, the equation can be used to compute the value Y if x represents the year 1999, which would have a code number of 32. The code number of 32 is obtained by extending the years and their corresponding code numbers (see Table 7.2) to the point where the projection is desired. Another way of making a projection would be to extend the graph, from which a crude estimate could be made; however, it is actually easier and more accurate to compute the projection.

$$Y = 6.4 + .07(32)$$

$$Y = 6.4 + 2.24$$

$$Y = 8.64$$

Since each whole number in the data represents 100 pupils, a value of Y of 8.64 would mean that 864 pupils would be projected for 1999. Based on the above calculations, there would be 864 pupils if all variables were to remain constant. The same calculations, using a code year of 28, could be used to get a projection of six years, or the projected enrollment for 1995, which would be 836 pupils.

The *least squares* method of determining a secular trend and making projections is also a common approach found in practice. The least squares method is a bit more involved and believed to be more refined and somewhat more reliable than the selected points method. The least squares method is, like the selected points method, applicable in determining trends and making linear projections for such information as test scores, population, and school attendance.

The kinds of data used to compute the linear equation in the least squares method should be in the same format as data employed in the selected points method. Amounts, representing such information as numbers of students, are recorded for specified and equal time intervals. The data may be displayed in a table (see Table 7.3). Once the data have been placed in a table, they are ready for computation.

Each year, or time interval, is given a code number starting with zero. The column containing the code numbers is identified as X. The column containing the values, or attendance figures, is identified as Y. A third column in Table 7.3 is the product of XY. Note, the first code number is zero so the first XY value is zero. The final column of the computation table is the square of X (X^2). Each of the columns headed X, Y, XY, and X^2 is summed. The mean of the code years (X) and of the attendance (Y) is computed. When computing the means, the actual number (n) of years always exceeds the last code year number because the code year numbering starts with zero rather than one.

The computations used to make projections from data in Table 7.3 are shown in the formula displayed in Table 7.3.

Previously, with the selected points formula, the equation was

$$Y = 6.4 + 0.7x.$$

The equation using least squares formula is

$$Y = 6.3 + .09X.$$

Table 7.3
Attendance Trend Line Using Least Squares Method

Year	Coded Year X	Attendance Y (hundreds)	XY	X^2
1968	0	4.13	0.00	0
1969	1	5.47	5.47	1
1970	2	6.53	13.06	4
1971	3	5.40	16.20	9
1972	4	6.75	27.04	16
1973	5	7.44	37.20	25
1974	6	7.46	44.76	36
1975	7	7.55	52.85	49
1976	8	9.10	72.80	64
1977	9	8.33	74.97	81
1978	10	7.07	70.70	100
1979	11	8.40	92.40	121
1980	12	7.80	93.60	144
1981	13	6.18	80.34	169
1982	14	8.12	113.68	196
1983	15	8.35	125.25	225
1984	16	9.07	145.12	256
1985	17	6.72	114.24	289
1986	18	6.07	109.26	324
1987	19	7.83	148.77	361
1988	20	7.52	150.40	400
1989	21	7.55	158.55	441
22 years	$\Sigma 231$	$\Sigma 158.81$	$\Sigma 1746.66$	$\Sigma 3311$

When calculating the student population for the year 2034 (Code $X = 71$), the following would be indicated:

$$Y = 6.3 + .09(71) \cong 1,269 \text{ students.}$$

The following projection would result if the year 1999 (Code $X = 32$) were used:

$$Y = 6.3 + .09(32) \cong 918 \text{ students.}$$

It may be of interest to note that the estimated enrollment for the year 2034, based on the selected points method, was 1,144 pupils as contrasted to the projection of 1,269 pupils by the least squares method. The projected figure for 1999 by the selected points method was 864 pupils and 918 by the least squares method. Variations between the selected points and least squares computations are reflected by these differences; the fact that one or both of the methods contain a degree of error is also suggested.

The positive value of .09 for b in the least squares trend line equation indicated (1) a positive trend and (2) the fact that the increase in number of students per year during the period was .09 in hundreds of units, or about nine students annually.

Limitations to time-series or linear projections are quite real. Innumerable factors, in which the future of a population is influenced, cannot be taken into account through time-series trends and projections, whether school enrollment or community, region, or state population. Human behaviors, values, expectations, or wants cannot be factored into the mathematical processes for projections. Economic and political considerations are very real; however, there is no way to take such future variables into account by a mathematical projection. Trends do change, as illustrated by recorded population figures. The historical aspect of a trend can be explained. For example, rural populations have declined in many states, while an increase has been shown in urban population figures. The shift in population, brought about by population mobility, economic opportunities, and personal preferences, can be seen in census figures, which show fewer people living in some rural areas. A rather clear picture of the developing patterns in the rural to urban shift in population is given in time-series analyses. When projections are made, however, the social, economic, and political variables that influence the mobility of a population are not taken into account in the linear nature of the process.

Linear projections, especially in situations involving small numbers, are subject to distortion. As an example, until a large electric power-generating plant had been built in a rural area, the K-12 enrollment in the school district ranged from approximately 340 to 390 pupils. School enrollments increased significantly when people moved into the area to build the power plant; enrollment remained at the inflated level in the district for the duration of the construction project, or approximately five years. Upon the completion of the power-generating facility, construction crew members left the area and took their children with them when they moved to another location. If a trend line were computed, in which the construction-inflated population for the school district were reported in the last few years of the time series, astronomical growth in the district would be seen through the inflated figures (see Figures 7.4 and 7.5). If a trend line were determined, projections made, and the construction bulge in population placed at the early portion of the time series in the time span being computed, the trend line and projections would point downward with such a radical decline that a zero population in a relatively short number of years would be suggested. Judgment on the part of an observer will not accept the fact that the population would totally disappear in a rural community when a construction project was finished. The question could persist regarding the number of pupils the school officials would need to provide for when the population returned to "normal."

Judgment calls and manipulations may be required to make the time-series computations work and not give misleading information. In the illustration of the rural school district, in which there was an influx of students for a short number of years, several ways of making adjustments to give more usable

Figure 7.4
The Impact of Inflated Numbers on Trends and Projections

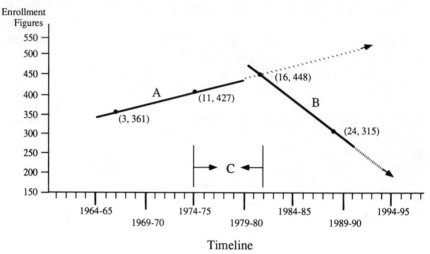

Timeline

Note: A = The trend line for the period 1964–1965 through 1979–1980 for the Sutherland public
school enrollments; B = The trend line for the period 1979–1980 through 1989–1990 for
the Sutherland public school enrollments; and C = Years when enrollments were inflated.
Trend Line = ————————
Projection = — — — →

results could be utilized. One approach would be simply to truncate the inflated
years and make a least squares trend or a selected points trend analysis and
projection. A distortion could still be apparent in the computations, because the
time intervals would not be equal if a set of scores was omitted. A second
approach would be to take the average enrollment for a few years before the
inflation of population occurred and a few years following the inflated period
and substitute the average population figure for the construction-influenced period, rather than the actual inflated population figures. Distortions could also
be apparent in this approach. In a third approach, an actual count of students
who were "permanent" residents and students who were from families of construction workers could be obtained. By excluding the actual number of pupils
who came from homes of construction workers, we could reach an approxi-
mation regarding the trend and projected enrollments. Even the latter process
could be distorted unless care were taken to consider the "locals" employed
on the construction project.

The actual process of computing trends and making projections can be accomplished with the assistance of computers. Microcomputers and software are
available that can be used to compute trends and projections and to present the
information in tables or graphs (see Figure 7.6). Quite obviously, the computer
as a tool can be of great assistance in making a time-series analysis. There are

Figure 7.5
Computer-Generated, Spreadsheet Projection of Enrollments

	A	B	C	D	E
1	SUTHERLAND ENROLLMENT HISTORY & PROJECTIONS				
2	Enrollment for 1964-65 thru 1988-89				
3	Projections for 1989-90 thru 1996-97				
4					
5	Least Squares Method of computing				
6	Trend and Projections				
7					
8	Year	Enrollment			
9	64-65	353			
10		341			
11	66-67	353			
12		365			
13	68-69	373			
14		380			
15	70-71	389			
16		383			
17	72-73	386			
18		395			
19	74-75	373	74-75 through 78-79		
20		373	are estimates based on		
21	76-77	373	average enrollments for		
22		373	71-72, 72-73,73-74 &		
23	78-79	373	80-81, 81-82, 82-83.		
24		378			
25	82-83	351			
26		343			
27	84-85	335			
28		340			
29	86-87	322			
30		276			
31	88-89	318			
32		311	Projected enrollments for		
33	90-91	297	1989-90 through 1996-97.		
34		277			
35	92-93	256			
36		233			
37	94-95	207			
38		179			
39	96-97	174			

Figure 7.6
Computer-Generated Histogram of Enrollment Projections

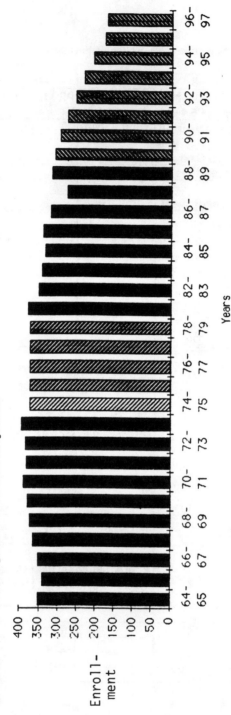

Note: The numbers of students for 1974-1975 through 1978-1979 are estimates based on the average enrollments for years 1971-1972 through 1972-1973. The estimated enrollments were used to replace dramatically inflated temporary enrollments. Projections from 1988-1989 were computer-generated based on the Least Squares Method, taking into account years 1964-1965 through 1988-1989.

various spreadsheets and software packages for the Macintosh (EXCEL Spreadsheet Software) or the IBM or IBM compatibles (Lotus 1,2,3 Software) available for use when making time-series studies and projections.

Persons interested in examining the topic of time-series studies more closely may find it helpful to examine the works of DuBois,[1] Kazmier,[2] or Stevens.[3]

PROJECTIONS BASED ON COHORT SURVIVAL RATIOS

In the cohort survival ratio method, student enrollment figures are taken for a period of 10 to 15 years, and the ratio of students who progress from one grade level to the next is computed. Ultimately, an average of the survival ratios is determined for each grade level. Projections can be made about student enrollments from the average of the cohort survival ratios. The cohort survival ratio method is used extensively when planning for school facilities, since planners can be provided with enrollment projections that are fairly reliable.[4] In actual practice, a relatively high level of accuracy has been demonstrated in the projections made by the cohort survival ratio method. It is not uncommon to have an error factor in which 93 percent of the 10-year projections fall within a plus or minus 4 percent error margin. The error margin can be looked upon with concern as the planners realize that an error of 4 percent could be costly, not to say anything about being embarrassing. The flip side of the coin is that without a means of making enrollment projections, such as the cohort survival ratio method, the margin of error will typically be much greater. The only saving grace for the planner who wants to trust instincts without data is that in all probability that person will be gone in a few years and thus avoid accountability for instinct-generated building plans that were wide of the mark. By contrast, the planner who accepts a projection without questioning it is also in danger of missing the mark by a considerable distance. All mathematical projections, the cohort survival ratio method included, need to be juxtaposed to various other sources of data so there are several comparisons upon which judgments are made.

To compute a cohort survival ratio, preschool census data are customarily collected for a period reaching back 10 to 15 years. School enrollment figures, listed by grade level, are needed for at least 10 years. The survival ratios can be computed for each year, and an average survival ratio for the 10 years of historical data can be determined by using census and enrollment figures.

In some states, the collection of preschool census data is not required, and consequently such information is often hard to obtain. In such instances, the person making a cohort survival ratio projection must rely upon the number of births in the district, reported by place of mother's residence. The number of births is generally available from the local recorder of vital statistics. Even if the office of the superintendent of schools has preschool census figures, the number of births by place of mother's residence should be obtained for com-

Figure 7.7a
Fremont Enrollment History, Age 1 Through Grade 6, for 1979–1980 through 1988–1989

	A	B	C	D	E	F	G	H	I	J	K	L	M	N
1	FREMONT ENROLLMENT HISTORY FOR 1 YEAR OLDS -6TH GRADE													
2														
3														
4														
5														Total
6	YEAR	1Yr.	2 Yr.	3 Yr.	4 Yr.	5 Yr.	Kinder.	1st Gr.	2nd Gr.	3rd Gr	4th Gr	5th Gr.	6th Gr.	K-6th
7	1979-80	165	334	368	345	357	328	361	370	397	411	376	360	2603
8														
9	1980-81	127	256	316	351	326	382	336	354	359	403	400	370	2604
10														
11	1981-82	107	260	258	318	347	337	392	326	341	355	397	393	2541
12														
13	1982-83	126	281	294	304	306	376	311	390	307	325	346	390	2445
14														
15	1983-84	134	250	303	316	305	391	355	325	358	300	333	370	2432
16														
17	1984-85	142	300	289	327	363	377	368	324	319	344	286	322	2340
18														
19	1985-86	155	260	309	282	319	425	353	354	313	321	332	279	2377
20														
21	1986-87	174	294	302	338	304	393	391	362	336	311	309	321	2423
22														
23	1987-88	160	297	318	323	374	403	384	381	352	334	298	317	2469
24														
25	1988-89	136	260	303	331	319	433	381	384	384	338	354	300	2574
26														

Figure 7.7b
Fremont Enrollment History for Grades 7–12, for 1979–1980 Through 1988–1989

	O	P	Q	R	S	T	U	V	W	X
1	FREMONT ENROLLMENT HISTORY 7-12									
2										
3										
4										
5							Total	Total	YEAR	
6	7th Gr.	8th Gr.	9th Gr.	10th G	11th Gr	12th Gr	7-12th	K-12th		
7	300	319	355	430	417	408	2229	4832	79-80	
8										
9	318	305	347	403	360	411	2144	4748	80-81	
10										
11	323	335	343	392	339	388	2120	4661	81-82	
12										
13	345	324	339	368	333	338	2047	4492	82-83	
14										
15	358	369	355	351	319	319	2071	4503	83-84	
16										
17	315	362	386	335	308	319	2025	4365	84-85	
18										
19	282	311	381	391	322	305	1992	4369	85-86	
20										
21	287	296	331	393	360	312	1979	4402	86-87	
22										
23	316	278	302	341	376	343	1956	4425	87-88	
24										
25	298	306	312	294	312	350	1872	4416	88-89	
26										

parison purposes. A need for reconciliation may be suggested by a discrepancy in the two sets of figures.

To understand the computations for a cohort survival ratio, first examine the enrollment history presented in Figures 7.7a and 7.7b. The enrollment history presented in Figures 7.7a (one-year-olds through grade 6) and 7.7b (grades 7 through 12) is for a school district with a stable population and enrollment pattern; the district included one senior high school, a junior high school, ten elementary attendance units, and one alternative learning center.

The computation of survival ratios is accomplished by computing the percentage of the number of students enrolled at one grade level who remain the following year at the next grade level. An illustration can be seen in Figure 7.8, in which information from the Fremont public schools for students, kindergartners through grade five, are taken from the enrollment history reported in Figure 7.7a. There were 382 five-year-old children enrolled in kindergarten in 1980–1981 (cell L 9). By following that group of kindergartners diagonally down and across to the year 1981–1982, when they were in the first grade, it can be seen there were 392 students (cell N 11). By dividing cell N 11 (392 students) by cell L 9 (382 students), a survival ratio for that grade level, involving the years 1980–1981 and 1981–1982, can be computed and is 1.03

(cell M 10, shown in italics). By following the same group of student enrollment figures on to the second grade level in 1982–1983, which is shown in cell P 13 (390 students) and repeating the process of dividing cell P 13 by cell N 11, the survival ratio is computed as .99, as shown in cell O 12 in italics. By reading down and across Figure 7.8, the survival ratios for the group of students is .92 in cell Q 14, .96 in cell S 16, and .97 for cell U 18. In each case, the enrollment of a given year or cell is divided by the enrollment figure from the preceding year, when that group of students was in the previous grade level.

The computations of mean survival ratios for a ten-year period are computed for kindergartners through grade five, as shown in Figures 7.9 and 7.10. The survival ratios for all grade levels and years, kindergarten through fifth grade, are shown in Figure 7.9. When all survival ratios have been computed, a mean survival ratio for each grade level can be determined that will serve as a base for making projections. By referring to cell M 28 in Figure 7.10, a mean survival ratio of .96 can be observed. The mean survival ratio in cell M 28 was computed by adding all the survival ratios in column M and dividing by 9, which is the number of ratios in that column. Following across row 28 in Figure 7.10, the mean survival ratios can be seen as .99 in cell O 28, .96 in cell Q 28, .98 in cell S 28, .98 in cell U 28, and 1.00 in cell W 28.

Projections are computed by starting with mean survival ratios and the last figure from a column in an enrollment history, multiplying the enrollment figure by the mean survival ratio, and projecting that figure into the next grade level as a projected figure for the next year. The computation for making a projection can be seen by referring to cell L 25 (see Figure 7.9), which has a figure of 433 kindergarten students attending in 1988–1989. By multiplying 433 by .96, the mean survival ratio for column M, a number of 416 is projected for the year 1989–1990, as shown in cell N 29. To make the projection for the number of second-graders for the year 1990–1991, the number projected as shown in cell N 29 (416) is multiplied by .99, the mean survival ratio as shown in cell O 30. The result of multiplying cell N 29 times .99 (cell O 30) results in a projected number of second-graders of 409 for the year 1990–1991, as shown in cell P 31 in Figure 7.10.

A ten-year projection can be computed by taking the mean survival ratio and using it to compute each additional year of a projection, as numbers from the previous grade level are fed into the spreadsheet. By looking at the pattern of third-grade enrollments as shown in Figure 7.10, column R, there are 370 students projected for 1989–1990 based on the mean survival ratio of .96 contained in column Q. Third-grade projections for the year 1990–1991 are reported in cell R 31 based on a projected number of 375 second-graders as shown in cell P 29. By following down column R, a projected enrollment of 394 can be seen in cell R 33, again based on .96 times the second-grade enrollment of 409 contained in cell P 31. In cell R 35, a projected enrollment of 342 was derived from multiplying .96, the mean survival ratio, by the amount in cell P 33, or 355. In this manner, the projections for the third grade continue

Figure 7.8
Computing Cohort Survival Ratios

	J	K	L	M	N	O	P	Q	R	S	T	U	V	W
1														
2														
3														
4														
5														
6	5 Yr.		Kinder.		1st Gr.		2nd Gr.		3rd Gr.		4th Gr.		5th Gr.	
7	357		328		361		370		397		411		376	
8		1.07												
9	326		382		336		354		359		403		400	
10				1.03										
11	347		337		392		326		341		355		397	
12						0.99								
13	306		376		311		390		307		325		346	
14								0.92						
15	305		391		355		325		358		300		333	
16										0.96				
17	363		377		368		324		319		344		286	
18												0.97		
19	319		425		353		354		313		321		332	
20														0.97
21	304		393		391		362		336		311		309	
22														
23	374		403		384		381		352		334		298	
24														
25	319		433		381		384		384		338		354	
26														

Note: C L9/Cell N 11 = SR or 382/392 = 1.03; Cell N 11/Cell P 13 = SR or 392/390 = 0.99; Cell P 13/Cell R 15 = SR or 390/358 = 0.92; Cell R 15/Cell T 17 = SR or 358/344 = 0.96; Cell T 17/Cell V 19 = SR or 344/332 = 0.97.

Figure 7.9
Fremont Cohort Survival Ratios for Age Five Through the Fifth Grade

	J	K	L	M	N	O	P	Q	R	S	T	U	V	W
6	5 Yr.		Kinder.		1st Gr.		2nd Gr.		3rd Gr.		4th Gr.		5th Gr.	
7	357		328		361		370		397		411		376	
8		1.07		1.02		0.98		0.97		1.02		0.97		0.98
9	326		382		336		354		359		403		400	
10		1.03		1.03		0.97		0.96		0.99		0.99		0.98
11	347		337		392		326		341		355		397	
12		1.08		0.92		0.99		0.94		0.95		0.97		0.98
13	306		376		311		390		307		325		346	
14		1.28		0.94		1.05		0.92		0.98		1.02		1.07
15	305		391		355		325		358		300		333	
16		1.24		0.94		0.91		0.98		0.96		0.95		0.97
17	363		377		368		324		319		344		286	
18		1.17		0.94		0.96		0.97		1.01		0.97		0.98
19	319		425		353		354		313		321		332	
20		1.23		0.92		1.03		0.95		0.99		0.96		0.97
21	304		393		391		362		336		311		309	
22		1.33		0.98		0.97		0.97		0.99		0.96		1.03
23	374		403		384		381		352		334		298	
24		1.16		0.95		1.00		1.01		0.96		1.06		1.01
25	319		433		381		384		384		338		354	
26														

Note: Enrollment figures are in bold print; projections are in italics.

Figure 7.10
Projections Based on Mean Cohort Survival Ratios for Kindergarten Through Grade Five

Row	J	K	L	M	N	O	P	Q	R	S	T	U	V	W
26														
27	5 Yr.		Kinder.		1st Gr.		2nd Gr.		3rd Gr.		4th Gr.		5th Gr.	
28	338	**1.18**	375	**0.96**	416	**0.99**	375	**0.96**	370	**0.98**	378	**0.98**	333	**1.00**
29		1.18		0.96		0.99		0.96		0.98		0.98		1.00
30	326		398		360		409		362		364		372	
31		1.18		0.96		0.99		0.96		0.98		0.98		1.00
32	299		383		382		355		394		355		358	
33		1.18		0.96		0.99		0.96		0.98		0.98		1.00
34	**304**		**351**		368		376		342		388		350	
35		1.18		0.96		0.99		0.96		0.98		0.98		1.00
36	304		357		**337**		362		362		336		382	
37		1.18		0.96		0.99		0.96		0.98		0.98		1.00
38	304		357		343		**332**		349		356		331	
39		1.18		0.96		0.99		0.96		0.98		0.98		1.00
40	304		357		343		338		**320**		343		351	
41		1.18		0.96		0.99		0.96		0.98		0.98		1.00
42	304		357		343		338		326		**315**		338	
43		1.18		0.96		0.99		0.96		0.98		0.98		1.00
44	304		357		343		338		326		320		**310**	
45		1.18		0.96		0.99		0.96		0.98		0.98		1.00
46	304		357		343		338		326		320		315	
47		1.18		0.96		0.99		0.96		0.98		0.98		1.00
48		1.18		0.96		0.99		0.96		0.98		0.98		1.00

Note: Mean survival ratios are shown in Columns K, M, O, Q, S, U, and W. Computed projections, based on mean survival ratios, are shown in columns L, N, P, R, T, and V.

to the bottom of the spreadsheet in column R as 362 (cell R 37), 349 (cell R 39), 320 (cell R 41), 326 (cell R 43), 326 (cell R 45), and finally 326 in cell R 47. As shown in Figure 7.10, this process is computed for all grade levels. A summary of projected enrollments based on the cohort survival ratio method for the Fremont public schools is depicted in Figure 7.11, in which the history of enrollments for ten years for K–6 and 7–12, as well as K–12, can be compared to the ten-year projection made for the district.

The use of a spreadsheet makes computing the projections with the cohort survival ratio method a rather simple process. By entering the enrollment history data for preschool and school attendance for a ten-year period, we make available the needed information from which the projections can be computed. To insert the formula to compute a given survival ratio in a spreadsheet is a simple process: M8 = N9/L7. (The illustrations given for computations when using a spreadsheet were used with the EXCEL program on a Macintosh.) That formula can then be extended down through column C and the process repeated in columns D, G, H, etc., until all the grade levels are computed. To arrive at a mean cohort survival ratio on a spreadsheet is equally simple. Carrying over from Figure 7.9 to Figure 7.10, the nine scores printed in italics in any column can be totaled and divided by nine to compute the mean, for example, cell M 28 = SUM(M 8:M 24)/9, which in this case resulted in a mean survival ratio of .96.

There are obvious variations or even inaccuracies that emerge when looking at preschool census figures and school enrollment histories. It is common for the data on one-year-olds to be inaccurate. Census figures become more accurate when two-year-olds through five-year-olds are reported. Because of these common variations, a survival ratio of 1.95, as shown in Appendix C-1, cell C 28, is not totally unexpected when going from one-year-old preschool census figures to two-year-old census figures. Thus, making projections of one-year-olds demands a judgment call or an estimate, since it is not possible to interview all women of childbearing age to determine their intentions for the future. One way to project how many one-year-olds to expect is to look at the history of the number of births by place of mother's residence and make a linear projection based on that history. Another means of arriving at a number to use in making projections is to look at the ten-year history of census figures for one-year-olds and make a projection, using the least squares or selected points method, described previously, to arrive at a set of figures for projection purposes. In the illustration of the Fremont school system, the number 136 was determined to be a reasonable projected number of one-year-olds based on the history of the community. Since the census history was reflecting a stable population pattern, with obvious minor fluctuations, the number 136 was used for all projections. If, however, the pattern of births showed an upward trend, the number 136 would have to be adjusted to reflect that growth. By contrast, if the people in an area were experiencing a decline in birthrates, a decline in fertility rates, and a corresponding decline in population, it would then be necessary to com-

Figure 7.11
Summary of Enrollment History and Projections for Fremont Schools

	AL	AM	AN	AO
5	HISTORY SUMMARY			
6	Total K-6	Total 7-12	Total K-12	Year
7	2603	2229	4832	79-80
8				
9	2604	2144	4748	80-81
10				
11	2541	2120	4661	82-82
12				
13	2445	2047	4492	82-83
14				
15	2432	2071	4503	83-84
16				
17	2340	2025	4365	84-85
18				
19	2377	1992	4369	85-86
20				
21	2423	1979	4402	86-87
22				
23	2469	1956	4425	87-88
24				
25	2574	1872	4446	88-89
26	PROJECTION SUMMARY			
27	Total K-6	Total 7-12	Total K-12	
28				
29	2599	1798	4397	89-90
30				
31	2595	1812	4407	90-91
32				
33	2598	1853	4450	91-92
34				
35	2531	1904	4435	92-93
36				
37	2485	1933	4418	93-94
38				
39	2449	1955	4403	94-95
40				
41	2381	2030	4412	95-96
42				
43	2365	2008	4373	96-97
44				
45	2330	1983	4312	97-98
46	0			
47	2307	1914	4221	98-99

pute a projected trend that would determine future estimates of one-year-olds that would show a decline from 136 with a fixed percentage of decline.

To make such estimates requires the use of more than numbers on a given spreadsheet. Demographic data regarding the growth or decline patterns in an area are essential. Hard data, when available, are much more important than using wishful thinking on the part of some overly enthusiastic community promoters. Information, such as the number of deaths per 1,000 persons per year, is available and can be studied. New building permits and plans by commercial interests either to cut back or to expand are also variables to be considered. When all is said and done, it is still a judgment call. But as said before, a judgment based on the best data available is better than a judgment based on wishful thinking of one person. (For a complete example of an enrollment history and set of projections, see Appendix C-1.)

NONLINEAR PROJECTIONS OF GROWTH CURVES

Growth curve formulas commonly used are

1. $\text{Log } Y_T = \log L + \text{Log } a(b)^x$

2. $Y_T = L/1 + 10a + bx$

Nonlinear curves possess mathematical properties that logically correspond to the process of economic growth in a firm or industry or perhaps educational tax projections. Lower and upper limits are indicated by the growth curves. In other words, zero would be the lowest limit or the general starting point, and the maximum or saturation point would be represented by the upper limit. The upper limit is generally never 100 percent. The upper limit may be expected to vary with the nature of the data being studied. The number of computers in a school serves as an example. Zero is easy to understand. When there were no computers in a school, that point was the starting or zero point. If every student and faculty member had a personal computer, the maximum limit would be achieved. The reality, the upper limit, would probably be based on a different assumption that every student and faculty member did not have a computer. In this case, the upper limit would be viewed quite differently than if the expectations were for every person to have a personal computer.

In computing nonlinear growth curves, the selected point method may be used. A minimum of three points is plotted, and L constant represents the upper limit. The growth curves can be used for short-term forecasting. Long-range projections based on the growth curve, however, are risky, because the assumption cannot always be made that future growth will occur at the same rate as in the past. Examples of two growth curves are shown in Figure 7.12.

The S curve has been used when studies have been conducted to determine the rate of innovation adoption. At one time, observers suggested it would take

Figure 7.12
Nonlinear Projections

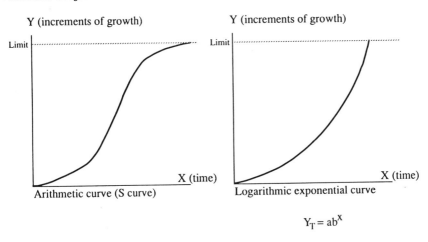

approximately 30 years for an innovation, such as kindergartens, to be fully adopted. The S curve is plotted by recording the frequency, or the number of schools in which an innovation was adopted, on an annual basis over an extended period of years. In practice, there is a saturation point or a maximum percentage of schools that can be expected to adopt any given innovation. The pattern observed with the S curve, or, as it is often referred to, "the adoption curve," is that at the time when an innovation is introduced, there is a very gradual increase from one year to the next in terms of the number of schools in which the adoption is made. An acceleration in the rate of adoptions is then observed, as more people become aware of the innovation, or as a band-wagon effect is noted. After a period of rapid growth, as the saturation point is neared, the number of new adoptions of the innovation declines and eventually levels off.

The amount of time in which innovations were adopted in education was greatly reduced in the late 1960s with the advent of the large sums of federal funds that poured into curricular materials and staff development programs targeted by the National Defense Education Act. The time period for adoption of an innovation can be influenced by numerous variables, such as funding or the mood and expectations of citizens. During the 1960s, full limits of implementation were reflected in some adoption curves in less than a ten-year period, as contrasted to the previously held view that innovations in education could be completed in only a 30- to 50-year period.

The S curve has value in providing a means of observing and ultimately making predictions about when an innovation will be fully adopted or, more accurately, when an innovation will reach a saturation point at some level less than 100 percent.

Bad decisions can stem from the failure to understand the S curve. An example of such a failure can be found in the case of an electronics firm that manufactured citizen band (CB) radios to be installed in trucks and cars. During the CB craze, as managers of the electronics firm observed the acceleration portion of the S curve, they perceived the market to be unlimited and constantly growing. The managers failed to realize there was a limit to the number of trucks and cars in existence and a limit to the number of drivers who were interested in owning a CB, despite the large growth in sales. Consequently, production schedules in the electronics firm were geared to a projected growth pattern based on the period of acceleration on the S curve, and the fact that there would be a saturation point and a leveling off for the demand for CBs was ignored. The end result was that the electronics firm became overextended; in approximately two years its managers were in bankruptcy court. Of course, the suggestion can also be made that the situation was exacerbated, and the fall of the electronics firm was hastened, because of the fad involved in the public interest in citizen band radios. The fact that fads come and go simply suggests more than one form of data is needed in making projections.

The S curve is frequently used for a projection by plotting the data along standard time intervals from the early period of gradual acceleration into the midrange portion of the S curve, and then in anticipation of reaching or nearing the saturation point of the growth curve, a projection is freehanded. The projection may be crude; yet, in some situations, it is more appropriate than a linear projection based on a mathematical formula. Perhaps the most important benefit derived from the S curve comes from the realization that the rate of growth will go through three periods along the total S curve: (1) the introductory period of gradual acceleration, (2) the period of rapid growth in the central portion of the curve, and (3) the period of declining growth as the saturation point is reached.

The logarithmic curve is the second nonlinear projection that can be used to make predictions based on the exponential factor. The exponential trend curve is determined, as explained in specialized textbooks, by presenting growth along the Y axis and time along the X axis. The exponential trend curve is typically applied to a time series in which a constant rate, or percentage, of growth during a series of years is reflected. The exponential trend curve has been used to depict the growth of compounded interest income. The exponential trend curve has been used to depict the growth of recorded knowledge since the beginning of history. Suggestions have been made that within each three years the amount of accumulated knowledge is doubled or grows by the exponential factor. A period of very gradual growth is typically depicted in charts, gradual acceleration is shown with the dawning of the Renaissance, and the curve turns upward on the chart as the exponential factor is fed larger numbers in the twentieth century, seemingly pointing to the top of the page. Unlike the S curve, there is no period of deceleration and leveling off. (Commonly used formulas for projections are included in Appendix C-2.)

SUMMARY

Throughout the discussion on making projections, repeated warnings have been given not to overinvest in a linear projection and to hedge projections by using multiple sources of data to make comparisons. Not uncommonly, projections from one source of information are in conflict with other projections. Patterns need to be identified for use with comparisons and verification of projections. When studying demographics, one should note such information as the shift from rural to urban areas, fertility, and death rates. A host of demographic data is available, and the planner should take into account as much verified and confirmed information as possible to substantiate enrollment projections. The planner must also know the tools for making projections, their capabilities, and their limitations. Good planning is accomplished more frequently when adequate data are available than when needed data are not in hand. The accuracy of data input for computations is, however, essential.

NOTES

1. Edward N. DuBois, *Essential Statistical Methods for Business* (New York: McGraw-Hill, 1979).

2. Leonard J. Kazmier, *Basic Statistics for Business and Economics* (New York: McGraw-Hill, 1979).

3. D. J. Stevens, "Trend Analysis" (University of Nebraska, Lincoln, Nebraska, 1988).

4. Basil Castaldi, *Educational Facilities Planning, Modernization, and Management*, 2nd. ed. (Boston: Allyn and Bacon, 1982), 397–410.

8

Group Processes

INTRODUCTION

Planning is primarily a human endeavor. At certain stages of the process there are formulas and computers used to assist in the management of data and the development of techniques and materials. The technology and the mathematical approaches are, however, used only to support the human efforts of planning. No formula or computerized data base can be called upon to make judgments or determinations. Data, as vital as they are to the planning process, are appropriate only as they contribute to human beings who make judgments and decisions. The manner in which individuals and groups of people function becomes paramount, because data can be avoided, rejected, or misused by people. Of course, any tool or process can be misused in the planning process. If the contention that the human dimension emerges as the most significant element in the planning process is accepted, it follows that planners need to know how to work effectively with individuals, small groups, and large populations. Planners must be knowledgeable and competent in the management of human resources. Planners need to be people-oriented.

As groups of people have worked together, not uncommonly the proverbial committee will build a camel or discover another wheel. In fact, not too infrequently persons have suggested that a proven strategy to avoid getting anything done is to appoint another committee. Some conflicting information about the effectiveness of group decision making can be found in the literature. While the preponderance of research on decision making and group processes points to the fact that two heads are better than one, a dissenter can be found now and then who suggests that group performance is inferior to the best individual working alone.[1] The findings suggested by Price are in stark contrast to the hundreds of applications, which have involved several thousand subjects and extended over a decade of use, of exercises such as *"Lost on the Moon"* or "The Project Planning Situation," processes to demonstrate group decision making. In-depth studies and developmental efforts have been completed, and general users of various group processes, as well as those who have developed and advocated group approaches, have demonstrated that group decision making and planning can be far superior to the work of individuals if sound, tested group processes are appropriately employed and not misused. Administration has entered an age of "maximum feasible participation" in both public and private organizations.[2] Yet, as suggested by various authorities on group dynamics and group functioning, the individual's characteristics brought into a group as well as the group processes themselves are fraught with dysfunctional potential, if not properly understood and managed. Therefore, planners must understand the techniques that facilitate optimum group potential and consensus.

Group processes for decision making and planning have attracted a considerable amount of attention. Numerous approaches or techniques have been developed and tested. The variations in the application of group processes, some of which have been intentional and some apparently unintentional and even misguided, are numerous. A combination of approaches, or the selection of the best from one process and putting it with the best from another approach, has intrigued many planners and resulted in what has become known as the "eclectic approach." Group processes have been devised with specialized applications and intent, such as Quality Circles, used primarily in manufacturing firms to foster better quality control. Quality Circles has, like many processes or techniques initiated in business or industry, been adapted for educational institutions. Effective schools and site-based management advocates have proposed the use of Quality Circles to facilitate how staff should be chosen and how they should function in an educational setting as well as to determine the advantages and outcomes to be achieved.[3]

Group processes are designed and applied in an effort to capitalize on the human potential. Individuals in a school system and community have many talents and capabilities. Leaders—planners—need to employ techniques to bring out the talents of human minds so that all concerned in the planning process can benefit. Only planners who have confidence in people and who are secure within themselves can fully capitalize on the human potential.

Group processes are essential not only as a means of bringing out the best decision-making and planning efforts. They serve another vital function; they can be a strong force to develop ownership among opinion leaders and stakeholders. As group processes involve people and develop leadership, they become a valuable tool that can contribute to the management of change.

BRAINSTORMING

Brainstorming is used for group problem solving. A long list of ideas or proposed solutions is generated by setting a stage for members of a small group to input ideas with no opportunity for rejection, regardless of how unusual the idea may seem to others. Brainstorming is most effective when a group of five to nine persons is involved in a setting where the group can work uninterrupted for approximately one to two hours.

In step one at the opening of the brainstorming session the facilitator explains the problem to be addressed and explains the ground rules. The ground rules state: (1) no criticism is permitted during the idea-generating session; (2) no comments or discussion favoring an idea are permitted during the idea-generating session; (3) any and all ideas of a participant should be presented no matter how unusual the idea may seem at first appearance, since one idea may trigger another; and (4) the first priority is the quantity of ideas generated.

When all ideas the members of the group can think of have been generated, in step two the facilitator can ask participants to formulate potential alternate solutions based on the ideas presented in the first activity. As the case in the first idea-generating session, the second phase of the brainstorming process requires that ideas be synthesized or combined without critical debate regarding the merit of ideas. As a result of the second phase of the process, the list is generally shortened and suggested solutions are stated more clearly.

In step three participants in the group are asked to select the best ideas for solving the problem or meeting the prescribed need. Various selection methods can be employed by the facilitator in leading the group to determine the best solutions. Acceptance of solutions may be based on a simple yes/no vote by each participant; consensus-seeking methods may be employed; solutions can be placed in rank order; or the participants may be given a rating scale that could generate a list of preferred or recommended choices and in which two or more choices could have the same rating.

If a large number of participants are involved in a brainstorming effort and divided into small groups for deliberations, it may be possible to bring all the groups together and have a representative from each small group present an idea to the combined groups. A round-robin of ideas could be presented until all ideas or solutions are presented and a refined and combined list is generated. At that time the leader could guide the participants in a process to select the most highly recommended solution and to set priorities.

One of the primary concerns of the brainstorming process is the avoidance of a dominant person or persons who unduly influence the total process or tie up the effort in debate. Consequently, the group facilitator should exact discipline in the process to avoid such abortive and disruptive behavior of individuals.

NOMINAL GROUP TECHNIQUE

The Nominal Group Technique (NGT) is perhaps the most commonly known and used group process. The NGT is a means for structuring small group meetings in which "individuals work in the presence of others but do not verbally interact for periods of time."[4] The NGT is designed to encourage pooling of individual judgments in settings where "uncertainty or disagreements exist about the nature of a problem or possible solutions."[5] The NGT is a structured process designed to capitalize on the collective mental power of a small group of people.

The NGT has gained popularity and has been perceived as useful in problem identification, exploring outcomes and possible solutions, setting goals, and determining priorities. The NGT is acclaimed as working well with "strange groups" of 5 to 12 persons where it is important to neutralize status differences and "verbal dominance among group members."[6]

How to Conduct the NGT Process

There are some preliminary considerations that should be noted when preparing to employ the NGT. Three general givens are considered prerequisites: (1) a question carefully crafted that provides clarity and elicits specific responses; (2) a group of individuals who are focused or task-oriented and who have some prior knowledge or expertise relative to the topic; and (3) a group leader who has mastered NGT procedures and who will "act as a process facilitator, not a substantive expert."[7] Facilities needed for the group activity consist of a small room in which there are comfortable chairs, tables upon which participants can work, flip charts and marking pens (avoid marking pens that bleed through the newsprint and stain walls), masking tape (to paper the walls with items generated in discussions), possibly a chalkboard, and 3 × 5 cards and pencils. A word processor and a keyboard operator in the room and an electrostatic copy machine nearby to reproduce a summary document for participants right on the spot have also proven helpful, but not essential. If the planning team is made up of 21 persons, it would be necessary to have three or four small rooms with a complete set of materials and supplies and a facilitator assigned to a group of 5 or 7 persons in each room. The small rooms should afford privacy for each group.

Prior to the gathering of participants the group leader will need to write a carefully phrased yet simple and clear question or statement that is presented on the chalkboard or at the top of a sheet of paper placed on the table in front of each participant. All the supplies will need to be assembled and flip charts strategically placed toward the front of the room. Tables need to be placed in a U shape so that all participants have the best possible vantage point to see the front of the room and to face each other. If a computer operator-recorder is to be involved, that person needs to be instructed regarding the task to be performed and must understand that he or she is not a discussion participant.

The group leader should start the meeting at the scheduled time. Being prompt will avoid wasting time and will help set the tone for the group to see that the process is a work session of importance and not simply another opportunity to build a camel. The group leader should make an opening statement in which greetings or introductions are made and the importance of the task and the unique contribution expected from each participant are underscored. The desired outcomes or goals of the meeting, how the results of the deliberation will be used, a brief overview of how the meeting will be conducted, the steps involved, and the projected time of completion should all be reiterated.

The NGT includes several elements: (1) initial thoughts, (2) round-robin, (3) idea structuring, (4) discussion and synthesis, (5) voting, and (6) closure.

Initial thoughts are generated by individual participants and written on the 3 × 5 cards provided. The generation of initial thoughts or ideas to be presented is done without discussion. Each participant has been oriented to the task by having the topic or question under discussion presented on the paper provided by the facilitator and by the oral review of that question prior to generating ideas. In response to the question posed by the facilitator, each participant, in a time period of five to ten minutes, writes ideas on 3 × 5 cards for consideration. There should be no talking during the time individuals generate ideas. Each idea should be written on a separate card. As the facilitator observes the members of the group working individually at the task of writing ideas, he or she is able to determine how much of the maximum time allotment of ten minutes is needed. If the members of the group demonstrate by their behavior and body language that they have finished the task before the time limit is reached, the facilitator simply calls the session to an end and announces the next phase.

During the process of developing initial thoughts, it is not uncommon for one or more participants to want to reopen discussion and seek further clarification of the question to which they have been asked to respond. As participants have started directing their attention to the task at hand, there may be those who start to read between the lines or think, "Yes, but what if?" Should such questions be asked, the leader should quietly respond to the individual in a general way and tactfully encourage the participant to respond to the question as stated. By following this approach, the leader avoids shaping or giving direction to individual responses. It is also important not to distract the total group and veer off on some unscheduled tangent.

The *round-robin* is the second step in the process and is structured to map the thinking of the group. The facilitator can begin by turning to any member in the group and asking the participant to pick one of the topics he or she has generated and written on a 3 × 5 card and present it orally in a concise phrase or brief sentence without elaboration or justification. As the idea is presented, it is recorded on a flip chart by the facilitator precisely as the person has presented it. No discussion of ideas is allowed at this point. The facilitator will then go to the next person and ask for that person's idea, which is recorded on the flip chart. This process is used to work around the table so that each person in sequence is afforded an unobstructed opportunity to present an idea for consideration. The procedure continues to cycle around the table until all ideas have been recorded. After a round or two, some individuals will indicate that they have no more ideas or that their remaining ideas have already been presented. Once all ideas have been exhausted, the procedure is considered complete.

As the round-robin process unfolds, there will probably be items mentioned by some presenters that are similar but not exactly like an item presented by another participant. This occurrence gives the facilitator the opportunity to encourage participants to build on the ideas presented by others and to add new items, even if the items were not written on a card during the generation of initial thoughts. Members of the group may elect to pass a turn at any time but may also reenter a cycle at any time their turn comes around.

As the facilitator writes each idea presented by a participant on a flip chart, there should be a concerted effort to record the idea in the exact words of the presenter. Each idea is numbered by the facilitator as it is recorded. Some participants may have presented ideas in rather lengthy statements that are too long to afford easy recording. In that case, the facilitator should ask the presenter to reword or to summarize the idea so it still contains the meaning and can be recorded on the flip chart. If the restatement of an idea causes a delay, the facilitator should move on to the next presenter in sequence and indicate to the presenter who is editing or rewriting an item that the item can be presented in the next round so there will be no loss of thoughts or time. Another time-saving technique is for the facilitator to ask a participant who is not presenting an idea to take the first full sheet on a flip chart and tape it on the wall as the facilitator moves to a second flip chart and continues to record ideas. All items on flip charts need to be displayed throughout the round-robin so all participants have reference to them. At the conclusion of the round-robin all ideas generated by the group should be displayed.

As items are presented, the word processor operator should record each item as presented and numbered. Unless the facilitator sees a need to keep items in their original form, there is no need to keep a separate draft of the originals, but in subsequent deliberations the word processor operator can simply edit each item as agreed upon by the participant.

Idea structuring is the next step in the process. The facilitator should explain to the group what will be taking place. Idea structuring is used to clarify and focus each item presented and not to debate the merit of the item. The first idea that was presented by a participant is read by the facilitator, and comments are invited from anyone in the group. Generally each member comments and gives a brief expansion of the item simply for sake of clarity. Any member in the group can then ask questions or make comments as long as the comments are not evaluative or argumentative. Idea structuring is not a time for debate, but a time for clarification. If an argument does arise about the merit of an idea, the facilitator must intrude and indicate the focus of idea structuring and keep the group on task.

The facilitator should take an active role in encouraging members of the group to view the list of ideas as belonging to the group. It should be made clear that any person in the group can comment on or clarify any item under discussion. When a member of the group asks for clarification of an item, it is often productive for the facilitator to solicit responses about the meaning of the item from other participants. The group leader can restate or summarize in an effort to clarify by saying, "To me this means. . . . Is that how others see this?" As items are restated or modified for clarification, the word processor operator should input the changes in the original draft.

The facilitator should, in advance of the idea-structuring task, identify the number of items presented by the group that need to be considered and estimate the amount of time needed. Such an estimate can be made by multiplying the number of items to be considered by 2 minutes, the approximate amount of time needed to consider each item. If the group process is being conducted under a strict time limit or constraint, it may be necessary for the leader to look at the prescribed adjournment time, save 15 minutes for the voting process, and allow the remaining time for idea structuring and discussion and synthesis to be divided equally. Using this latter time frame, the facilitator can determine how much time can be allotted to clarifying each item.

Discussion and synthesis can follow idea structuring. At this point participants are to enhance ideas or to combine or synthesize concepts or ideas. No idea is to be eliminated. Participants should be encouraged to bring up points for consideration that can focus, consolidate, or blend ideas into more meaningful statements. If the originator of an idea finds suggestions objectionable or feels they take away the intent of an item as presented, that item should be kept in its original form. The facilitator should ask the originator of an item that is being considered for combining with another item, "How do you perceive the combination of these two items? Is your original intent preserved in the combined statement?" If the presenter of the original item is in agreement, the items can be combined or reshaped into a new statement. The group should be asked if such changes are clear and if they see any loss of an item in the combining or synthesis process. The word processor operator will need to capture the newly stated items and edit them as the individuals in the group reach agreement. All unedited items would remain as originally inputted. The number for each item may need to be changed as a result of discussion and synthesis.

The group has been working and concentrating on the task at hand for a considerable amount of time when the discussion and synthesis process is completed. It is appropriate to give a short break to participants. (If you are in a setting that is new or unfamiliar to members of the group, give instructions where the restrooms and other facilities can be found.) The word processor operator should, during the brief break, obtain enough copies of the edited list of numbered items so that each member of the group has a copy.

With the group called back to order and with the list of clarified and consolidated topics in the hands of each participant, the facilitator can again ask for a review of items by group participants and questions or comments for clarification. Each member may speak to clarify a topic or to ask a question. This is not a time for debate or rebuttals.

Voting and setting priorities remain to be accomplished by the participants of the group. Nominal voting simply means that participants put in priority, or rank order, their personal view of the most important items generated by previous deliberations. The facilitator should determine in advance if each participant will be asked to select the top five or top seven items from the total list. If five items are to be selected, participants are instructed to write the number of the item chosen from the list on a card and then to place their number of rank ordering on the card and circle the rank-order number so it can be distinguished from the number of the item that was chosen. The first item of importance should be given a ranking of five, if five is the number each person is to select from the total list. The second most important item should be given a weighted ranking of four, and so on until the last of the five items is given a weighted ranking of one. The reverse numbering system in terms of most important to least important will ultimately make easy work of computing the scores to identify the importance group participants attach to each item. Each item selected from the total list by each participant should be placed on a separate card; thus, each participant will have five (or seven, if that is the number to be selected) cards on which one number representing an item appears and on which a circled number representing the weighted ranking is written. Putting a circle around the rank-order number is simply a means of helping the facilitator distinguish between the number representing the item selected and the number representing the ranking of the item. The selection of the top items and placing them in rank order are done by each individual working independently. No discussion should be permitted during the process of selecting and rank ordering items.

A technique to help participants place the five, or seven, cards in priority is to instruct them to place all their cards, on which they have identified the items selected by number, in front of them so they can see all cards. This step is to be done prior to placing weighted ranking numbers in circles on each card. Participants are then instructed to select the card representing the item of highest priority in their mind from the five they have selected and place a five (5) in a circle on the card and then select the card representing the least important of the five items selected and place a one (1) in a circle on the card. Such a distinction may not be easy for participants to make because all five (or seven, if that is the number to be chosen) are items seen as important and differentiation in terms of importance may be difficult. After the first and last items in importance are identified, the highest-ranked card with its score of five and the lowest-ranked card with its weighted ranking of one (circled) are turned face-down. Three cards will remain faceup in front of each participant. Participants are then to select the most important and the least important of the three remaining cards and place a circled four on the card of the item with the most importance and a circled two on the card representing the item of least importance. When this step is done, cards given weighted priority of two and four are turned facedown. One card is left, on which the participant places a circled three and thus ranks that item at the midpoint of the five chosen as most important from the total list.

The facilitator collects all cards from all participants and shuffles them so that any sequence in which the cards were collected is not seen as a way of identifying who chose a given item or how any person ranked any item. Anonymity is important. The rankings are then reported on the flip chart or chalkboard on which the numbers of all items generated at earlier stages of the process were listed. Participants may also record the votes, or rankings, on the individual sheets of paper that was provided by the word processing operator and on which the items and their numbers were listed.

An example of a tally sheet, containing 22 items originally generated by the group, can be seen below.

Item No.	Tally Rankings	Item No.	Tally Rankings
1	3, 4, 2, 3, 3, 4	12	3, 5, 5, 5, 5
2	5	13	1, 3, 2, 2, 1
3		14	
4	4, 5, 5	15	
5	1	16	3, 1, 1
6	3, 1	17	1
7		18	2, 1
8	1, 3	19	
9		20	
10	1	21	2, 5, 3
11	5	22	

After the rankings are tallied, the facilitator leads a discussion on the voting patterns. The number of votes an item received is an important indicator; it is also important to review items that may have had fewer votes but received a higher overall ranking because of the high ratings given by respondents. For example, item number 1 had the most votes (6 votes), and items number 12 and 13 had the second most votes (5 votes each). The weighting of items 1, 12, and 13, based on the weighted rankings given by participants, ranks item 12, with a rating of 23, above item 1, with a ranking total of 19, and item 13, with a total of 9 points. Both the frequency of votes and the weighted ranking scores are important to consider.

If the voting generated a list of items for which there was no clear priority, a second voting can be conducted on those items that received the most votes in the first balloting. The second round of voting would be conducted in a similar manner as the first round. An option that can be used to select the items upon which a second vote is to be taken is to pick the five items that have the highest total ranking scores and have the members of the group rank those five items, using the same method of voting or ranking as before; however, all members would be ranking the same five items. After the participants placed the number representing the items on five different cards, they would again assign numbers from five for highest priority to one for lowest priority to the cards. The cards would be collected by the facilitator and shuffled to ensure anonymity, and the results would be tallied on a clean flip chart or chalkboard as the group observes the results. Based on the final pooled rank ordering of items, the group consensus and recommendation can be determined. Note the word *recommendation*. The group involved in the NGT is generally not a decision-making group with official authority and the responsibility for accepting accountability. The NGT is typically used as a means for arriving at a recommendation, not an official decision.

Advantages and Limitations of NGT

Any tool, such as the NGT, has its area of applicability and its limitations. NGT is a process that demands a facilitator who is able to ''facilitate'' and not dictate or manipulate. The facilitator needs to be sufficiently familiar with the process so the group of participants can demonstrate their best thinking within the framework of the process. There is a discipline required of the facilitator and the members of the group; as they work through an NGT effort, it is essential that the process be trusted and adhered to if it is expected to work. If the facilitator permits modifications that pollute or dilute the process, only by chance will the results be satisfactory, and it is very unlikely the participants will be satisfied with their work.

The success experienced by a group of participants when solving a problem and using about any process is generally proportionate to the amount of time spent on the problem. The suggestion has been made that ideas are significantly better when ''generated in the final third period of an individual's independent thought on a topic than in the first two-thirds of the period.''[8] Therefore, the facilitator is well advised to stay on the course and retard speedy decisions; he or she should also create a ''problem-solving'' versus a ''solution-mindedness'' pattern among the members of the group. The NGT is a tool that assists in achieving the problem-solving mind-set by stressing problem centeredness through task assignment that focuses group members' attention to problems and delays selection of a solution.[9]

Group size is an important consideration. There is a direct relationship between the number of persons in a group and the amount of participant input and interaction. In larger groups, some participants are more restrained. In fact, in a group of 12 or more persons, some participants typically become nonparticipants and turn into observers. In larger groups in which some members of the group fall silent, those persons who are inclined to speak out can begin to dominate the conversation. The NGT, by its structure, avoids the loss of member participation and the dominance of some individuals. NGT achieves the desired result of getting all participants involved only when adhering to the process. While it is easy for a group to contain too many people, by contrast, a sufficiently large number of people are necessary so that there are ideas to exchange. Some experts suggest that from 5 to 7 persons is the right number. Others have suggested different numbers and indicated that up to 9 persons can be effective. Certainly, at least 5 persons are needed to generate sufficient interaction. It has also been demonstrated repeatedly that 12 becomes a maximum that should not be exceeded. Seven to 9 may well be the optimum number. The groups should be kept within the general parameters suggested, the results should be studied, the amount of time for groups to achieve closure when different sizes are employed should be measured, and feedback should be gathered from participants. Each facilitator can see what fits and works best within the parameters that have been suggested by various group dynamics specialists.

As a general rule, NGT imposes structure while limiting and directing discussion in the interest of effective decision making. The procedure is designed to reduce the loss of group production due to social interaction and lack of task understanding and orientation.[10] In what has become a familiar scene at typical committee meetings, the group is often dominated by some loudmouth. The NGT avoids this unproductive behavior. Consequently, some persons who would be political or who are classified as controllers have a definite dislike for the structure displayed in the NGT.

One of the downfalls of many groups is "group think." Group think is a condition in which the majority of the group participants may go along with what some dominant personalities suggest and propose rather than voicing an opinion that they think will be rejected. If individuals in a group believe it is easier to go along with the group, even if it is known that the direction may not be productive, a symptom of group think is evident. The structure of the NGT is an effective means of avoiding group think. The NGT allows members time for uninterrupted thought without recriminating influences from would-be dominant members of the group. A social atmosphere that allows, even demands, total member participation and at the same time tolerates minority opinions is also established. The very structure of NGT fosters the generation of ideas from socially awkward, reticent, or shy members. The NGT actually imposes a structure that "assures more nearly equal participation" from all participants.[11]

The voting process in NGT, which provides for anonymity, tends to minimize the potential for individual domination and intimidation. In this respect, the NGT not only avoids, but precludes much of the potential for group think.

The structured method in which individuals provide input and structured responses and then vote provides virtually equal access for all participants, even those who wish to present minority views. While it is not possible for any process to avoid hidden agendas totally, the NGT does circumvent the insidious nature of the hidden agenda to a major degree. The potential for personality differences or status differences that cause conflict is reduced if the NGT process is adhered to by the facilitator and the participants.

Lest a person who has never been introduced to the NGT begin to perceive it as a fail-safe tool, a few cautions should be mentioned and limitations recognized. Suggestions have been made that one of the acclaimed advantages of the NGT may contain a limitation of some proportions in the process. That is, although the structure limits conflict, domination, and intimidation, at the same time creative problem solving may actually be limited. The process requires a knowledgeable and rather strong group leader or facilitator. Not any person off the street is capable of directing a NGT process. The rigidity of the structure may frustrate some people who perceive themselves as "free thinkers" and who, with little or no concern for controlled outcomes, will often rebel at the NGT structure.

Perhaps one of the greatest limitations of the NGT is the potential for overuse. It is a bit like the proverbial "retreat for planning." One retreat may be great, and everyone gets excited and applauds the results. The first retreat may, in some instances, be viewed so positively that there may be a hue and cry for a second one falling on the heels of the first. Too many retreats, or retreats scheduled too close together, soon lose much of their luster. The same is true for the NGT.

IMPROVED NOMINAL GROUP TECHNIQUE

There are so many different types of group processes that it is impossible to list all of them. Various modifications of the NGT have been designed and tested. Different kinds of group processes have been developed for use in different settings when the intended purpose to be served is quite different or specialized. No effort will be made to list all the different kinds of group processes that have been developed and tested. The novice is cautioned to stay with a process that has been thoroughly developed and tested. Following the tried and true is generally much better than getting a wild idea and jumping into some scheme that has been proposed because someone thought it would be "fun to try" or because it "just seemed like a good idea." Developmental work is important but may be a poor substitute for a proven process when results are needed.

One modification of the NGT is the Improved Nominal Group Technique (INGT), proposed by William Fox.[12] Fox took some of the concepts that had been developed by persons in the Rand Corporation who introduced the Delphi technique and blended those concepts with the NGT to originate the INGT.

There are premeeting steps in the INGT, which include the following items.

1. The purpose of the meeting is determined.

2. Persons who will be participants are selected and identified, and their consent to be involved is obtained.

3. The purpose is communicated to participants in advance of the scheduled group meeting, and they are requested anonymously to submit ideas focused on the topic on 3 × 5 cards.

4. After the deadline for receiving the cards, the facilitator numbers each card and makes a list of ideas submitted with no changes or editing. The list is duplicated, and a copy is distributed to each person who will be participating in the INGT. Participants are instructed to note on the list any changes in the wording or the combining of any items they wish to make. After the prospective participants have gone over the materials given them by the facilitator, they may have further ideas. They are, therefore, requested to note any additional ideas they may have for consideration on 3 × 5 cards, without their names, and return them with the other suggestions they have for refining the previous list to the facilitator.

5. The facilitator now has the job of producing a refined list of topics, which may include new items for consideration. The refined list of topics for consideration will be made available at the first group meeting.

6. The next step to be completed by the facilitator is the arrangements for the room or rooms (as demanded by the number of participants) and the equipment and supplies. As with the NGT, the availability of a word processor and person to input information and make copies of materials can be a valuable asset. The room arrangements described in the NGT process apply to the INGT. The premeeting steps described above are more elaborate than is the case with the NGT. The concept of anonymity and the use of controlled feedback, as suggested by the developers of the Delphi, are incorporated in the INGT. If the participants are from diverse groups and do not know each other, nameplates should be prepared and placed on the table in front of each person.

The INGT meeting is directed by a facilitator in a manner similar to the manner in which a facilitator directs the NGT process. Topics or issues for discussion were, however, gathered prior to the meeting, and some noticeable variations occur in the actual meeting at the level of generating items for group consideration.

1. After needed introductions have been made, the facilitator should review the procedures and the purpose to be accomplished with the members of the group. The refined list of topics is then distributed to each member of the group. If an assistant is available to input data into a word processor, the refined list should have been entered prior to the meeting.

2. Participants are given 3 × 5 cards. The facilitator should conduct card collection

rounds to gather additional topics or issues for discussion. The collection of ideas generated by participants is done by instructing members of the group to place a card facedown upon the table. If a participant has no additional ideas to submit, that person should place a blank card on the table. The facilitator gathers the cards, shuffles them to ensure anonymity, and records and numbers each item on a flip chart. The process of card or idea submission is repeated until all participants have indicated, though submitting blank cards, that they have exhausted all their ideas. All flip chart pages, with additional topics listed, should be displayed for the group participants to view. Each participant can now study the items on the flip charts and the items listed from the pre-meeting input of participants.

3. The facilitator annnounces there will be a five- to ten-minute period of silent writing, in which the participants are to list any additional items that have come to mind as a result of reviewing all the items listed prior to the meeting and those items that were introduced at the beginning of the meeting and recorded on the flip charts. This additional silent writing period and time for reflection are to bring out every possible idea of the participants and be sure that a thorough and creative list of topics has been generated. Unlike other input rounds in which each participant places one card facedown at a time, in this exercise it has been suggested that a participant may write as many ideas as desired on one card. Participants who contribute new ideas are instructed not to identify themselves.

The facilitator collects, shuffles, and enters the content from the cards collected from the participants onto flip charts. At the same time, the information is inputted by the word processor operator.

4. As the expanded list of items is displayed on the flip charts, any participant may propose the rewording of an item, the combination of two or more items, or the elimination of duplicate items. In this period of the INGT, however, debate does not take place. If any participant objects to a proposed change at this juncture of the process, the proposal is blocked. All changes that are agreed upon, or not blocked, are noted on the flip charts and by the word processor operator.

5. When all items are displayed on flip charts and on the duplicated list provided participants at the beginning of the meeting, the facilitator introduces the participants to the discussion phase of the process. The group is informed that although it is entering into discussion, participants can still add to the list of items to be considered as the discussion unfolds.

If a word processor is available, the group can be given a short break while electrostatic copies are made of the entire list of items for all participants.

Discussion of all the topics or issues follows these steps.

1. Discussion is introduced and directed by the facilitator, who goes through the entire list of items. At this point, the facilitator should determine if the number of items for consideration exceeds the time limitations of the group. If there are too many items for consideration within the time available for the group, the facilitator should determine the wishes of the members of the group with respect to extending the time of the meeting or scheduling a second meeting.

2. When the discussion is set to proceed, the facilitator reviews with the participants several guidelines to govern the discussion process.

a. The discussion is for seeking and giving clarification and is not intended for debate.
b. Needless repetition is to be avoided.
c. The discussion is not designed as a means of reaching agreement.
d. It is not essential for participants to discuss any item, but there is an opportunity for any participant to deal with any item.
e. At any time a participant can return to an item previously discussed if the purpose is not a matter of reiteration but an exploration of new information as a result of other materials discussed, provided the total discussion time does not exceed agreed-upon limits.
f. The facilitator reviews and summarizes the refined list of items and asks for any additional changes or combinations for which no objections are raised. The final list is then ready for voting.

Voting steps in the INGT have been designed to assure anonymity. If a word processor operator is available and each participant has a copy of the list of items, that list can serve as a guide to voting. The voting process is a means of setting priorities from the total list of items generated by participants. If an extensive list of topics has been generated, it may take as many as three rounds of voting to narrow the list and identify the top priorities.

1. Each participant is instructed, independently and without discussion, to select a given number of items from the list that he or she views as most important. The number of items to be chosen should be five, seven, or nine. Each participant is to prioritize the items in the same manner described previously in the NGT.

2. Votes from the participants are recorded on cards; the number of the item chosen is placed on the upper left corner of the card, and the weighted priority number given the item is circled and placed in the lower right corner to separate it from the number identifying the item. In the event a copy of the computer-generated list is duplicated for each participant, the lists can serve as a ballot in place of the method using cards. The participant can simply place the priority number by the item on the ballot.

   Experts in the use of the INGT have suggested that 15 percent of the items generated is a sufficient amount to consider as high-priority items. Thus, if approximately 35 items are generated by the participants of the group, the top 5 items would be prioritized. If there are 50 items, approximately 7 top items would need to be identified. If there are more than 60 items generated in the INGT, 9 top priority items would be indicated, and if more than 60 items were generated, a situation that is not uncommon, a strong likelihood exists that more than one ballot will be needed to narrow the selection process.

3. The cards, or the computer-generated ballots, are gathered and shuffled to ensure anonymity, and the results are tallied for the group to see. Votes, or points, are tallied to determine the top 15 percent.

   If a second round of votes is needed, the participants are instructed to rank order the items that were prioritized in the top 15 percent. If there are seven such items, participants should be instructed to give a weighting of seven to the item of their first choice, a rating of six to the second item, and so on until they reach the seventh item, which should receive a weighted rating of one. Again, the cards or ballots are to be collected by the facilitator, and the votes are tallied for the group to see the final results.

4. After the voting process has been completed and the top priority items have been identified and placed in order from the first to the last in importance, group participants will generally want to discuss the results of their work. At this point, however, the results of the priority-setting process cannot be changed. Participants generally prefer to be able to reflect on, even object to, what has been accomplished. An expression of dissent is not totally uncommon and can serve as a release for some individuals.

5. Following the INGT, the participants should be thanked for their contribution, and the group is formally disbanded. Expense vouchers should be distributed to individuals who were required to travel to the meeting, and other information related to the next steps in the planning process should be made available to those involved.

Advantages of the INGT include the fact that input is obtained from participants in advance of the actual group meeting; such input not only gathers items for discussion but develops a mind-set on the part of the participants.

A conscious effort was made to incorporate some of the Delphi system in the INGT so that input from each participant is provided in an anonymous way to avoid political pressure or the undue influence of a dominant personality. While some NGT facilitators use oral input sessions in place of written, anonymous input cards, in the INGT process written cards are used, and the author of the idea is not disclosed.

Providing an opportunity for participants to input ideas in advance of the meeting and giving the facilitator the opportunity to compile the list of ideas prior to the meeting can save time for the group. The advance call for items can also give participants more time to state their topics more carefully.

Disadvantages of the INGT include the fact that it has some of the same limitations as the NGT, such as the frustration expressed by some individuals concerning the tight structure. The flip side of that concern is, of course, that distinct advantages can be derived from the tight structure. There is also the danger that the premeeting call for ideas may or may not involve all participants. Although a person could fail to respond with a list of items for consideration prior to the meeting, there is an opportunity for that same person to input items in the meeting. The opportunity for more thoughtful input and the opportunity to save time may, however, be lost in such cases.

LIVE MODIFIED DELPHI

An adaptation of the Delphi has been employed and tested with a large group of people in a live setting, in which there were large group presentations used in conjunction with individual deliberations and extensive small group discussions for consensus building. The intended outcome of the Live Modified Delphi (LMD) process has been to gather the best thinking of opinion leaders to provide input for policymakers regarding the place of technology in education.

In step 1 of the LMD, what is to be studied is determined or clarified, and outcomes needed from opinion leaders are outlined. Such topics as preschool child care, providing options to deal with spiraling energy costs in school systems, how school personnel should face the issue of broken homes, or technology in education could be addressed by opinion leaders in a school district, a region, or even an entire state.

In step 2 of the LMD, as is the case with the typical Delphi approach, the persons to be involved in the LMD process are identified. The area to be considered and the identity of the opinion leaders or experts should be established to generate a list of prospective participants. The selection of participants may be based on several criteria, such as (1) geographic distribution, (2) rural or urban representation, (3) representation from major political parties, (4) representation of experts recognized for their work in the discipline being considered, (5) representation of stakeholders, and (6) representation of legislators. All significant experts or opinion leaders who are viewed as occupying a position in which they make a meaningful contribution or who have benefits to be derived from the deliberations should be considered for representation. With the criteria for selection determined, known opinion leaders in each of the groups identified should be asked for nominations of individuals perceived to be influential or recognized as opinion leaders in their field. From a master list of all persons suggested, a representative group based on the established criteria can be formed.

In step 3 of the LMD, invitations are sent to opinion leaders to become participants. A large number of persons can take part in an LMD. With proper facilities and trained personnel, 1, 2 or 300 persons can be involved in the LMD. Specific information about the purpose for holding the LMD or conference and an explanation of the arrangements with respect to time, place, housing, meals, and costs should be included with the letter of invitation. If a letter of invitation can be sent out with the signature of a well-known and respected official, there may be a greater possibility to attract the opinion leaders who are desired.

Some areas of under representation may be identified when responses are received from the participants. Consequently, a second letter may need to be mailed to alternates so that the best possible representation is achieved.

In step 4 of the LMD, the conference is scheduled, and arrangements are made for the facilities. The LMD may be scheduled over a period of several days. It is possible to accomplish desired outcomes in a two-day period. Each participant should receive a packet of information in advance that contains preregistration materials and copies of articles, reports, or scenarios intended to supply information and ''prime the pump.'' A detailed schedule should also be enclosed, and each participant should be identified with, or assigned to, a small group for discussion purposes. The small groups should be structured so that in each group of 7 to 12 persons various groups are represented in the LMD process. By intent a heterogeneous mix of opinion leaders should be found in each small group.

Facilities needed for conducting the LMD are those typically found in most conference centers. Housing is needed for overnight participants. Meals will be required. An auditorium large enough to hold the total group of participants is needed, and a sufficient number of rooms for small groups will be required. Dividing the total number of participants by the number for each small group will determine the number of small group rooms and small group facilitators and recorders needed for the LMD process.

The equipment needs for conducting an LMD are, as with many conferences, rather standard items. Overhead projectors or television monitors for large group viewing may be needed. Public address equipment may also be needed. In small group meeting rooms it is helpful to have a chalkboard, flip charts, and a microcomputer for the recorder. A copy facility will also be needed to produce multiple copies on short notice for conference participants.

A sample schedule for a one and one-half–day LMD process could be structured as shown below.

Sample Schedule for a One and One-Half–Day Live Modified Delphi Conference

First Day

Welcoming Comments	8:00 A.M.–8:30 A.M.
An Overview of the Conference, Process, and Intended Outcomes	8:30 A.M.–10:15 A.M.
First Discussion Group (generate key issues and generate an accompanying rationale statement for each issue)	
Coffee Break	10:15 A.M.–10:30 A.M.
Second Discussion Group (review and revise issues and statements of rationale generated in first discussion group)	10:30 A.M.–11:45 A.M.
Luncheon and Speaker	12:00 P.M.–1:30 P.M.
Third Discussion Group (make further refinements in issues and statements of rationale generated in the second discussion group)	1:30 P.M.–2:45 P.M.
Coffee Break	2:45 P.M.–3:00 P.M.
Continuation of Third Discussion Group (make final editorial changes in issue and rationale statements, put the issues in priority, and suggest strategies for accomplishing recommended outcomes)	3:00 P.M.–4:45 P.M.
Dinner and Presentation of Related Information; Informal Discussions with Resource Persons or with Persons from Similar Backgrounds	5:30 P.M.–7:00 P.M.

Second Day

Present Composite Listing of Key Issues to all Participants	8:30 A.M.–9:30 A.M.
Discussion of Participants with Like Interests (review and suggest strategies for achieving recommended outcomes)	9:30 A.M.–10:30 A.M.

Coffee Break	10:30 A.M.–10:45 A.M.
Continuation of Discussion (decide what agencies, groups, or individuals are to be suggested to carry the responsibility for accomplishing the recommended outcomes	10:45 A.M.–11:45 A.M.
Lunch and Final Reporting Session	12:00–2:00 P.M.

At the final reporting session, following the luncheon, the recorder assigned to each group would be responsible for reporting the deliberations of the last discussion session to the total group.

In step 5 of the LMD process, small group facilitators and recorders are selected and briefed. The briefing is needed in advance of the conference to explain the purpose for conducting the planning conference and the process to be employed. The function and techniques to be used by small group facilitators need to be explained in detail. All small group facilitators should be chosen with the task they are to perform in mind so that only those persons adept at the small group process are enlisted. Small group facilitators should be assigned to a specified group and meeting room and provided with materials such as flip charts and marking pens and, of course, a detailed schedule.

A recorder should be assigned to each group. The recorders should be capable of using a microcomputer as a word processor and will be responsible for keeping a summary of deliberations in the small groups to which they were assigned. A format for recording the deliberations of each small group can be very helpful and make it possible to have a standardized set of data at the conclusion of each session; in this manner the final compilation process can be facilitated, and the conference coordinators can be assured that complete information is available.

Step 6 of the LMD is kick-off time. As the time to begin arrives, all participants, small group facilitators, and recorders should meet in an auditorium for the introductory comments and an overview of what is to take place during the ensuing days. Appropriate dignitaries may be called upon to make introductions and to be introduced to lend credence to the importance of the task at hand.

A futurist or specialist, acknowledged as an expert in the area under consideration, may be a keynote presenter for the audience of opinion leaders in the planning conference. The intent of having a keynote presentation is to set the tone and to provide the participants with some additional factual information about the topic under consideration.

Step 7 of the LMD starts the active participation of the opinion leaders. Participants are instructed to move to their assigned groups for their first small group task. There are, as previously suggested, 7 to 12 persons assigned to each small group, as well as the facilitator and the recorder. The facilitator is to explain the task and the process to be followed in the first small group activity. Participants are to identify as many issues, needs, or concerns as they can regarding the topic under consideration and write their topic on a 3 × 5, or 5 × 8, card. The facilitator then collects and shuffles the cards, and the topics are listed on the flip chart used to record for visual support while the recorder inputs the same information in the word processor. The second portion of the session is built upon the anonymous inputting of issues for consideration. Items generated during the input session are discussed, using group process techniques, to arrive at a list of issues perceived by the group to be of high priority or significance. The participants are to be led in the small group process to produce a list of issues upon which they can agree and to give with each issue a brief rationale, of one or two paragraphs, supporting the inclusion of the issue.

During time for a coffee break the recorders can edit for correct form, while protecting the intent of the participants, the final list of issues that were identified. The recorder then needs to run 15 copies on a photocopier.

In step 8 of the LMD, the materials, issues, and their accompanying rationales are moved to a new group of opinion leaders for their consideration. The live Delphi, unlike a traditional approach, has a portion of the deliberations, as shown in the first small group sessions, where opinion leaders work face-to-face in developing a rationale statement for each issue. It is recognized that the face-to-face portion of the small group discussion violates standards of the Delphi approach. The general concept of providing for anonymity is repeated in the second small group activity, as a cycle of moving materials from one group to another is set in motion. The list of issues and their accompanying rationale statements generated by group A are passed on to group B, and so on until the final group's materials are given to group A. A sample rotation schedule for an LMD conference in which there are 80 participants would have three rotations as shown below.

First Small Group Discussion	Second Small Group Discussion	Third Small Group Discussion
A	B	C
B	C	D
C	D	E
D	E	F
E	F	G
F	G	H
G	H	I
H	I	J
I	J	A
J	A	B

The issues and accompanying rationales from group A are handed to members of group B, and materials generated by group B are sent to group C.

Finally, the materials prepared by members of group J, the last group, are given to group A for the second-round discussion.

When the second small group session is called to order, each participant is given a copy of the issues that had been generated in the group next to his or her group in the alphabetical listing. (This is the copy the recorder was busy preparing when participants were on their coffee break. The reason the recorders need to prepare 15 copies is to provide some spare copies for the program coordinators.)

Facilitators in the second group work session should see that each participant has a copy of the issues and rationale statements that have been received from the preceding alphabetical group. Participants are to study the list of issues they receive, discuss them, and determine what refinements they would make in the issues and the rationale statements. Participants are given the option of combining issues, editing, or even deleting issues if they can give a reason or justification for the deletion. As group B examines the list of issues generated by group A, and so on through the various groups, definite areas of duplications and congruence will be found in some areas of groups' thinking. As one group works with the issues generated by another group, refinements and greater clarity and insights will emerge. The adage of two heads being better than one will surface as the structured process unfolds.

During the second round of discussions, an interesting set of forces may be observed. Quite simply, it is one of the purported advantages of the Delphi technique: the avoidance of face-to-face lobbying or the power of personalities or a position unduly influencing the process. Some bigwig in group A could have added an idea to the list of issues in the first input and discussion session, but when that idea reached group B at the second discussion level, no one in group B knew whose ideas had influenced the rationale statement, nor did they care. Ideas can be taken at face value with no political implications or personal persuasions involved. The end result of the second discussion session should be a set of issue statements that are more focused and succinct and supported by a sounder rationale. There will be, as a result of opinion leaders in one group discussing the issues generated by opinion leaders of another group, some obvious and clear modifications as an issue is added, some issues are possibly combined, and others are expanded or clarified; the group process will reinforce consensus positions and provide a platform for the development of sounder justifications or rationale statements.

During lunchtime, another speaker may give brief comments and present material explaining still another facet of the basic topic of deliberation. It is time for lunch for everybody in the Live Modified Delphi except the recorders, who may be given a cold snack while they work at cleaning up the draft of the deliberations of the second discussion sessions and make 15 copies on the photocopy machine, which will be passed on to members of the next group in the rotation schedule for still further deliberations. (See round three of the rotation schedule.)

More than idle curiosity and friendly prattle may be experienced among the participants as members from one group, for example, group C, mingle with members of group D, who were the recipient of the first group's original deliberations. Opinion leaders, being human, may seek out information to learn how the issues generated by their group fared in the second round of deliberations. A considerable amount of thoughtful discussion can be conducted on an informal basis, and a fruitful exchange of ideas can occur as individuals join in informal discussions and react to presenters. One by-product of the process that can emerge at this stage of the Live Modified Delphi process is an increased understanding of the views of opinion leaders from different segments of the population.

Step 9 of the LMD takes place following lunch. The third small group work session is convened by the facilitators and the materials that were developed in the second round of discussions are handed to a new group. The materials generated in the first brainstorming session by group A are moved to group B for refinement, and in the third session the materials from group A that group B refined are moved on to members of group C. In the third round of deliberations in small group settings in the Live Modified Delphi, the task is to make further refinements in the materials and to place the issues in order of importance. The participants are instructed to give their attention to refinements and clarification of issues rather than throwing the issues out and starting over again. Statements of rationale are to be further clarified and, if necessary, expanded, and the statements of issues are to be given further scrutiny and refinement. Members of discussion groups may be given the latitude to make further additions or combinations of items; however, rather than making sweeping deletions, they are simply to change the rationale to explain why an issue might not be worthy of consideration or at least might occupy a place of lesser importance in the pattern of deliberations.

The facilitator directs the deliberation in the third discussion group, and the recorder continues to keep a record of the deliberations. As in previous discussions, the recorder is provided a format to follow in setting up the record of discussions. At the end of the third discussion session, the recorder should make approximately 15 copies of the deliberations.

Coffee breaks come in the schedule for everyone except the recorders, who are to put final revisions of issues and statements of rationale into a prescribed format. The copies of the third group deliberations will be used.

As the afternoon discussion group reconvenes, participants are given the printed statements upon which they had been working prior to the coffee break. Their task in the extended session is twofold. First, they are to review, edit, and make any corrections they feel are necessary. This process is conducted in a controlled format to avoid the problems of having a committee edit a camel. Second, the participants are to give consideration to the identification of strategies for implementation. Such questions as who should be responsible for dealing with an issue and what kind of resources will be needed should be considered.

In step 10 of the LMD, a composite list of issues that have been developed by all the group discussions in the conference is compiled. This task is accomplished by a team of recorders and conference coordinators. The process of synthesizing and combining issues may take time and careful thought. The task of making a composite of the rationale statements may be an even more arduous undertaking. Keeping the intent of the issues clear and unchanged in the translation process is key to the process of synthesizing and developing a list of issues. Many duplications will likely be found, as one group in its deliberations will have identified the same topic or topics that other opinion leaders in other groups had identified. Consequently, the process of combining may be, in some instances, only a matter of minor editing. In other instances, the various topics may, in the way they have been stated, suggest combinations of two or more issues into one. If the opinion leaders have been placed in a process that has given them strong background information and adequate resource persons and if the structured LMD has been well organized and properly focused, there will be common themes and agreement among the participants on some issues. The discussion process and the movement of materials from one group of opinion leaders to another group are designed, as in a standard Delphi process, to generate focus and refinement on issues. It is the task of the conference coordinators to pull out the essence of the total set of deliberations and to: (1) generate a composite list of issues and place them in order of importance; (2) develop composite rationale statements; (3) prepare a suggested set of strategies for meeting needs or issues; and (4) summarize a listing of persons or agencies recommended as the logical ones to carry out the tasks required to achieve the recommended outcomes.

It will have been a long day, and while conference coordinators are developing the composite list of issues, participants who have been in a structured setting that was eliciting responses and demanding their undivided attention will be ready for a change of pace. The group may be held together by providing a banquet where designated leaders or political figures are given an opportunity to express views. Informal discussions may follow as an extension of the day's deliberations.

Step 11 of the LMD process is designed to provide opinion leaders an opportunity to move to groups of their own choosing, where people of like interest can consider the issues and the recommendations for action. The second day of the LMD may begin with all participants meeting in an auditorium in which the coordinators present the results of the first day's deliberations. The steps may be reviewed, and the details of how many topics or issues were generated and how they funneled into the final list of issues may be described. Each participant should have a hard copy of the issues, the rationale, the level of importance, suggested strategies for implementation, and what persons or agencies are recommended to carry out the implementation process. There will undoubtedly be questions and points raised for clarification. The final list of issues is used to identify topics for discussion. In other words, an issue or several issues dealing with the same theme become the topic for a special interest group discussion.

Participants of like interest may self-select by area of interest and move into small group meeting rooms where they are to undertake the task of making final revisions and suggestions for improvements in the materials that have emerged from the deliberations of the previous day. The opinion leaders are to make suggested refinements and editorial changes in the draft they have been presented. Some revisions and editorial changes are to be expected. If no suggestions for improvement are forthcoming, possibly the groups are not giving the process their best shot. What can be expected is that the final deliberations will generate refinements and even some possible modifications; however, the integrity of the document with which they have been presented will be, for the most part, maintained with only slight revisions and improvements. It is only natural that topics or issues generated by opinion leaders from various backgrounds, when placed under the scrutiny of opinion leaders viewed as specialists in the area being discussed, would be revised and refined.

During coffee break recorders will once again prepare a revised draft of the deliberations and make sufficient copies so that all members of the self-selected group will have a hard copy to review when the group reconvenes. Following the coffee break, groups composed of opinion leaders of similar interest will return to their chosen small groups and the task of making final editorial changes and suggestions for refining the document. The work of the recorder, facilitated by the availability of word processing and copying equipment, will be called upon for the last round of editorial changes.

Step 12 of the LMD is the final reporting session. Thank-you speeches are given by various dignitaries at the luncheon, and the live Delphi comes to the closing session. By the end of the luncheon session, a copy of the final draft should be made available for all participants.

The coordinators for the live Delphi conference will need to take all materials from the conference and prepare a final edited copy for general distribution. The conference proceedings, containing the names of all participants and the usual thank-you letters, should be sent to each participant. News coverage may be warranted, and a mailing list of targeted audiences may be identified to receive copies of the proceedings.

The effectiveness of the LMD process as described above is difficult to determine. There is speculation with respect to its impact. It is easy to identify the fact that a document may be produced and distributed to a given number of persons. A report may be prepared indicating the total cost of conducting such a conference. It is much more subjective to make a determination about what influence the effort of a LMD process may have on a legislative body or community leaders. The LMD process could create an awareness on the part of officials that in turn could lead to improved or expanded efforts. It may be even more difficult to see if there were any links between the deliberations of an LMD conference and what children and youth learn in schools. The most definitive assessment may come in the form of feedback gathered from the participants. Although it is difficult to determine the LMD process's impact on strategic planning, it may be equally or more difficult to prove that such a process had no impact or that it led educational planners astray.

Advantages and Disadvantages of LMD

The use of the Delphi process has been acknowledged by observers to have definite advantages and also to demonstrate some limitations.[13] The same is true for the LMD. Admittedly, the LMD must bring a group of specialists or opinion leaders together for a meeting; thus, the advantage of the Delphi, which may involve persons who are geographically distant, is lost. As Van Nostrand and others have suggested, the Delphi eliminates the sometimes harmful psychological barriers often found in groups and allows each participant an equal opportunity. The LMD, especially if involving opinion leaders, is designed to place some controls and limitations on dominating individuals but does not manipulate that variable to the extent found in a regular Delphi process. The LMD does permit anonymous input and responding and uses an idea evaluation stage.

One of the disadvantages of the Delphi process is that it involves a considerable time commitment for each participant. The end result can be a high rate of attrition as the cycles progress. This disadvantage of the Delphi is largely reduced with the LMD. Although it may be difficult to attract experts or opinion leaders to attend a two-day session, once a person has accepted the task, the participant usually will not leave before the process is completed. The Delphi requires a higher level of writing skill on the part of participants than does the LMD. Less competent writers are not at a disadvantage in the LMD. While the Delphi does not provide any social interaction, obviously the LMD, with scheduled coffee breaks, lunches, speakers, and an evening for visiting and exchanging ideas, is able to capitalize on social interaction. The Delphi fails to provide an opportunity for verbal clarifications while the LMD incorporates group processes to clarify and refine ideas and at the same time afford verbal compromises in thinking.

DIRECTING SMALL GROUP ACTIVITIES

When planners consider the use of one or more small group techniques, it is important to have a specific outcome in mind. Small groups should not be used just because "everybody else is doing it" or because "it seems like a good idea." Very explicit goals for a small group activity need to be determined before the group is called together. The planner needs to develop a clear and precise statement of the purpose for conducting a group activity and communicate that statement of purpose to those who will be participating. It has been suggested that acceptance of goals results in an increase in group decision-making quality and ultimately a higher level of acceptance of the group solution.[14]

"Group think" is an insidious condition that can result when members of a group acquiesce to a dominant view and agree just because it is easier to agree than disagree or when they are indifferent and vote in agreement with something on which they do not agree just so they can "get on with it." Brightman pointed out that "highly cohesive and long-lived groups are susceptible to group think . . . [and a] . . . consensus-at-any-cost mentality that produces a serious deterioration in a team's problem-solving capabilities."[15] When group think is in evidence, members suppress their personal beliefs and criticism of ideas to let the group reach what appears to be agreement. Such false agreements do not generate acceptance.

At the signs of group think, the planner should give careful consideration to the size and composition of groups. The most appropriate size for a group is needlessly debated by those who seem to want to forge ahead without listening to researchers who have conducted studies on the topic. While there is some latitude in the number of persons who can work effectively in a small group, there is evidence to suggest that as group size increases from 3 persons to 5, the quality of their decisions improves. Some experts suggest that once a group surpasses the number of 5, there is a gradual decline in the efficiency and effectiveness of the group.[16] The decline of effectiveness is quite sharp when there are more than 12 persons in a group. Quite simply, if there are more than 12 persons, some individuals do not participate to any significant degree even if they wish to take part. As a general rule of thumb, planners who intend to work with small groups for decision-making activities should consider group numbers ranging from at least 5 persons up to 9, and never more than 12.

The composition of the group is also an important consideration for the planner to address. Homogeneous groups will be less inclined to generate conflict, but they are much less likely to generate any worthwhile results. Heterogeneous groups are more inclined to be productive, to come up with more creative options, and to be less protective. In the Live Modified Delphi described above, all participants were placed in assigned groups prior to the starting of the planning effort to ensure that individuals of like background or from one organization were not in the same group. There is a flip side to the coin that suggests heterogeneity. If a group is so "strange" that it has no common base from which to operate or if there are individuals who are so at odds that they lose their ability to communicate, the groups can be torn apart by incompatibility. Actually, there is much less danger of such an occurrence than some would like us to believe. It is uncommon for differences in groups to render them impotent. Heterogeneous groups, when given a clear charge and structured in a way that has been proven to be effective, can and will generally come to decisions that are superior to decisions reached by any one individual or by a group that is noted for its homogeneity.

Groups cannot work in a vacuum. Leadership in structuring the group and in directing or facilitating the work of a group is an essential ingredient. Unstructured and nondirected groups left to wander about some vague arena are generally like any nondirected activity—aimless. Groups can and do waste time if not structured and disciplined in their task. The discipline for group effectiveness, while it can be fostered by individual group members who are sensitive and informed about group processes, must ultimately come from the facilitator or person responsible for directing the entire planning effort. If a planning process involves a large number of people who are to be assigned to work in small groups, the person responsible for the overall planning process is responsible to see that group facilitators are instructed in what outcomes are sought and the group process to be employed. Uninformed or errant small group facilitators can make a major dent in the results of group activities.

It is not uncommon to hear an administrator comment that small group activities may be all right if you have time for them, but if you want to get things moving, "somebody has to make a decision." The cost-time effectiveness question is not an easy one to answer. How much time should be invested in letting a group become involved? How many people should have input? These and many other questions have been asked many times. Part of the difficulty in arriving at a clear answer regarding the cost-time effectiveness question is that it does not yield simplistic answers. When the planning process is followed and little or no input is gathered from stakeholders, the end result is often a failure to find commitment on the part of the staff or to get a majority vote at the polls on a bond election. But even when such failures do occur, some persistent controllers who fear the involvement of significant others seek shelter by claiming there is no clear evidence that the lack of involvement made the difference, and "anyway, the neighboring district tried to get a lot of people in the act and their bond issue went down." The rationale is strong and the evidence is clear that the involvement of people can make a major difference. The way to achieve that major difference is to involve people appropriately and in so doing gain their thinking and their support.

SUMMARY

Many references can be found that deal with various approaches to group processes, and numerous expert practitioners can be identified who have exceptional skills in managing group activities in decision making. Only a few approaches have been suggested in the limited space of this planning guide. Planners who have an understanding of human motivations and who are competent in the area of interpersonal skills can, by employing any of the approaches described above, move effectively into group decision-making activities. Group techniques, like any tool, must be chosen to meet a specific need. Thus, the planner must determine what outcomes are sought and which group approach will best meet the identified need. One group process may have a particular appeal to a novice planner and consequently seem very attractive. The selection of the process to be used should, however, not be based upon attractiveness or appeal, but rather it should be based on fit. Will the process yield the desired results?

As planners work in the role of group facilitator and gain confidence and experience, a clear understanding of the discipline required in working with groups will be developed. For the most part, a safe rule of thumb is that once a process has been chosen for a group process in decision making, it is advisable to stay the course. Trust the process and employ the discipline of that process in facilitating the work of a group. While the process is important, and it can be argued that it is also important for the participants to feel positive about their group effort and experience, results are essential.

Members of effective groups exhibit several behaviors. They know where they are going and how to get the job done; "examine the validity of opinions and assumptions; are . . . rigorous in evaluating solutions and comparing solutions to the stated goals; base their decisions on reasonable facts, inference, and assumptions; have influential members who exert a positive facilitating influence";[17] demonstrate open communication patterns; and show respect and trust.

It is possible to infer, as well as observe, what can be expected in groups that are ineffective. They (1) seek status over quality; (2) have hidden agendas; (3) are often tardy or absent; (4) rarely challenge ideas and treat opinions as facts while placing pressure on dissenters; (5) may evaluate solutions in a perfunctory manner; (6) ignore basic assumptions or data underlying issues being discussed; (7) lack a clear direction or employ an incomplete definition of the problem; (8) have individual members who inhibit or stifle; and (9) focus on only one alternative and have no contingency plan.

Several of the characteristics of ineffective groups are associated with group think failures as members of the group harbor a shared illusion of unanimity.

NOTES

1. K. H. Price, "Problem Solving Strategies: A Comparison by Problem Solving Phases," *Group and Organization Studies* 10, no. 3 (1985), 289–299.

2. A. H. Van De Ven, *Group Decision Making and Effectiveness* (Kent, Ohio: Kent State University Press, 1974), 6.

3. Merrell J. Hansen, "Site-Based Management and Quality Circles: A Natural Combination," *NASSP Bulletin* 74 (October 1990), 100–103.

4. W. G. Cunningham, *Systematic Planning for Educational Change* (Palo Alto, California: Mayfield, 1982), 128.

5. C. M. Moore, *Group Techniques for Idea Building* (Newbury Park, California: Sage, 1987), 24.

6. Ibid., 24.

7. Ibid., 25.

8. Van de Ven, *Group Decision Making and Effectiveness*, 20.

9. Ibid., 20.

10. P. S. Goodman et al., *Designing Effective Work Groups* (San Francisco: Jossey-Bass, 1986).

11. W. B. Eddy, *The Manager and the Working Group* (New York: Praeger Press, 1985), 171.

12. William M. Fox, *Effective Group Problem Solving* (San Francisco: Jossey-Bass, 1987).

13. Arthur B. Van Gundy, *Techniques of Structured Problem Solving*, 2nd ed. (New York: Van Nostrand Reinhold, 1988), 327.

14. I. M. Lane, "Making the Goals of Acceptance and Quality Explicit: Effects on Group Decisions," *Small Group Behavior* 13, no. 4 (1982), 542–554.

15. Harvey J. Brightman. *Group Problem Solving: An Improved Managerial Approach* (Atlanta, Georgia: Business Publishing Division, Georgia State University, 1988), 47.

16. Phillip Yetton and Preston C. Botber, "The Relationships Among Group Size, Member Ability, Social Decision Scheme, and Performance," *Organization Behavior and Human Performance* 32, no. 2 (1983), 145–159.

17. Brightman, *Group Problem Solving*, 22.

9

Surveys

INTRODUCTION

Planners are frequently faced with the task of gathering information so they can make informed decisions. One of the cardinal sins in planning is demonstrated when would-be planners plunge ahead blindly and make decisions based on preferences or hunches while lacking the information to make informed decisions. A tool that can help provide information is the survey. "Surveys are frequently conducted for the purpose of making descriptive assertions about some population." [1] There are times when planners need to know descriptive characteristics, such as age, sex, place of residence, or other demographic information. At other times, planners need to know what people are thinking, what their opinions are, or what expectations they may have. Thus, surveys may be used to provide explanatory assertions about a population or to explore or inquire in an effort to better understand people's stance with respect to issues or perceived needs.

SURVEY RESEARCH CONSIDERATIONS

While "survey research" has been considered to be less sophisticated than "basic research" in some circles, it does serve a definite need. The quality of the survey methodology does, however, become an issue; if poor methodology is employed, and the data collected and analyzed are questionable, results will be misleading and possibly detrimental. Surveys are used with a rather high level of frequency in practice and have often been taken for granted. There has been an assumption that anyone can throw a survey together and get the needed information; after all, if some researchers perceive the survey methodology to be simple and of a menial quality, any plodding individual could conduct a survey without giving the process any major thought or planning time. Wrong! Only well-planned surveys can provide solid, usable data. Like any tool, the survey can be misused more easily than it can be used properly.

Perhaps one of the best illustrations of how a segment of the population in the United States relies on survey data can be found in the political arena. Politicians live and die by the results of the polls. There are numerous illustrations of politicians who have announced they are "studying the issue before announcing their position." Loosely translated, that statement often means, "The polls are not in, and the wishes of the voters are not yet identified; as soon as that information is collected, I will announce where I stand on the issue." The way to learn where the population is going is to take a poll or conduct a survey. The value of the survey technique has been perceived, and a major industry has been established to meet the survey needs of the nation.

Various kinds of surveys have been developed to serve differing needs. The *cross-sectional* survey is perhaps the most common. In the cross-sectional survey, information is gathered from a specified audience or sample at a specified time in order to describe some larger population. In one way, it can be compared to a snapshot in contrast to a moving picture, since it captures information at a specified time. The cross-sectional survey may be used to describe a population, to gather selected descriptors, or to determine perceptions held by people in the sample. Such surveys can also be used to gather information to make comparisons between groups of people or to discover relationships between variables. Perhaps the best known survey group in the United States is Selection Research-Gallup, Inc.; staff members are continually polling groups to gather information regarding education, marketing, politics, or any topic about which people wish to know the opinions of some group or population in America.

Another form of survey is the *longitudinal* study, in which information is collected over an extended period of time. Longitudinal surveys may be descriptive or exploratory. Generally, longitudinal surveys are used in conjunction with trend analyses. In some longitudinal surveys, data are gathered from data banks rather than starting from ground zero and developing an entirely new data base. The Phi Delta Kappa Gallup Poll, which elicits Americans' view of education in any one year, is a cross-sectional survey. As such data from several years have been gathered, however, the cumulative information allows for longitudinal analysis. *Panel studies* are a form of longitudinal surveys in which individuals in a given sample are polled each year over a number of years. For example, questions have been raised about parents' involvement and level of satisfaction in the education process of their child. A panel survey could be undertaken in which a selected group of parents could be identified as their children entered kindergarten. The sample could be polled to gain information concerning their perceptions regarding the quality of the educational experience provided by the school and to determine the amount and nature of parental involvement in school. If the study is extended for a period of eight years, it would be possible to "follow" the selected panel of parents through primary grades and on into the middle or junior high schools. Information from the panel group could provide insight into the question of parent involvement that could benefit planners. Because of the obvious time requirement for conducting such a longitudinal survey, the method could be used only in limited situations. Persons needing information regarding parental involvement might need to search for another approach for gathering needed data.

Definitions

As might be expected, a number of terms and definitions are used by experts on survey methodology. Fortunately, most terminology used in conjunction with surveys is rather straightforward.

The *sample frame* "is the list, indexes, or other population records from which a sample is to be selected."[2] The sample frame is the population or the set of people who have a chance of being selected to be a part of the study. The planner needs to understand three characteristics of a sample frame: (1) any sampling scheme needs to assure comprehensiveness or the representative nature of a sample to know the extent to which segments of the population may be excluded; (2) each individual in a sample frame should have an equal opportunity to be selected; and (3) consideration should be given to the efficiency with which the sampling is performed.[3]

The *universe,* as used by pollsters, "is the theoretical and hypothetical aggregation of all elements, as defined for a given survey."[4] It is a broad and encompassing concept or set of parameters that generally takes in more than the limits needed for a given survey.

The *population* or *survey population* is that portion of the universe or the aggregation of elements from which the survey sample is actually selected.

A *unit of analysis* is the "thing" being studied.

An *element* of a sample is "that unit about which information is collected and which provides the basis of analysis,"[5] for example, a family, parents, social groups, church memberships, or employees in a given firm.

The *sample unit* is that element of a population to be selected as the final group of persons to be surveyed. In a simple or single-stage sample, the sample unit is identical to the element involved in the study. "In more complex samples, however, different levels of sampling units may be employed. For example, a researcher may select a sample of census blocks in a city (primarily sampling units), then select a sample of households on the selected blocks (secondary sampling units) and finally select a sample of adults (final sampling units) from the selected households."[6]

The *sampling frame* is a list of actual sampling units from which a planner may select a sample. The sampling frame, in a single-stage sample, is often synonymous with the "population." A planner can begin with the "universe" or "population" in mind and determine the sample frames contained in the population. A determination can be made to draw a sample from the total population or to stratify the sample by drawing subsamples from identified and chosen sampling frames.

Observation units are the units for data collection. An observation unit is an element or aggregation of elements from which information will be collected in a survey. A survey may be directed at the head of a household (the observation unit) to gain information about the children in the household (the unit of analysis).

Random sampling is the most commonly used approach to draw a representative group from a total population. In random sampling, "the selection is made in such a way that each element of the population has a known probability of selection, although not necessarily an equal chance."[7] More information will be presented on this popular means of sampling, as well as other forms of sampling, later in this chapter.

Systematic sampling is a process of selecting units from a population based on set intervals. For example, every 4th person from a list could be drawn, or every 10th or 15th person could be selected depending upon the number and percentage of the population used in the sample.

Quota sampling is a form of systematic sampling in which the person conducting the interviews selects, within prescribed parameters, the persons to be contacted rather than having the names generated by the planner of the survey.

Stratified random sampling is a process in which the population is categorized into subgroups or strata, and a random sample is then drawn from each stratum based on a predetermined set of proportions. For example, if it were known that 73 percent of the adults in a community did not have children attending school, a subpopulation of adults without children in school could be identified; 73 percent of the total sample would be drawn from that subpopulation, and 27 percent of the stratum of adults with children would constitute the balance of the sample.

STEPS USED TO CONDUCT A SURVEY

The steps involved in most surveys generally follow a sequence of activities or tasks similar in nature. Every survey should, however, be individually designed and structured in a way to achieve desired results. Typically, no two surveys will be the same. A generic list of tasks used to conduct a survey could include the following items (see Figure 9.1).

1. Determine or clarify the need to be met or the purpose for conducting the survey.
2. Determine what to ask for in the way of information.
3. Develop the individual items or questions to be asked.
4. Pilot and revise the instrument.

5. Determine who to go to for the needed information.

6. Select the sample.

7. Determine how to get the information from the sample.

8. Plan the data collection process.

9. Collect the data.

10. Code and tabulate the data.

11. Analyze the data.

12. Prepare the report.

Determine Purpose for Conducting a Survey

Careful thought needs to go into determining the need for a survey. The need or purpose for conducting a survey must be clearly specified and focused. By refining the need, the planner is able, in subsequent steps, to direct and focus the efforts to ensure that the basic questions will be answered. Lack of specificity can cause people to wander into blind alleys and become involved in fruitless meandering. An imprecise needs statements can result in a failure to find answers, a source of frustration, and a lack of confidence. (For an example of a survey project, see Appendix D-1.)

Determine What to Ask

The purpose of a survey is not to answer one question by gathering responses to a single item. In developing a survey, the purpose or need is broken down into parts that can be listed as the questions for which answers will be sought in the survey. In turn, the basic questions may be divided into many items to be considered for inclusion in a questionnaire. The purpose of a survey should be a broad or general intent that can be broken down into more focused survey questions and eventually into specific items for respondents to answer.

Develop Questions

Guidelines for framing questions for a public opinion questionnaire were suggested years ago by Nunnery and Kimbrough.[8] These early guidelines have been used with only minor modifications to aid planners and pollsters for approximately two decades. Minimal guidelines that have been suggested for questionnaire item development include the following:

1. Make the questions brief. If questions are long and complex, the respondent can become confused or withdraw from the process because of an excessive time commitment.

2. Use words that are easily understood and commonly used. If the syllabic intensity is above the level of the respondents, confusion and resistance can build between

Figure 9.1
Steps in Conducting a Survey

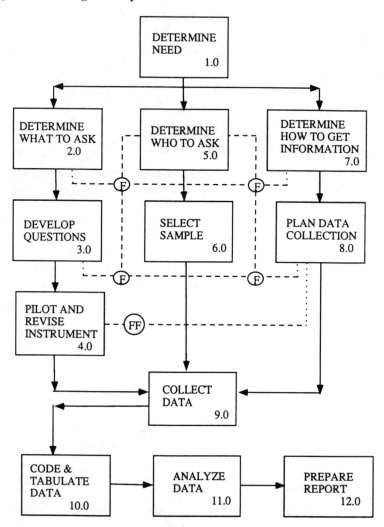

the researcher or planner and the persons from whom information is sought. Formulas can be applied to measure syllabic intensity and assure that the items are
targeted to the least literate respondents.

3. Always avoid leading questions. Neutrality in the wording of items for a questionnaire is important. For example, a question would possibly "lead" a respondent if
it was stated that "evidence has been gathered that to compete in the world market
bilingual business people will be required, so would you favor expanding the modern foreign language curriculum in the school?" Another illustration of a leading

question would be, "Do you want your child to have the limited advantages of an outstanding music program?" Obviously, such a question would influence the respondent to give an affirmative or positive response. After all, would any caring parent want a child in a music program that was not outstanding?

4. Avoid questions that contain two concepts or that are double-barreled. Double-barreled questions are actually two questions in one and, as such, require two answers. An example of a double-barreled question is, "Do you favor expanding the vocational curriculum in the high school and including a work-release program?" A respondent might favor expanding the vocational curriculum but not favor a work-release program.

5. Avoid ambiguity in terms used in the survey or the use of double negatives. Ambiguity frequently occurs when terms lack precision and are open to different interpretations from different individuals. For example, if a question was stated, "Do you think students should appreciate the accomplishments of Martin Luther King?" there could be some debate over the meaning of the word *appreciate*. Words that are included in lists of ambiguous terms are appreciate, feel, enjoy, understand, believe, and comprehend.

6. Avoid words that carry emotional connotations or that are biased, emotion-laden, or value-laden. References are made to "liberals" and "fundamentalists" in religious discussions. Consequently, a question in which the respondent was asked for an opinion about the influence of "fundamental religious church members" in a community could get a different set of responses than if only the words "church members" were included in the question. Terms that label groups of people often generate connotations because of social conditions and perceptions of people. Again, as an illustration, different sets of responses could be received if a question asked, "Do you think bail should be increased for terrorists accused of threatening the safety of innocent and unarmed airline passengers?" as contrasted to a less value-laden item, "Do you think bail should be increased for persons accused of threatening the safety of airline passengers?"

7. Refrain from the use of embarrassing questions as a general rule. If an item is a potential source of embarrassment for respondents, it can be a cause of a low response pattern. People generally do not like to divulge information about their income, their sex life, or many of their personal and private thoughts. If data pertaining to such items as personal income or the amount of money given to support the church are needed, the pollster should design the items with considerable care or consider searching for such information through alternate sources.

8. Avoid colloquialisms or words that may have specific meanings in certain geographic areas or with selected minority groups. "Street talk" may be acceptable and have a clear meaning for some groups of people and, by contrast, be completely unacceptable to other groups. In a recent television advertisement, a food product was referred to as "very bad" when the intent, or the meaning, of *bad* was actually given a reverse translation to that found in a standard dictionary. While a reverse connotation may serve to attract attention in a television advertisement, reverse connotations are not recommended for items in a questionnaire.

9. Keep the instructions and format simple to avoid overloading the mind or intimidating the respondent. If respondents are expected to read lengthy sets of instruc-

tions before answering questions, a strong likelihood exists that the response percentage will be low. If respondents are preoccupied with the complexity of instructions, they may not give enough attention to the content of the questions. Clarity and simplicity of instructions become a prime consideration when developing a questionnaire.

10. Design questions that respondents can be expected to have appropriate knowledge to answer. If a respondent is expected to conduct an investigation or to delve into old records for information, this expectation can lower the percentage of responses.

11. Obviously, questions must be developed that will elicit the responses needed to answer the basic purpose for conducting the survey. It is often tempting to include a few "interesting" questions that fail to contribute to the data base needed to meet the purpose for conducting the study. The persons responsible for developing items for the questionnaire should examine each item and determine how the responses to the item will be analyzed and will be used to contribute to the study.

As survey techniques have been refined, there have been several types of questions that have become recognized for their discreet nature and applicability. The question types that are most frequently found in questionnaires include closed-end questions, open-ended questions, rating questions, and demographic questions.

The *closed-end question* is used to guide the respondent when selecting one of several options. The closed-end question may be designed to involve a dichotomous set of "yes" or "no" responses, or it may include a number of options (see examples 1 and 2 in Figure 9.2). In the most frequent form of the multiple-response item, a Likert scale, which generally has five options, is used (see examples 3a and b in Figure 9.2). When the closed-end question is used, the respondent is generally not asked for a justification or rationale for the answer. It is possible, however, to combine the closed-end question with an open-ended question (see Example 4 in Figure 9.2).

The *open-ended question* is designed to give the respondent complete discretion in providing an answer. No categories are provided from which the respondent is to choose. Questions are intended to elicit responses that are more detailed than simple "yes" or "no" answers. Opinions, feelings, insights, or judgments are sought in many open-ended questions. In some instances, an open-ended question has been used to ask for the names of people who are perceived to have specified characteristics. An open-ended question can also be used to determine what agency or organization is perceived to possess certain identified characteristics (e.g., What baseball team during the decade of the 1950s was the best? What professional organization provides educational administrators with the most progressive point of view in its publications?). In the case in which a name of a person, team, or organization is sought in an open-ended question, the analysis is accomplished by a simple tabulation and count or frequency of responses. In other open-ended questions in which opinions, feelings, insights, or judgments of a more involved nature are sought, a more sophisticated process for analysis should be employed. With the current

Figure 9.2
Sample Survey Questions

EXAMPLE 1

Should interscholastic soccer be added to the list of sports available for students in Centerville High School?

_____ Favor _____ Oppose

EXAMPLE 2

Do you feel elementary school facilities should be used for child care in the afternoon after classes are over for the day?

_____ Yes _____ No _____ No Opinion

EXAMPLE 3

Place an "X" in the space that matches your opinion regarding the following statements. (SA = Strongly Agree; A = Tend to Agree; NO = No Opinion; D = Tend to Disagree; SD = Strongly Disagree.

	SA	A	NO	D	SD
1. The official communications sent from school to parents and guardians regarding school matters are clear and informative.	—	—	—	—	—
2. School officials have been fair and honest in their communications with me as a parent or guardian.	—	—	—	—	—

EXAMPLE 4

Would you approve or disapprove of a plan to require high school students to stay at school during the lunch hour?

_____ Approve _____ Disapprove

Please state your reason _____

_____

surge of interest in qualitative research methodology, there has been a more sophisticated approach to content analysis than was often used in past decades. The analysis and interpretation of open-ended questions are more time consuming, and the process is subject to faulty analysis unless the researcher is well-versed in the process.

The novice confronted with the task of conducting a survey may be of the opinion that a closed-end question procedure is easier and perhaps better than an open-ended approach. Other persons conducting a survey may take the opposite point of view. The choice of the type of question should not be determined by the likes or dislikes of the persons conducting the survey; the type of question should be chosen that solicits the data needed. Some data that are needed can be gathered with closed-ended questions and some with open-ended questions. If a survey were to be developed to determine if high school students had used marijuana and if not, why not, it would be appropriate to have a dichotomous question followed by an open-ended question in the following manner.

Have you ever smoked marijuana? Yes—— No——

If your answer was "No," please explain why you made the decision not to smoke marijuana.

Rating questions, in a variety of forms, are frequently used in questionnaires. Rating question responses are ordinal in nature and thus the responses are subject to statistical analysis designed for such data. Rating questions may be dichotomous, a Likert type scale, a scale measuring intensity, interval data, or ratio data. The rating question provides some parameters or forced choices for the respondent. The analysis of data gathered by means of a rating question is generally accomplished by reporting frequencies, percentages, measures of central tendency and, in some instances, measures to determine if there are significant differences between groups of respondents.

Demographic questions are used in almost all questionnaires. The purpose of gathering demographic data is to relate findings to certain characteristics of the sample or sub-samples. There is a tendency on the part of some persons responsible for developing a survey instrument to ask for more demographic data than is necessary. There should be a clear rationale for the inclusion of every demographic item on a questionnaire. Common demographic information sought can include sex, age, marital status, occupation, number of years of employment in current job, highest educational grade completed, number of persons in the family, race, religion, political party affiliation, and income. Some demographic information, such as sex, is generally or with a few exceptions not controversial. By contrast, the level of income is less willingly given by many respondents. There is a natural tendency on the part of some people to want to protect their privacy and consequently to be reluctant to divulge information about themselves. When designing a survey, the researcher should consider gathering as much demographic information about a sample as possible from other sources, such as available voting lists or other public records.

Pilot and Revise the Questionnaire

The questionnaire should be piloted when all items have been developed. It is very unusual for a questionnaire to go through a pilot unscathed. Planners will find that nearly all pilot efforts will generate suggestions for clarifying and improving the items on a questionnaire and the format in which the questionnaire has been constructed. Persons who are asked to respond to a questionnaire when it is in the pilot stage of construction should be asked to (1) answer each item as if they were actual respondents; (2) make notations indicating questions, ambiguity, or any confusion they might experience with an item; and (3) record the time that it took them to complete the instrument. From the information received from pilot study respondents, the items and format of the questionnaire can be revised and improved; such revision can assure that there will be a better rate of response and that the data to be collected can be analyzed and will contribute to the purpose for conducting the poll or survey.

Questionnaire revision is generally a simple matter of studying the responses from persons in the pilot group to each item and the total format to determine changes that, based on the feedback and the judgment of the designer of the questionnaire, will enhance its quality. The editorial changes can be incorporated, and a final draft is prepared. The final copy of the instrument, especially if it is to be a mailed questionnaire, should be proofread by at least two different proofreaders. Proofreaders are to proof, not edit; editing is to be accomplished prior to the final drafting of the questionnaire. Extreme care should be taken when proofreading so that no misspelled words or typographical errors can be found in the final product. A proven process for proofreading is to have one person ''read'' the final draft to a proofreader who follows along on the draft copy. It is also advisable to have the product read by at least one proofreader who is not familiar with it. Persons who wrote or inputted the questionnaire on a word processor are often the poorest persons to proofread; psychologically they do not, at least in their subconscious mind, want to find errors and are the most likely persons to overlook mistakes.

Once the final draft is free of errors, it is ready for reproduction. With current word processors and electrostatic copiers, the final draft of a questionnaire can be produced that is professional in appearance and of the highest quality. High-quality questionnaires, especially for mailing purposes, are essential in a society in which expectations are high due to the available technology displayed in the area of mass media.

The format of a questionnaire will vary depending upon whether it is to be used for a telephone interview or a face-to-face interview or mailed to respondents. The instructions for the telephone or face-to-face interviewer will be written and displayed differently than when the questionnaire is mailed. In mailed

questionnaires, the spaces used by participants to check answers should be formatted for the convenience of the respondent. In cases involving telephone or
face-to-face interviews, the spaces for answers can be designed for the convenience of the interviewer. The instructions and spaces provided for responses
in mailed questionnaires should be self-contained. The training process for projects
in which interviewers will be collecting information over the phone or in face-
to-face settings will allow questions and discussion about the instrument and
how it is employed that cannot be duplicated in mailed questionnaires.

Determine Who to Ask

The purpose for conducting a survey is to get unbiased information about a
given topic or set of questions. If unbiased opinions are to be sought, it is
important to determine who has the needed information; thus, questions can be
posed to appropriate individuals to collect desired information or views needed
to answer the basic questions of the survey. The selection of persons to answer
questions leads to the topic of sampling.

Select the Sample

Sampling becomes a major emphasis within the total purview of conducting
surveys. Since a total population is typically much too large to ask every person
the questions for which answers are being sought, a sample must be drawn
from the total population. The planner must strive to achieve representativeness; that is, the sample should mirror the characteristics of the total population. If the sample does not represent a cross section of the population, it will
be inadequate and generate sampling error, and the results will have little value.
A brief summary of causes of errors may be worth inclusion to forewarn those
conducting surveys. Errors can be identified at the sampling stage of a survey
if the sample is drawn by faulty methods, if the list of persons constituting the
population is incomplete or inaccurate, or if the population has not been clearly
defined. There may be temptations to take shortcuts in sampling, which can
cause serious sampling errors. For example, a researcher may be inclined to
take a sample consisting of persons from one agency with a sample frame
encompassing numerous agencies and rationalize the selection based on the
convenience of persons chosen, while disregarding the fact the population was
not representative of all segments. There are also instances where a sample was
used that consisted of persons who were not appropriate for inclusion in the
sample but were chosen simply because of convenience. A disproportionate
number of subsamples, again drawn because of convenience, can distort the
results. In several ways, sampling may be one of the most difficult steps to
complete correctly in a survey.

In spite of the complexity of sampling, the concept underlying the process is
rather straightforward: sampling is an effort to select a portion of a population

that, in aggregate, represents as accurately as possible the characteristics of the total population. There are several types of samples used in surveys: (1) random samples, (2) systematic sampling, (3) stratified samples, and (4) cluster samples.

The *random sampling* technique is the most frequently used form to select samples. In a random sample, a predetermined number of subjects are drawn from a population, in which the selection is made in such a way that each element of the population under consideration has a known probability of being selected. Once a determination has been made about the size of the sample drawn from a population, the planner uses a computer, or a table of random numbers, to select the subjects. In simple terms, each individual in a population is numbered. If there are 7,000 voters in a school district and it has been determined that a sample of 250 persons will be drawn, 250 numbers would need to be identified from the table of random numbers. To identify or select the numbers from the table of random numbers, the planner must select by a random process a row or a column from a table, using a random process. As shown in Figure 9.3, columns in the table are headed 1–4, 5–8, 9–12, 13–16, 17–20, 21–24, 25–28, 29–32, 33–36, and 37–40, for a total of ten columns. If ten numbers were put in a cap and one drawn, it could be used to identify a starting point on the table for selecting the random numbers. Let us assume that drawing a number randomly from a cap yielded the number three; the third column containing numbers 9–12 would be identified. Since the number of voters in the district is 7,000, or a four-digit number, the columns in the table of random numbers that contain four digits could be used. Starting at the top of column 9–12, or the third column, and moving down will enable the planner to start generating the 250 numbers needed to form the sample. The first number in column 9–12, as shown in Figure 9.3, is 5454, the second number is 1454, the third is 3551, and the fourth is 1446—all of which can be used in the sample. The fifth number in column 9–12 is 9318, and the sixth number is 9914; both are larger than the population size of 7,000, so neither can be included in the sample. The seventh number in column 9–12 is 0690, or 690, which can be included in the sample. This process continues until the end of the table is reached. At that point, another column number is drawn from the cap. For the sake of our illustration, let us assume the number two, representing column 5–8, is drawn. Again, starting at the top and working down, the process is continued. Note that in the second column numbered 5–8, when you get down to row 8, the number is 0087. That would mean the person with the number 87 in the population would be chosen in the sample. When the number desired in the sample, which in this case is 250, is reached, and when a check has been made to be sure no duplicate numbers were drawn (which is always a possibility), the sample has been identified. It is then a simple matter to go to the list of numbered voters and pull out those identified by the numbers selected in the sampling process.

If computers and appropriate software are available, the parameters can be

Figure 9.3
Sample Table of Random Numbers

Fifty-third Thousand

	1-4	5-8	9-12	13-16	17-20	21-24	25-28	29-32	33-36	37-40
1	31 25	81 44	54 54	67 03	24 44	15 18	33 87	87 72	65 38	75 32
2	14 96	99 80	14 54	30 74	38 89	92 30	23 98	15 98	39 47	69 17
3	49 05	49 56	35 51	68 36	65 12	83 12	92 83	66 63	86 06	95 80
4	99 67	57 65	14 46	92 88	05 55	25 91	83 07	52 80	59 48	78 69
5	54 14	95 34	93 18	78 27	55 58	86 51	76 79	99 83	55 28	89 22
6	57 50	34 89	99 14	57 37	66 77	82 88	79 57	08 99	19 18	76 84
7	98 67	78 25	06 90	39 90	20 75	54 02	81 68	16 01	08 30	75 44
8	40 99	00 87	90 42	88 18	07 16	03 73	65 61	08 55	36 54	59 97
9	20 82	09 18	84 91	64 80	84 60	96 63	24 26	28 16	12 63	84 30
10	78 84	39 91	16 08	14 89	71 27	05 63	11 40	88 16	94 37	04 95
11	94 31	64 58	04 34	13 15	05 60	33 47	61 89	09 91	94 64	06 98
12	57 36	99 81	96 68	61 78	55 79	58 85	36 32	90 43	69 89	41 40
13	95 36	39 25	35 17	89 06	19 43	81 86	19 10	19 18	85 07	09 13
14	10 31	73 43	80 00	37 14	07 05	24 50	15 98	02 14	45 75	20 63
15	10 28	21 65	63 18	39 40	27 05	06 38	96 06	84 09	22 72	24 67
16	53 56	01 55	85 12	61 01	08 62	16 21	27 97	88 36	94 67	36 45
17	58 41	12 39	38 85	03 36	27 69	30 76	99 28	64 78	06 83	14 71
18	06 32	39 32	71 62	02 95	92 07	23 02	40 74	34 21	15 94	59 97
19	49 53	01 98	62 37	00 67	70 82	69 78	03 50	12 51	82 12	65 37
20	15 89	46 59	06 81	36 06	09 34	92 81	94 95	51 76	61 59	23 45
21	78 02	07 68	29 05	72 99	90 56	26 96	05 13	16 87	79 59	98 82
22	99 06	46 04	54 49	23 11	76 19	74 95	55 88	13 68	19 89	95 50
23	48 71	67 46	86 41	86 85	36 56	69 40	29 77	85 13	50 71	96 53
24	67 96	52 73	11 13	49 24	63 93	68 33	52 63	96 89	31 12	18 18
25	87 50	50 70	52 03	10 21	67 66	26 02	12 07	44 56	92 86	76 93

Fifty-fourth Thousand

	1-4	5-8	9-12	13-16	17-20	21-24	25-28	29-32	33-36	37-40
1	93 27	85 30	20 07	36 93	95 13	96 69	43 83	76 37	72 96	56 67
2	69 08	04 12	28 62	78 03	33 79	54 03	04 28	08 85	39 52	80 09
3	25 11	31 99	22 71	91 35	55 53	50 91	13 10	49 57	96 35	03 17
4	82 68	55 15	18 69	01 95	95 73	45 72	68 18	57 89	75 04	69 85
5	37 68	95 64	81 54	71 23	65 37	01 92	31 38	00 20	62 44	33 61
6	67 35	34 52	87 50	54 86	04 13	88 57	72 76	98 78	75 61	27 56
7	92 14	20 18	47 86	82 25	72 84	72 05	72 58	77 42	13 69	79 93
8	07 40	62 86	54 57	35 30	07 77	11 73	40 70	64 91	65 91	52 47
9	06 12	36 52	09 69	16 32	51 17	77 46	95 23	82 88	66 36	78 18
10	88 73	49 54	02 71	97 79	43 21	40 69	19 70	72 02	75 28	35 84
11	81 13	35 09	43 56	49 81	80 18	86 36	72 88	75 03	81 03	91 65
12	07 45	97 17	25 73	69 15	62 35	08 58	26 78	78 40	57 69	23 89
13	50 26	11 88	08 91	31 93	66 22	80 99	12 56	55 03	02 33	
14	13 40	43 79	22 94	78 43	00 35	87 30	33 54	84 52	58 33	02 99
15	03 65	18 67	47 54	73 44	57 61	57 61	50 81	78 76	47 97	56 37
16	28 88	90 79	87 68	97 64	09 91	29 99	21 30	13 12	90 03	23 24
17	32 04	54 90	93 99	39 93	38 42	76 30	28 25	13 51	67 16	02 40
18	78 02	21 02	15 57	77 73	86 35	18 04	78 81	61 65	50 04	41 03
19	57 57	79 86	32 35	37 93	15 24	54 66	48 61	33 43	74 20	07 25
20	63 35	23 04	26 98	48 94	43 44	91 94	01 57	91 32	64 54	46 67
21	36 92	05 70	79 21	12 32	35 92	21 31	75 53	40 18	34 71	71 18
22	14 45	76 61	79 36	72 87	45 46	68 29	21 65	20 65	64 93	44 54
23	60 04	93 93	24 69	95 35	21 29	97 39	41 64	10 66	88 82	81 40
24	60 72	12 34	81 91	59 49	50 13	49 77	01 64	34 93	60 77	40 14
25	35 46	84 82	49 35	61 47	58 94	29 39	13 31	69 41	31 53	86 66

Source: Wilmer Bugher, "Sampling," *Polling Attitudes of Community on Education Manual.*
Bloomington, Indiana: Phi Delta Kappa, 1980, 35.

entered, which in this case are a population size of 7,000 and a sample size of 250; the random numbers will then be generated and printed by the computer. The computer-generated list of random numbers may be preferred to doing it the "old-fashioned way." Selecting the numbers by hand using a table of random numbers may be less precise, may contain small errors, and certainly takes longer to accomplish in most instances.

Systematic sampling is a process in which, once the population has been defined and the sample size determined, a specified number of subjects are drawn by selecting them on regular intervals. If a population consisted of 300 subjects, and a determination is made to draw a sample of 50 by a systematic sampling process, then every 6th subject would be drawn for inclusion in the sample. The cycle to be used for making the selection is determined by dividing the number in the population by the number to be included in the sample.

Systematic sampling is not the equivalent of random sampling. A biased sample can result if a population is listed in such a way that it is associated with some characteristic being considered. If a sample of students is to be drawn from a population in which there are 11 gifted students and 8 with learning disabilities and if the student population categorizes students in the gifted and special needs areas, a sample list could be generated that contained distortions with respect to the representativeness of the sample. It would be possible, due to the starting point on the student roster, to eliminate either all of the gifted or all of the special needs students by using the systematic sampling process. To illustrate, assume the population consisted of 160 pupils, and the cycle or interval selected was every 8th person. The starting number for choosing subjects was determined by a random process, and the first number in the sequence was 5; thus, the first subject to be chosen would be number 13 (you started with subject number 5 and counted off 8, or the cycle size.) Such a systematic sampling process could eliminate all the learning disabled students (8) from consideration in the sample.

Systematic sampling is most appropriate in the selection of subjects to be contacted in a community survey in which the blocks and the residences are numbered. A map of a survey area, which could be an entire community, is used, and each city block identified as residential is given a number. A determination of the number of residential blocks desired in the survey is made. If there were 100 city blocks and the decision was made to select 25, the systematic sampling process could be started with some random number between 1 and 4. If that random starting number was 3, the person conducting the survey would start with block number 3 and count off every 4th block, or 3, 7, 11, 15, etc. until 25 blocks were chosen by the systematic sampling process.

Once the 25 sample blocks are identified, the average number of residential dwellings per block can be determined by counting or studying census data; in 1970, authorities indicated there were 13.69 dwellings in an average city block.[9] If a sample of 100 heads of households was wanted, it could be determined by multiplying the number of blocks (25) times the number of dwellings in an average block (13.69), which would provide a list of 325 residences. The 325 residences, divided by the number of desired heads of households, or 100, would suggest that every 3rd residence should be selected from each of the 25 sample blocks chosen by the systematic sample.

To choose every third residence in each of the 25 residential blocks selected in the sample, the planner must draw a random number between one and three. The planner can then start with the residence in the northwest corner of each block and make systematic sample selections of four dwellings in each block. It actually does not matter if those canvassing the selected blocks use the northwest corner, the southeast corner, or any other corner, as long as a standardized method is used in each block.

Once a residence has been selected, the person to be interviewed, such as the head of the household, is contacted by the interviewer. If a house is vacant or if a given subject refuses to be interviewed, a random means of selecting an alternate dwelling, either on the right or the left of the dwelling originally chosen, can be employed to ensure that the size of the sample is achieved and the integrity of the sample is not compromised.

Stratified samples are employed when a population is made up of distinct subgroups. Males and females are one of the most obvious examples of subgroups. While a random sample can be used adequately to select subjects from a population in which men and women are represented equally, it is often suggested that sampling should be done with consideration given to the composition and the percentage of the total population taken into account when the sample is drawn. It may be known that a certain percentage of a population are Republicans, Democrats, and Independents. With this knowledge, a proportional sample can be drawn from each category. The total sample could be composed of strata commensurate with the total strata of the population. To select a stratified random sample, the person conducting the survey should have knowledge of each stratum of the population; one source for such information is voter registration lists. The appropriate percentage of the sample can then be drawn randomly from within each stratum. People who use the stratified random sample argue they are getting the best of two worlds; they are ensuring that predetermined strata will be included in their sample, and the subjects within each stratum are randomly selected.

Cluster sampling is used when standardized random or systematic sampling is not practical because of the population distribution or if distance becomes a time and cost factor that precludes using random methods. At other times it may be necessary to sample a population for which there is no adequate descriptive information, and individuals cannot be contacted in specified groups. Such could be the case if a large migrant work population moved in and out of a school district with the harvest season. To reach migrant workers and to tap the information they possess, a survey may be required in which randomness or systematic sampling is disregarded. It may be possible to get the needed information by contacting everyone within a targeted population in a given area. Some marketing research has been conducted by means of "target groups," a method that is not greatly different from selecting a sample by means of a cluster group. The use of a cluster group is not generally advised, unless the conditions needed to draw a more defensible and adequate sample are not present. The cluster method of sampling should never be done as a matter of convenience.

Sample size raises a question in which all kinds of suggestions are generated. Various tables and formulas and good and poor judgments have been used to determine sample size. An interesting and homely analogy regarding the adequacy of sample size was given by Bugher when he wrote: "When a cook, for example, wants to test the quality of soup, he or she tastes only a teaspoonful or two. The cook knows that if the soup is thoroughly stirred, one teaspoonful contains all of the ingredients in amounts that are proportional to those in the larger container, no matter what its size." [10]

By going beyond the quaint analogy of soup tasting, it is possible to verify different parameters for sample size. Borg has suggested that every major subgroup in a sample should contain approximately 100 subjects as a minimum; minor subgroups should contain 20 to 50 subjects. [11] If there are fewer than 20 subjects in a cell, statistics become more of an academic exercise and less applicable to problem solving in real-life settings. If a simple correlation is to be considered, a minimum of 30 subjects is considered essential.

Conditions that suggest an increase in sample size are the following: (1) the nature and parameters of a population are unknown or poorly defined; (2) subgroups are used in the statistics; (3) a very high level or powerful test for significance is used; (4) numerous variables are involved; and (5) there is a high probability of a small or limited return rate.

A procedure and a formula sometimes used to provide parameters to determine sample size have been discussed by Borg and Gall. To provide a "rough estimate" of appropriate sample size when two groups are to be compared to determine any significant differences, the following formula has been suggested:

$$N = 2s^2 \times t^2/D^2$$

N = number of cases needed in each group to achieve a difference that is significant at the .01 level;

s = standard deviation;

t = t-test value needed for significance at .01 level when approximately 45 cases are involved;

D = estimated difference between mean scores of experimental and control groups.

A table to establish the sample size for a correlational study has been referenced by Borg and Gall. A crude determination of a sample size may be established by reading down a column of correlation (r) values until the desired r is reached and across to the number (N) required in the sample to meet the desired level of the correlation.[12]

Telephone surveys are becoming more popular, especially in larger school districts where information is gathered from citizens on a continual basis or at frequent intervals. The method of drawing the phone numbers from the phone book is rather simple. More information about the steps involved in a telephone survey is presented later in this chapter.

Determine How to Collect Information

Survey data can be collected in various ways. Most data are collected from primary sources; that is, if a planner wants to know how first-grade teachers perceive a given topic, first-grade teachers are asked the questions. The information collected from the first-grade teachers in a sample would be "primary data." There are certain types of data, however, that may be drawn from existing sources or data banks. Data drawn from existing sources that may have been analyzed and documented are classified as "secondary" data. For some surveys, primary data are essential; in other instances, secondary data are appropriate. If, for example, information is needed about the level of education of the citizens in a given county, such information could be obtained from data banks in which census information is stored. As a general rule, it is best to draw upon existing data sources, when it is perceived that such sources are accurate, rather than asking people in the community to give data they have previously volunteered in some other survey.

If existing sources of data are not available to answer the questions in a survey, the planner has several means of collecting information. One method of conducting a survey is to collect information in a *face-to-face interview;* a trained interviewer asks a subject a specified list of questions and records the information as it is collected. There are advantages of the interview as a means of collecting data, and there are some obvious limitations.

Potential advantages of the interview method of data collection are that (1) the interview is often the best way to solicit cooperation from some subjects; (2) the interviewer can answer or clarify questions for the respondent; (3) multimethod data collection can be conducted at one time, as questions are answered by the subject, and the interviewer "observes" and records information, such as the location of the television or possible socioeconomic indicators; (4) for surveys with long lists of questions, the face-to-face approach may enable the interviewer to get complete data where other methods might not "hold" the subject to completion; and (5) the interviewer can build or develop a rapport and level of confidence with the subject that can foster accurate and complete reporting.

The limitations of the face-to-face interview are real and need to be taken into account. The limitations include the following: (1) face-to-face interviews are costly and often time-consuming; (2) interviewers need to be trained and monitored; and (3) some samples are inaccessible for face-to-face interviews.

To capitalize on the potential of the face-to-face interview method and avoid or overcome some of the limitations, the persons directing the process should consider several factors: (1) a straightforward plan and procedure should be developed to identify the persons to be interviewed and (2) interviewers should know how to (a) reach persons to be interviewed, (b) ask questions and record answers in a standardized and consistent way, (c) ask appropriate, probing questions, (d) relate to respondents in such a way that they are motivated to complete the interview, (e) record information accurately, and (f) terminate the interview and leave the respondent in a positive frame of mind.

The *telephone interview* is another option available for gathering data. In recent years, the use of computer assistance in conducting telephone interviews and recording information has enhanced the procedure. Telephone interviews are applicable in both urban and rural areas as a means of reaching samples that might be inaccessible for face-to-face interviews. When an initial contact gets no response, a callback can be made with relative ease and limited expense. The cost of conducting a telephone interview is one of its attractions, and it is frequently a more rapid process than a face-to-face interview.

Computer-assisted telephone interviewing (CATI) has emerged as one of the technologically assisted approaches and seems to have some distinct advantages. Advantages of CATI include the elimination of recording the data in the wrong places and the avoidance of asking the wrong question and possibly missing a question.[13] Question "branching" can be controlled by CATI as it provides a crutch for the interviewer and helps avoid interviewer error. Monitoring the interviewer's work is made easier with CATI, and callbacks are possible with minimal time and effort. In school districts where the telephone is used extensively and repeatedly for conducting interviews, the CATI method can become a valuable tool that is cost-effective.

The telephone interview procedure, like other data collection approaches, has its limitations. As telephone marketing has become widespread, a negative connotation and resistance to the "intrusion" of the unwanted telephone call into the home have developed. Consequently, it takes a highly skilled person to be successful in conducting telephone interviews; therefore the person must be trained and monitored. There is also the reality that not all persons are included in the telephone directory. Some individuals have unlisted numbers, and other people do not have a telephone; therefore, it is not always possible to get a completely representative sample with a telephone survey. Answers to qualitative or comparative questions are hard to obtain over the telephone. It is also more difficult to generate a personal rapport between the interviewer and the respondent than is the case with a face-to-face interview.

Conducting telephone interviews is an involved process that should not be undertaken by untrained or inexperienced persons. A considerable amount of information has been developed to help persons conduct telephone interviews.

Some guides for conducting telephone interviews have been suggested by Bugher.[14]

1. Be sure the telephone directory used for the process is coterminous with the geographic area from which the sample is drawn.

2. When a respondent is reached on the phone, a question must be asked to verify that the person is eligible to participate in the study. For example, it could be possible to reach some respondent's relative who was visiting from another community or even from another state.

3. Realize that only 50 percent of the selected numbers from a telephone directory may be usable numbers. Some numbers are business numbers; others may be unanswered for various reasons. Consequently, the researcher must plan to select twice the number needed for the desired sample size.

4. When conducting a telephone survey in which several telephone directories may be involved, determine the number of contacts desired and select a number based on the proportionate percentage from the various directories. That is, if one directory contains 25 percent, a second directory 25 percent, and a third directory 50 percent of the phone numbers, draw the sample based on those percentages. If a sample of 200 is to be chosen and it is recognized that only 50 percent of the phone calls will generate responses, 100 should come from one directory, 100 from the second directory, and 200 from the third directory in order to generate twice the needed numbers of the desired sample size.

5. To select the sample from the phone directories it will be necessary to count the number of columns in each phone directory. If 100 numbers need to be drawn from one of three directories, in which there are 421 pages with 3 columns on each page, the numbers would be chosen from a total of 1,263 columns. Divide the number needed, in this case 100, into the number of columns. The result of the computation would be 12.63 or, if rounded off to the nearest whole number, 13. By this method, the researcher would choose a number from every 13th column in the phone book. By selecting a random number from 1 to 13, the researcher can identify the column from which the first phone number would be chosen. Start with the randomly chosen column and then select every 13th column to choose a number.

6. To choose a phone number from a column that has been systematically chosen, very simple devices can be employed. On a card that is the same length as the printed material on a phone page, mark off ten sections of equal size. Place the card by the numbers in the chosen column and by means of a table of random numbers or by drawing numbers from one to ten from a cap, select a number from one to ten. If the number drawn is seven, go to the space numbered seven and select any residential phone number from that space. Then move forward by the designated number of columns, which in this illustration would be 13, and repeat the process with the card and the random selection of a number from one to ten. When this process is repeated 100 times, the end of the phone book should be reached if the computations were correct.[15]

Random digit dialing (RDD) is a procedure that has been developed to provide a high level of assurance that every eligible person—those listed in the phone book and those with unlisted numbers—has an equal chance of being selected. Various computerized programs can be used to generate the list of numbers to be called by beginning with a list of working telephone exchanges in the area to be sampled. The last four digits are generated by a random procedure, which, when linked with the area code, gives the number to be called.

7. When the list of phone numbers representing the sample has been completed, the persons making the telephone interviews should be instructed in the method used to keep a complete record of the calls made and the calls completed. Persistence is the watchword. It is easy to give up on a number for a household in which one or more teenagers reside. If a number is busy, mark the sheet on which the numbers are listed by the use of a tally in a specified column. It is recommended that a waiting period of 10 to 15 minutes be allotted between dialing and redialing a busy number. If the number continues to be busy after ten redials, ask for directory assistance to determine if the number is working. If numbers are not reached during the first day, an effort should be made to reach a potential respondent on another day. A set of codes can be used to indicate the status of the telephone contact; for example, an A could designate a completed interview, a B could signify no answer, a C could indicate that an ineligible person, such as a babysitter, answered the phone, and an R could specify an eligible person's refusal to be interviewed.

Not only does the interviewer have to keep complete details of the contacts, but a complete and accurate recording of the data collected is essential. If an agency, such as a school system, has computer-assisted telephone interviewing, the system will keep records of all calls made and provide a guide for asking questions and recording answers received from each respondent. The telephone interviewing process is often attractive to people who have not become acquainted with all the intricacies and complexities of conducting such a survey; however, as suggested by various specialists, it is a complex process and, if misused, can generate useless or unreliable information and cause poor public relations.

The *mailed questionnaire* is perhaps the most common means of collecting information from a sample of people. It is the least expensive of the three methods described here and has the advantage of reaching out to disparate audiences. A sample that extends from Maine to California can be reached by a mailed questionnaire for the same amount of money as a sample drawn from one local school district. The questionnaire is a good device for posing questions that require some visual presentation or aid. In like manner, the questionnaire is the best method of presenting questions that require the respondent to make comparisons, to consider scales, or to collect data that may have to be gathered from files. When gathering some forms of sensitive data, such as political affiliation, personal income, or interaction with members of the immediate family, the respondent may feel less reluctant to provide answers on a questionnaire than if the questions were being asked in a face-to-face interview.

There are distinct limitations that need to be taken into account when preparing items and deciding the format of a questionnaire. The wording of questions is of utmost importance. Obviously, questions that are open-ended pose problems for the person who has to code and analyze the information. Also, it is not possible to use probing questions at selected points of the data collection process, nor can an interviewer clarify the meaning of questions or encourage the respondent. When a questionnaire is used, it is mailed and becomes your emissary; as such, it stands alone, unaided in the quest for information from a subject.

A modification of the questionnaire method to collect information is the use of a questionnaire in a group setting. Occasionally, portions of a sample population can be brought together and administered the questionnaire in a group setting, which has some distinct advantages. The rate of response is generally improved over individually mailed questionnaires. It is possible to clarify issues and respond to questions. There is also the sense of community upon which the person collecting the data can capitalize if the questionnaire is well constructed and the respondents do not feel they are coerced or taken advantage of because they are a captive audience.

Follow-up of questionnaires sent in the mail have proven to be both essential and beneficial in most cases. Low response rates can cause distortions to the information gathered and a loss of reliability and validity. The person collecting the information from a sample should strive to get the highest possible rate of return. When a questionnaire is put in the mail, several of the potential motivations for the respondent to complete the instrument have been lost. Causes of nonresponse are (1) questionnaires of excessive length, (2) complex or confusing instructions, (3) poorly worded questions, (4) questions for which the respondent does not have the information, (5) options that are not appropriate or force the respondent to answer inappropriately, (6) poor layout or a cramped format, (7) a lack of professional printing, (8) poorly defined or ambiguous terms, (9) questions that may be perceived as threatening or an invasion of privacy, and (10) poor timing, for example, mailing questionnaires to secondary school principals in the month of May. But even if a researcher can plead innocent to all the above transgressions, a follow-up may be necessary. One or two follow-up notes will generally yield additional responses and ultimately increase the level of reliability of the data. If, after one or two follow-up notes, the researcher has still not received a response, a telephone call can often be of benefit. To send follow-up notes, the person conducting the survey must have a record of persons in the sample and who has and has not responded. The need to be able to identify respondents leads into the proverbial question or debate about which type of survey will generate the highest response—one that is anonymous or one that is signed by a respondent. If deemed necessary, anonymity and a record of responses can be maintained at the same time. Anonymity, however, has not been as big a factor or positive influence on the rate of response as has been imagined by some persons.

Plan and Conduct Data Collection

The method selected for data collection—that is, the interview by phone, a face-to-face interview, or a mailed questionnaire—will determine the steps involved in planning for data collection.

If a face-to-face interview is to be used, a variety of points will need to be considered. (It is better to "over plan," if possible, than to take things for granted.)

1. Determine how many persons will be needed to conduct the interviews and how many interviews will be conducted by each interviewer. It is often wise to have a few alternate or extra interviewers.

2. Generate a list of names of interviewers and select those who are considered most capable and available.

3. Establish a time for conducting the training and interviewing.

4. Develop a thorough set of instructions for interviewers in which they are given detailed information about who they are to interview. If they are responsible for selecting random subjects from designated areas or blocks, they should be instructed how that selection is made and what kind of records are to be kept.

5. Provide training in how to conduct interviews. Simulations are often an excellent means of training interviewers. Nearly every facet of the interview process can be simulated, and when the training is finished, a person should be "certified" as a trained interviewer. If novice interviewers are involved, it is sometimes advisable to give them only part of their list of contacts. This practice will enable the coordinator to observe their work and determine if the novices are doing a satisfactory job of conducting interviews. Once it is acknowledged that interviewers are doing an acceptable job of collecting information, the complete list of contacts can be given to them. If an interviewer is not doing a satisfactory job of making contacts and collecting the needed information, the remainder of that person's list can be reassigned to interviewers who have proven to be satisfactory.

6. Monitor the interviewing process. Monitoring can be done by checking to see that all information for each interview is accurately and completely recorded. A review of problems or questions raised by the persons conducting the interviewing can also give the coordinator of the survey some insights into the process. Although interviewers are trained, they should be accompanied into the field and observed as they conduct interviews. Periodically, it may be beneficial to have all the interviewers meet in a group and discuss the progress they are making and the problems they may be facing. Group psychology can be a motivating experience, and the support interviewers can derive from one another can be a positive influence. Persons conducting interviews are sometimes placed in an "unfriendly" environment and may feel isolated. To help persons cope with such feelings, the person coordinating the survey should provide strong support and reinforcement.

7. File data and code for inputting and analysis. The coordinator will be responsible to see that all interview data are filed and made ready for coding and entry into the computer. Lists of contacts from each person responsible for interviewing should be checked to ensure that all work has been completed and no gaps exist. In some instances, the person responsible for coordinating the survey should make some phone calls to spot-check and verify that interviews have been completed.

The steps involved in collecting data when a telephone interview is used are similar to those when conducting face-to-face interviews. The forms and records will differ, but the basic steps and approach will be similar. The person coordinating the process should review records to make sure the persons conducting the telephone interviews are properly recording the calls and the information collected.

When the mail is used to distribute questionnaires and collect data, fewer people will need to be trained and supervised. A system should be maintained so a thorough record of all returned questionnaires is maintained. If responses involve confidential information, appropriate safeguards need to be established. The record of returned questionnaires becomes an essential for conducting a follow-up. As questionnaires are returned, each one should be checked for completeness, and, if completed, it should be determined if the information is properly presented and usable. A running total of the number of returns can be used to monitor the percentage of responses. Data from questionnaires should be inputted into a computer as they are received. If, however specialized personnel are to be employed to input the data, it may be appropriate to accumulate all the questionnaires and turn them over to the persons at one time.

As a general rule, if coding and tabulation of data are considered at the time the questionnaires are designed, the questions and the spaces for answers can be formatted in such a way to make the coding and tabulation of data much easier. In some instances, small data identification numbers may be inserted in the questionnaire as a guide to the persons inputting the information into a computer. The more straightforward and the less complex and confusing the coding system, the more likelihood the data will be inputted accurately into the computer.

Once the data are inputted, there should be some means of verifying that the raw data are accurate. One means of verifying input is simply to duplicate the inputting process, print out the results, and compare the raw data. Another way to verify is to "proofread" the results of the printout. Data should be proofread by having one person read the responses from the questionnaires while a second person reads the printout. If instruments have been designed to use mark-sense answer sheets, the process of verifying data is a simple matter. As a scanner "reads" an answer sheet, it is automatically inputted, and the results are considered foolproof.

Data may be analyzed once they are inputted and verified. The nature of the analysis will vary with the nature of the items and the questions. With the exception of very short and uncomplicated surveys, which may still be coded and analyzed by hand, standard means of data analysis and computerized programs are used by researchers. Software for desktop computers, minicomputers, or mainframes is abundant and used extensively for assistance in data analysis.

The written report, in which the results of a survey are presented, becomes an important communication document. The results need to be accurate and meaningful, but they should be presented in such a way that the intended audience can read and understand the analysis. Probably the biggest hindrance in the communication of survey results is the overuse of educational and research jargon. While jargon may make the writer of a report feel important, a survey report is not prepared for that reason. A survey report is intended to communicate to a selected audience, in many instances made up of laypersons, understandable answers to the questions asked in the survey. A good illustration of effective communication can be found in the results of a Gallup Poll in which straightforward questions are asked and, in similar fashion, clear, uncomplicated results are reported.

SUMMARY

The survey is a tool planners need to call upon at times to collect information to be used as a basis for planning. The information is only as valuable as it is accurate. Information that is inaccurate, incomplete, or biased can be damaging to a planning effort. To have some assurance that information gathered through survey methods is of value, the planner must be able to use appropriate survey methods and techniques for gathering and analyzing data. A planner must adapt survey methodologies to fit specific needs. It is even more essential, however, that planners know how to employ approved survey methods to gather information that will be of benefit.

NOTES

1. Earl R. Babbie, *Survey Research Methods* (Belmont, California: Wadsworth, 1973), 57.
2. Walter R. Borg and Meredith Damien Gall, *Educational Research,* 5th ed. (New York: Longman, 1989), 219.
3. Floyd J. Fowler, Jr., *Survey Research Methods,* rev. ed. (Newbury Park, California: Sage, 1988), 21.
4. Babbie, *Survey Research Methods,* 79.
5. Ibid., 79.
6. Ibid., 80.
7. Wilmer Bugher, *Polling Attitudes of Community on Education* (Bloomington, Indiana: Phi Delta Kappa, 1980), 4.
8. Michael Y. Nunnery and Ralph B. Kimbrough, *Politics, Power, Polls, and School Elections* (Berkeley, California: McCutchan, 1971).
9. Bugher, *Polling Attitudes of Community on Education,* 37.
10. Ibid., 3.
11. Borg and Gall, *Educational Research,* 223.
12. Ibid., 238–241.
13. Ibid., 458.
14. Bugher, *Polling Attitudes of Community on Education,* 63–70.
15. Ibid., 63–70.

10

Charts and Diagrams

WHY CHARTS AND DIAGRAMS ARE USED

Charts and diagrams are used by planners to communicate information about a plan or a process. It has been repeatedly suggested that one picture is worth 1,000 words. A parallel to that truism is that one chart or diagram is worth 1,000 words. Some individuals can grasp the gestalt of a process or a plan much more quickly when it is presented in diagrammatic form.

Another value of charts and diagrams, especially for the planner, is that they can be used to conceptualize how the parts of a plan go together. Some forms of a chart or a diagram can be used to assist the planner in developing a sequence of activities and revealing relationships among functions and activities. As suggested previously, the mind is the primary planning tool, and the ability of individuals to conceptualize how a plan is put together becomes a fundamental cranial process. If planners are able to go from the identification of the mission or purpose and determine the major parts of the plan, a means to improve the development of the mission profile is provided by diagramming the major parts. As the major parts of the plan are further divided, the functions are identified and can be diagrammed as subfunctions. Finally, the functions can be broken down into tasks to be completed. The process of moving from mission to mission profile, to functions, and ultimately to tasks is a sequence in the process of conceptualization that can be facilitated by diagramming the plan. As the conceptualization process is accomplished by planners and the diagram is developed, then the diagram moves from a tool to help in the process of conceptualization and becomes a means for communicating to significant others.

As plans and charts are developed, the planner can use them to show how one segment or step in the total process may relate to other steps in the process. The relationships of one part of a plan to another part of the plan can be presented to demonstrate how the different segments of a plan interact with one another.

Just as interrelationships of the various parts of a plan can be depicted in charts or diagrams, it is also possible to show how elements of a plan are sequenced. Diagrams can be "read" so they communicate which element of the plan is first, second, and so forth, until the last step of the plan is depicted.

Some charts and diagrams, once they are developed and the planning process is completed and moved forward to the implementation stage, can become management tools. As educational leaders progress from the role of planners to the persons responsible for conducting and managing the project, charts and diagrams can be used as a framework for monitoring what is being done and seeing that the sequence is followed and each segment is accomplished at the right time. Diagrams can be used as an aid to determine if resources need to be reallocated at crucial points in the program. Educational leaders who perceive a plan to be important will advocate the implementation of the plan; to implement a plan, leaders must work the plan, stay the course, and see it to completion. In the implementation of a plan, administrators will find various types of diagrams helpful.

Various types of charts and diagrams have been developed for use in the conceptualization, communication, and management of plans. As is often the case, the charts and diagrams used in education were originally developed in other fields, rather than specifically for education. The charts and diagrams presented here include those most frequently used in education: (1) flow charts, (2) Gantt charts, (3) LOGOS charts, (4) PERT, and (5) an eclectic or combination diagram. Capabilities and limitations are contained in each form or diagram. Consequently, the planner needs to select the chart or diagram that will best serve the needs of the project under consideration. As each charting or diagramming method is presented, capabilities and limitations are explained; hopefully, it will become apparent how each can best serve the needs of the planner.

With the advent of computer capabilities and accessibility of appropriate software, charting and diagramming have become much easier, and the end result of the planner's efforts can look much more professional, while providing clarity and readability. At one time, freehand diagrams, done with the style of an architectural draftsman, were often considered some of the better efforts to present such materials. Persons who, by their own admission, could not draw a straight line used ruler and templates to help in the process of making flow charts. One problem inevitably occurred when templates were used; the size of the figure traced from the template was either too small or too large. Consequently, professional draftsmen were frequently enlisted to make clear and professional-looking charts and diagrams. Microcomputer software has made

Figure 10.1
Flowchart Symbols

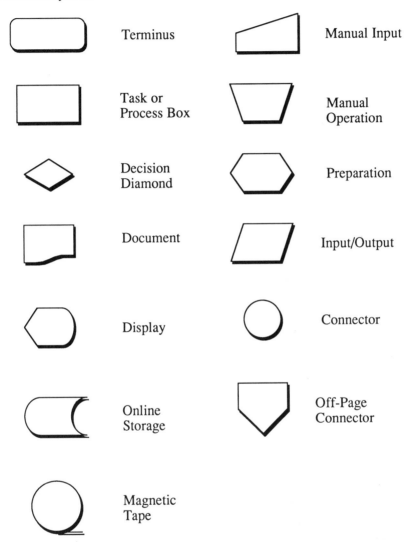

Terminus	Manual Input
Task or Process Box	Manual Operation
Decision Diamond	Preparation
Document	Input/Output
Display	Connector
Online Storage	Off-Page Connector
Magnetic Tape	

charting and diagramming much easier, and the results can be as professional as many costly jobs performed by highly skilled professional draftsmen or commercial artists. With the use of computer software, the planner is able to make figures larger or smaller, shadow figures, make uniform arrowheads, and include captions of any size and style of print. And, as is the case with various kinds of computer software, products can be edited with much greater ease than was the case prior to computer diagramming. Probably one of the most frustrating aspects of using computer software to generate charts and diagrams is keeping abreast of the latest versions of software.

FLOWCHARTS

Flowcharts are generally used to depict the steps, tasks, and functions involved in procedural activities. For example, with a flowchart a reader can be shown all of the steps to be completed in managing a payroll. Flowcharts consist of variously shaped objects, typically made of geometric shapes, and a specified meaning is denoted by each shape of object or icon. As flowcharting has progressed in recent decades, some objects have been deleted from the list of icons and new ones developed to accommodate newly developed techniques or tasks. In the 1960s and 1970s, a frequently used icon consisted of a rectangle with the upper left corner cut off so that it resembled the shape of a computer data card. As cards are no longer used and have been replaced with other means of storing data, the computer card icon has been deleted from the list of icons. Currently, the most frequently used icons for flowcharting are depicted in Figure 10.1.

Examples of flowcharts can be seen in Figures 10.2 through 10.5. In some instances the icons are shown with no shading, and in other instances they have been shaded.

Using the flowchart icons and arrows, various procedural activities can be depicted to communicate to the reader the necessary steps to be completed and in what sequence they are to be completed. Flowcharts should, as a general rule, begin at the top of a page so they can be read from left to right and from top to bottom. On occasion, the construction of a flowchart seems to defy what is seemingly a simple rule of placement on a page. When that situation occurs, the person making the flowchart should adhere as closely as possible to general guidelines but not be overcome or unduly restricted. Very little verbal communication is contained on most flowcharts. It is, however, perfectly acceptable to include notes for clarification. Flowcharts should also be accompanied by written documentation.

The written documentation contains the planner's explanation of a flowchart. The reader can gain a clearer understanding of a process if it is presented in chart form and supported with written documentation. Actually, the flowchart and the written documentation should be, by intent, redundant. Each should be understandable and "readable" in chart form or in written form. Since the same elements are contained in the flowchart and the written documentation, although the content is presented in different ways, they should be designed to support each other and clarify the message the planner intends to deliver.

Information about timelines is generally not included in a flowchart that stands by itself. Nor are planners able to present a simple and direct budget or cost control factors in parallel with the chart. Flowcharts can be an efficient tool for

Figure 10.2
Flowchart Example: Request for Information

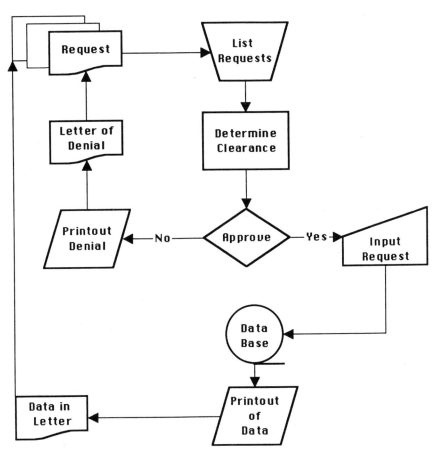

depicting the steps to be accomplished to meet a payroll, demonstrating the methods used to place an order for supplies, showing the procedures to follow to gain approval for a new course, explaining the steps to be accomplished in developing an Individual Education Plan (IEP), or demonstrating the many bureaucratic practices involved in managing an educational institution. Planners can use flowcharts successfully to explain tasks to be performed in selected administrative processes.

While most flowcharts are constructed with standard types of icons or geometric figures to explain specific steps or procedures, it is not uncommon to find artistically inclined planners who use various additional icons by which the steps in administrative procedures are depicted. Some computer programs have icons or pictures of filing cabinets, desks, computer terminals, and wastebas-

Figure 10.3
Flowchart Example: Preparing Hourly Payroll

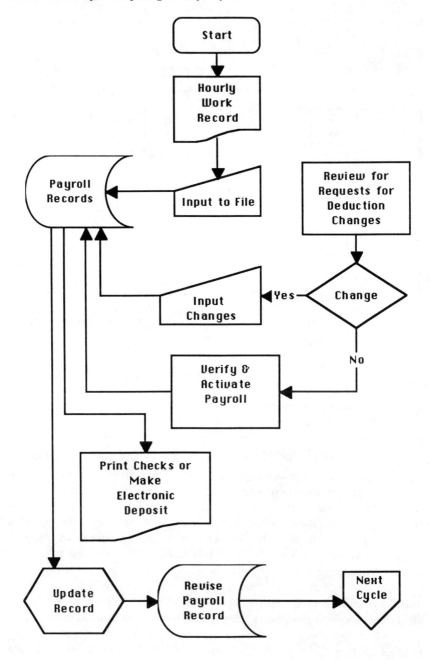

Figure 10.4
Flowchart Example: Hitting Fairway Shot

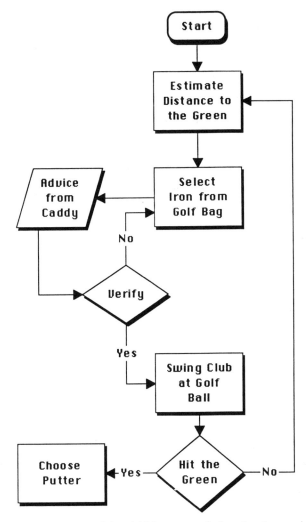

Note: Flowchart icons in Figures 10.2 and 10.3 were not shadowed as they are in Figures 10.4
and 10.5. Computer software affords the planner either option.

kets. By placing such icons on a page, connecting them with arrows, and affix-
ing key labels or descriptors, one can explain the steps that need to be completed in a similar fashion to the flowcharting process, in which more formal
and symbolic icons are employed.

Figure 10.5
Flowchart Example: Paying Monthly Bills

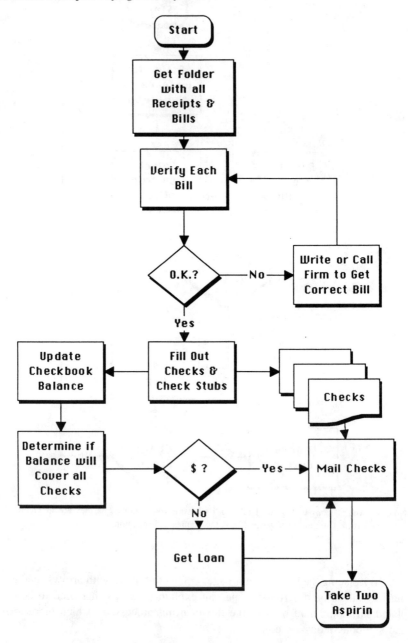

Figure 10.6
Basic Components in Constructing a Gantt Chart

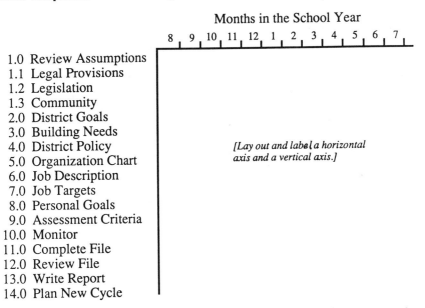

Months in the School Year

| | 8 | 9 | 10 | 11 | 12 | 1 | 2 | 3 | 4 | 5 | 6 | 7 |

1.0 Review Assumptions
1.1 Legal Provisions
1.2 Legislation
1.3 Community
2.0 District Goals
3.0 Building Needs
4.0 District Policy
5.0 Organization Chart
6.0 Job Description
7.0 Job Targets
8.0 Personal Goals
9.0 Assessment Criteria
10.0 Monitor
11.0 Complete File
12.0 Review File
13.0 Write Report
14.0 Plan New Cycle

[Lay out and label a horizontal axis and a vertical axis.]

GANTT CHARTS

William Gantt was an engineer who, during World War I, developed a method to keep track of major activities in a project and, at the same time, depict the time and sequence of activities in order to monitor a project. His plan, which was simple and straightforward, is a planning tool that has achieved widespread recognition and use. The plan has been applied in numerous and various ways, including such efforts as construction projects, steps to plan a conference, or possibly even schemes to spray fruit trees in a home orchard. Gantt's tool has become very adaptable and usable for planning.

To construct a Gantt chart, the planner begins with the placement of vertical and horizontal axes on a page. The vertical axis is placed toward the left side and the horizontal on the top of the page (see Figure 10.6). The various functions and tasks to be completed in a project are listed along the vertical axis. A timeline with measured increments is recorded along the horizontal axis. Typically, the scale or time calendar is shown at the top of the page. Each function or activity along the vertical axis, listed in sequence from first to last, is numbered. The time when the function or task is to begin and end is determined, and a line, usually a heavy or wide line, is extended horizontally from the estimated starting date to the time or date when the function or task is to be completed. The thickness or texture of the timeline can be varied to communicate different meanings to the reader (see Figure 10.7). Symbols can be

Figure 10.7
Basic Components for Constructing a Gantt Chart: Displaying Time Bars and Event Symbols

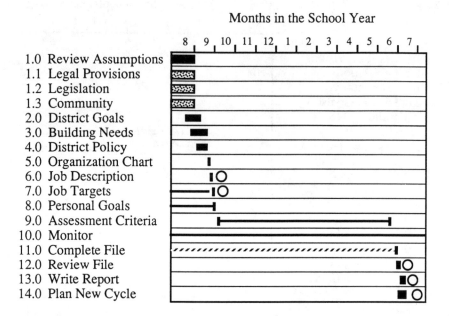

added to the Gantt chart that represent report documents or specified activities. Each Gantt chart is titled, and a key for symbols or the meaning of various lines, as depicted by different line widths or compositions, should also be included. Gantt charts can be constructed in various ways; in fact, variations are encouraged if such modifications help clarify the chart. In Figure 10.8, vertical lines have been added to show each month so the reader can determine more easily when activities are to start or end.

The final Gantt chart (see Figure 10.9) was designed to contain a title, the timeline, the functions to be accomplished, and the bars and symbols designed to show the activities or to depict when reports are to be prepared and due or when meetings will be scheduled. Finally, a key is included at the bottom of the figure to explain the "language" of the chart.

Typically, budget information is not contained in a Gantt chart. The documentation prepared to accompany a diagram contains the allocation of prime resources needed to carry out the processes depicted in a Gantt chart. In the Gantt chart shown in Figure 10.9, those responsible for performing the various functions should be identified. In the evaluation of a building principal, some tasks or functions would be done jointly by the principal and the person responsible for conducting the evaluation. Other tasks would be the responsibility of the person conducting the evaluation, and some responsibilities would be in the hands of the principal. While it would be possible to use varied types of timelines to depict such information, especially with the availability of com-

Figure 10.8
Basic Components for Constructing a Gantt Chart: Displaying Time Bars and Event Symbols with Explanations of Symbols

Months in the School Year

	8	9	10	11	12	1	2	3	4	5	6	7
1.0 Review Assumptions												
1.1 Legal Provisions												
1.2 Legislation												
1.3 Community												
2.0 District Goals												
3.0 Building Needs												
4.0 District Policy												
5.0 Organization Chart												
6.0 Job Description												
7.0 Job Targets												
8.0 Personal Goals												
9.0 Assessment Criteria												
10.0 Monitor												
11.0 Complete File												
12.0 Review File												
13.0 Write Report												
14.0 Plan New Cycle												

Notes: A solid bar on the chart represents a major activity. A line of a different texture may be used to indicate a supporting function. A finer line may be used to depict an ongoing function but one that is not a major function. A broken line may represent an intermittent activity. A circle, or various symbols, may be used to indicate the preparation of a document or a meeting to be scheduled. A key explaining the meaning of lines and symbols should be placed at the bottom of each Gantt chart. Vertical grid lines may be used as an option.

puter assistance, such information is generally placed in the accompanying documentation. The completed Gantt chart is primarily useful as a management device, since it is easy to see at a glance if appropriate progress has been made and all requirements met.

Documentation to accompany a Gantt chart is an important dimension of the total effort. Typically, the documentation accompanying a Gantt chart will have the same heading or title as the activities listed on the vertical axis of the chart. An introduction statement should be included, and each numbered line or item on the chart should be incorporated in the documentation, with the corresponding number used for each item.

THE LANGUAGE OF LOGOS

The acronym LOGOS is derived from ''A Language for Modeling Systems.'' For a LOGOS diagram to communicate a concept or a process accurately, the

Figure 10.9
Steps in the Evaluation of Building Principals

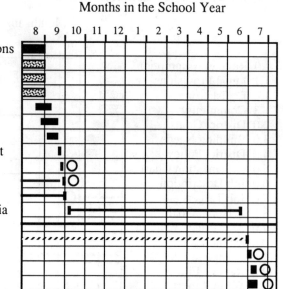

Months in the School Year

	8	9	10	11	12	1	2	3	4	5	6	7
1.0 Review Assumptions												
1.1 Legal Provisions												
1.2 Legislation												
1.3 Community												
2.0 District Goals												
3.0 Building Needs												
4.0 District Policy												
5.0 Organization Chart												
6.0 Job Description												
7.0 Job Targets												
8.0 Personal Goals												
9.0 Assessment Criteria												
10.0 Monitor												
11.0 Complete File												
12.0 Review File												
13.0 Write Report												
14.0 Plan New Cycle												

Key:
 Main Activity
 Supporting Activity
 Written Report Due   O
 Intermittent Activity
 Ongoing Support Activity

diagram must be conceptualized and depicted with precision. Any language can be distorted or used incorrectly. While modifications of all languages are continually emerging, it may be advisable for the beginning planner to adhere to the basic rules of the LOGOS language as it was designed and avoid the temptation to innovate until a considerable amount of experience has been accumulated.

LOGOS, by the way, should not be confused with the computer program called LOGO, developed by Pepard at MIT as a tool to help elementary children learn to reason. That ingenious software package is quite different from the graphic language of LOGOS.

LOGOS, as a graphic language, was developed to contain a sequence of steps and a pattern used by a planner to identify what is to be done and to conceptualize the gestalt of a complex system. LOGOS users employ both alpha and numeric characters. Words, numbers, rectangular-shaped boxes, and arrows, along with a few other symbols, constitute the basic elements of the

Figure 10.10
Function Boxes Used to Construct a LOGOS Diagram

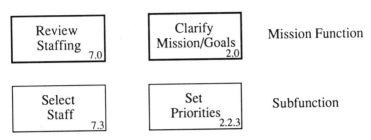

LOGOS language. By using the language of LOGOS, models can be constructed and presented diagrammatically in such a way that the conceptualization of the planner is communicated to the reader.

A *function* is the starting symbol of the LOGOS diagram. A function is represented by a rectangular figure and may be used to depict a mission function, a function or subfunction, or a task that is another layer of subfunctions.

A *function box* is a rectangle of approximately 5:9 proportions, generally placed so the long part of the rectangle parallels the top and bottom of the page. As demonstrated in sample LOGOS diagrams, however, function boxes may be of various sizes and shapes to accommodate several subfunctions. The function box, when representing a mission function (a major component of the total plan), has a border line that is heavier than boxes used to depict subfunctions (see Figure 10.10).

A *descriptor* is contained in each function box. The descriptor is generally centered in a function box if no other information, other than a code number, is to be contained in that box. If other subfunctions are to be inserted in the box, the descriptor is placed in the upper left-hand corner of a function box. Descriptors are made up of a few key words by which the function to be accomplished is conveyed to the reader. They are printed in uppercase and generally contain identifying nouns and action verbs (see Figure 10.10).

A *code number* is used to identify each function box. The point-numeric code is always placed in the lower right-hand corner of the function or subfunction box represented by the code. All major functions or mission functions are identified or coded as 1.0, 2.0, 3.0 . . . n. The mission function boxes depict the first level of detail in the LOGOS diagram. The second-level function boxes contain code numbers represented by such numeric values as 2.1, 2.2, 2.3 . . . n. Levels of function boxes can be broken down into subfunctions that follow the coding system reflected in numeric outlines used to depict levels of detail. The coding of function boxes follows the outline system depicted below. An illustration of how the code numbers are affixed to each function box is shown in Figure 10.10, and Figure 10.11 is presented to show how function and subfunctions are embedded.

Figure 10.11
Numbering Code for Functions and Subfunctions

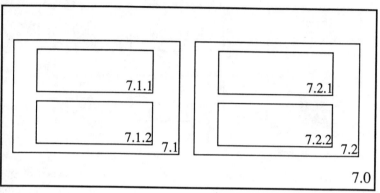

Level of Detail	Outline System and Coding Number
First level or mission function involving the mission analysis.	1.0
Second level of identifying functions or the function analysis is performed.	1.1 1.2 1.3
Third level of identifying tasks or in which task analysis is performed.	1.3.1 1.3.2 1.3.3 1.3.4
Fourth level of subfunction and further breakdown of tasks.	1.3.4.1 1.3.4.2
Fifth level of subfunction and further breakdown of tasks.	1.3.4.2.1 1.3.4.2.2 1.3.4.2.3

A *signal path* is depicted by the use of *input arrows* and *output arrows,* as shown in Figure 10.11. The arrows for input and output are solid lines by which the flow of thought or process moving from one function box to another is shown, ending with an arrowhead at the destination. As an arrow connects two function boxes, it represents an output path as it leaves the first of the two boxes, and it becomes an input path as it terminates at the second box. Generally, when constructing a LOGOS diagram, the arrow paths should make 90°

Figure 10.12
Input and Output Arrows for LOGOS Diagrams

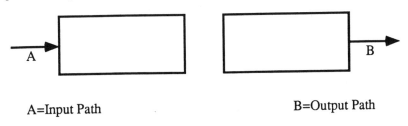

A=Input Path   B=Output Path

turns. It is then a judgment call as to whether arrowheads are to be used at the point of the turn. If the arrow turns with a short distance to traverse, no arrowhead is needed at the midpoint. For longer spans or distances, the reader can follow the arrow more easily if an arrowhead is placed at the point of the turn.

When several subsystem boxes are included, options can be used to depict the input and output arrows to convey a clear picture of the relationships between subfunctions (see Figure 10.12). If subfunctions within a function box can be performed in any sequence or as nonlinear subfunctions, the totality of the function can then be moved on as output to the next function box (see Figure 10.13). In Figure 10.13, the output arrow is started at the edge of the function box as a fat period or dot that is bigger than the width of the arrow. If, by contrast, a series of subfunctions in a function box needs to be accomplished in sequence or linear fashion, the diagram can be constructed with a directional arrow going from the last subfunction in a function box on to the next function (see Figure 10.14).

When it is necessary for arrow paths to cross and the crossing paths have no immediate relationship, the lines cross as shown in Figure 10.15. If, however, a relationship is involved as paths cross, an arrowhead at the point of intersection is used to indicate the relationship (see Figure 10.15).

A *feedback path* or loop is a key element of a LOGOS diagram. Feedback is generally represented by an arrow, in which an F is placed in a circle, continuing from one function box to another. In a generic, operational planning model, there is feedback between all segments of the system, as can be seen in Figure 4.1 (see Chapter 4) or Figure 9.1 (see Chapter 9). Through the feedback loop, the planner demonstrates a process in diagrammatical form for updating a plan and checking internal consistency. This process is the primary means to assure that a plan remains flexible and is never cast in stone. Plans that are afflicted with rigor mortis are quite obviously dead, even if the planner fails to recognize it.

Feedback is used to provide information for a succeeding subsystem while *feedforward* may be sent from one subsystem to a later subsystem. In the generic planning model, feedforward is depicted going from the establishment of assessment criteria (4.0) to the evaluation subsystem (8.0). Feedforward is rep-

Figure 10.13
**Connecting Function Boxes in LOGOS Diagram When Embedded Subfunctions in
One Function Box Are Not in Sequence and the Totality of the Function Is to be
Transmitted to the Next Function Box**

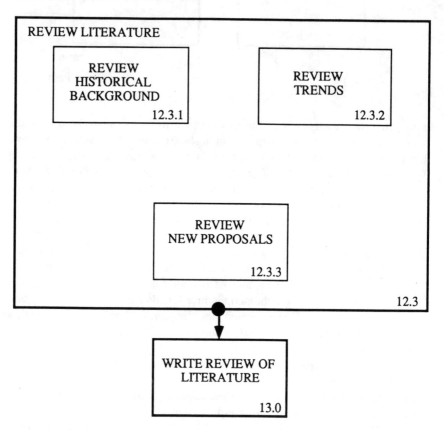

resented by a double capital F in a circle, as shown in Figure 4.1 (see Chapter 4).

Feedback and feedforward can connect all segments of a LOGOS diagram. All segments of a system should be connected to all other segments so that no subfunction is isolated or out of synchronization with the total system. Consequently, it is not inappropriate to identify all feedback and feedforward as one system depicted with a capital F in a circle at a midpoint of the feedback arrow. This latter option lacks some of the precision that can be shown by a diagram in which both feedback and feedforward arrows are used. The feedback system may be likened to the nervous system in a living creature. Through feedforward, a subsystem can be told to function in a given way; by feedback, all subsystems are kept synchronized and in tune, alerting the system if new information is received from an outside source or warning it if a malfunction is

Figure 10.14
Connecting One Function Box in Which There Are Embedded Subfunctions That Are in Sequence with Another Function Box

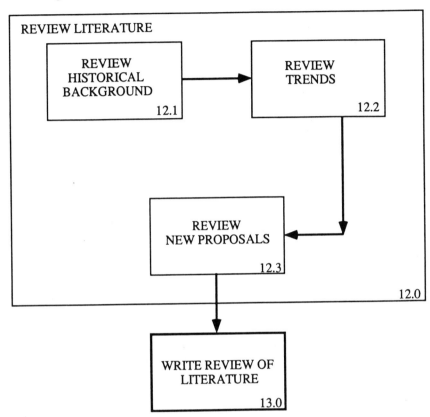

detected. The healthy body or healthy system can respond to input from outside sources and react to warning signals or malfunctions from within the system.

Feedback or the lack of it in a system determines whether a system is classified as an *open* system or a *closed* system. In some early explanations of open and closed systems, a semantic conflict emerged from culturally generated perceptions in the way the terms *open* and *closed* were used. Some pioneer planners suggested that a system with a feedback loop in which the last function of a linear system was connected to preceding functions was a closed system, as the loop was used to "close" the sequence. A system was said to be open if it was linear with no feedback loop. This use of the terms caused a semantic conflict in the minds of some planners and, more importantly, readers with whom they were attempting to communicate. As the terms were used in the manner just described, the confusion grew from the fact that an "open" system was not open to receive outside input, nor was it open to receive input

Figure 10.15
Merging and Crossing Arrows in LOGOS

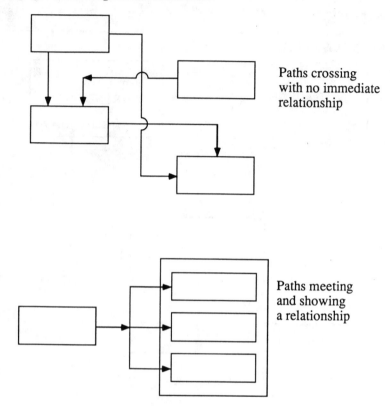

Paths crossing
with no immediate
relationship

Paths meeting
and showing
a relationship

from other segments of the linear system. By contrast, the early systems described as using feedback and thus "closing" the system loop, were not closed
to outside input nor to input from various functions and subfunctions within the
system. Possibly, less confusion would exist if open systems were referred to
as open-ended.

To be in tune semantically with the culture in which we live, an *open system*
is defined here as a system that contains feedback loops, as well as feedforward
loops. Through the feedback subsystem, a planner is able to input information
from outside the system and respond to internal input from one subsystem to
another. The system is open and even receptive to input from multiple sources.
By contrast, a *closed system* is one that is linear and has no feedback or feedforward loops. Consequently, a closed system can have a flow of information
only in a linear path, is not receptive to outside or internal input, and, because
of its closed nature, is not self-correcting. Thus, a closed system technically
can be perceived not as a whole system but only as a partial subsystem.

Good planners are good conceptualizers. Planners who have demonstrated high levels of skill can comprehend a mission statement and mentally identify the major components that go together to comprise the total mission. As a planner mentally depicts and organizes the major components of a mission statement, that person has actually performed a mental mission analysis. The mission analysis is the first level used in breaking the whole into meaningful and manageable parts, or mission functions. Each mission function, or major part of a mission analysis, can be broken down into functions. Functions, in turn, can be divided into the parts of which they are composed, called tasks. In some instances, planners even break tasks, which are subfunctions, into smaller subfunctions; thus, tasks can be further divided when needed. LOGOS is a tool that can be used by planners to help depict and support the mental process of conceptualization, in which a whole entity is reduced to its interrelated subfunctions. LOGOS is used by the planner to maintain order, logic, and relationships among subfunctions as a planner conceptualizes what is to be accomplished. Finally, LOGOS is a language to help the planner communicate what has been conceptualized.

PROGRAM EVALUATION AND REVIEW TECHNIQUE (PERT)

The Program Evaluation and Review Technique (PERT) was introduced by space engineers and originally used to help manage large projects in which there were literally thousands of tasks to perform. PERT was a valuable tool used by NASA officials to get a man on the moon. While PERT is used in the planning process, it has proven to be a most valuable project management tool. Desmond L. Cook took the concept from the space effort and applied it to education. PERT was an immediate success. There was a time when no self-respecting proposal writer seeking funds would think of sending a proposal to the Department of Education (even before it was a full-fledged department) without a PERT chart to explain the steps planned for the project. After PERT went through its cycle of popularity, it reached a level of use that reflects more selectivity and thoughtful applications. PERT is a good tool with definite applicability. As computer use has expanded and software has become more flexible, improvements have been seen in PERT, particularly in respect to tying the process into budget planning and management for a project.

PERT is a network. The PERT network is used in a graphic presentation to depict the activities to be accomplished in a project and to show the sequence and relationship of activities. Time estimates for each activity are included in the PERT network. From the accumulation and comparison of all time estimates, the longest path through the network can be determined. There may be many paths in a PERT network; the path that requires the greatest amount of time for completion is the *critical path*.

The PERT network begins, as all planning, by developing a clear definition of what is to be accomplished. The total project must be conceptualized, and

Figure 10.16
PERT Basic Building Blocks

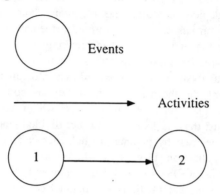

the various parts of the total project must be defined. Thus, once there is a clear agreement of what is to be accomplished, that total concept can be broken into its major parts or mission functions. Each mission function is further divided into functions, subfunctions, and tasks. According to PERT experts, this process is called the *work breakdown structure,* by which a top-down approach to planning is reflected. The work breakdown process continues until the desired level of specificity is achieved.

In progressing through a work breakdown structure, some mission functions without subfunctions or tasks do not need to be listed; the concentration should be on other mission functions and on breaking them down into very specific tasks. The PERT chart can be constructed to have much detail in some areas or along some paths and little detail in others. A PERT network can be developed for year one of a project, and the following years can be detailed as the time approaches for moving from year one on to the next phase or year. In projects in which multiple departments or agencies are involved, staff in one agency may develop a PERT network, while those responsible for other portions of the total project may not use PERT for management purposes.

Some basic building blocks are required when a PERT network is built. The components of a PERT network are not particularly numerous or complex. The tools and the language of PERT have been translated by Cook[1] from the conceptual structure of space engineers. So many manuals and books have dealt with PERT that many writers no longer feel a compulsion to footnote their work. In recent years, various microcomputer programs have been written to assist in developing PERT networks; in many instances, the addition of dimensions and budgeting capabilities through computer software has refined and exceeded capabilities of early PERT efforts.

A PERT network is composed of events and activities. *Events* represent the starting point or completion point for an activity; as such, events do not consume any prime resource, such as time, money, personnel, information, or

Figure 10.17
PERT Events and Activity Configurations

Events and Activities in a Series

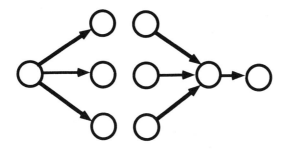

Events and Activities   Events and Activities
in a Burst Pattern   Converging

space. Events are defined as instantaneous points in time when an action or activity is started or completed.

Events are depicted in a network as circles placed at the end of a connecting line. Each circle contains a number corresponding to the number assigned to the event by the planner, or by the computer if computer assistance is used to construct a network (see Figure 10.16).

Since PERT charts have a number of different parallel networks running and sequenced together, *interface events* are needed to tie things together. An interface event is one that signals a transfer of responsibilty, information, or end

Figure 10.18
PERT Activities and Events in Parallel Paths

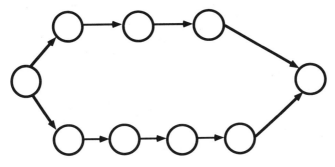

Figure 10.19
PERT Depicting Dummy Activities

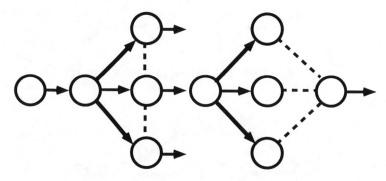

of a sequence related to or tied into other events or sequences. The subnetworks and series of events are tied together into a single system or structure by interface events in order to display the total program and internal relationships.

An *activity* is a task or job to be completed as one step in the project. Activities, unlike events, consume prime resources. Activities are work processes that lead from one event to the next event. The planner should define each activity as clearly as possible so persons involved understand what is to be done and how it is to be accomplished. Activities involve action; for example, they are used to compute, prepare, write, and sort. In other words, planners use activities to describe what action will take place. A realistic time estimate is required for each activity that, when placed in the total PERT network, will become one item of information to be used in computing the critical path (see Figures 10.17 and 10.18).

An activity is shown on a PERT network as an arrow connecting two event circles. There are, in addition to activities that consume resources, *dummy activities,* which use no resources—for example, no time or staff. Dummy activities are used to connect events and show relationships. Dummy activities do not designate action; they are not couched in action language. Dummy activities are distinguished from other activity arrows by the use of a dotted line (see Figure 10.19).

Various patterns of events and activities are found in the construction of a PERT network. Some activities are divided or fan out, run parallel, and finally converge. Patterns that fan out are referred to as *burst constructions* (see Figure 10.17). Some events and activities within a path are in a linear sequence. When events and activities are linear, they are referred to as *series constructions.* When events and activities come together, they are termed *merge constructions.* A merge construction can be found in two formats: (1) the activities come together in a merge pattern and (2) dummy activities are used to merge two or more parallel paths (see Figure 10.17).

When one constructs a network, there are many situations in which one ac-

Figure 10.20
PERT Event Symbols

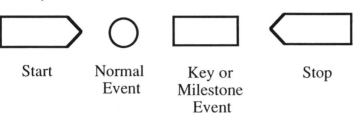

Start	Normal Event	Key or Milestone Event	Stop

tivity cannot be undertaken until a preceding activity is finished. Thus, the second of the two items is dependent upon the completion of the preceding item.

A planner who may wish to bring a series of paths together intentionally employs a *planned constraint* for the purpose of achieving unity at the chosen point in the total network. The use of a planned constraint might be appropriate at a point in the network where all conference arrangements will be completed on a specified date. The planner may be working alone late at night and say, "Let's see that we have everything ready to go on the Monday before the conference starts"; thus, a planned constraint is built into the PERT network. At the significant point in the network, a different symbol may be employed in place of the circle by which an event is signified. A key event may be depicted on a PERT network as a rectangle instead of the circle by which a regular event is denoted. Actually, various other geometric shapes have been used and incorporated into computer software for different kinds of events, as shown in Figure 10.20.

As mentioned above, there should be a reasonable estimate regarding how much time will be taken to complete each activity. A simple mathematical process is employed to arrive at time estimates that will be placed in the PERT network. In most situations, the planner should involve other people in estimating the amount of time needed; there may be experienced experts who would be able to give suggestions regarding the estimated time required for completion of an activity. The formula used to determine the amount of time required to complete an activity and to arrive at a realistic time estimate is explained below. The better the information that goes into the formula, the better the time estimate that will result from the computations. Like many other endeavors, if good quality raw materials are used in a product, the result will generally be a good quality product. By contrast, if poor quality raw materials are used, chances are the end result will also be poor. Good or even reasonable time estimates are essential if a PERT network is to yield a realistic set of time frames.

There are several time components shown on the PERT network that are used to arrive at the *expected elapsed time* (t_e) or the amount of time expected to complete an activity. They are most likely time (m), optimistic time (a), and pessimistic time (b).

Persons with some knowledge and understanding would define the most likely time (m) as the period that would be expected to complete an activity. The most likely time is a judgment call based on experience. Experienced persons would identify the optimistic time (a) as the earliest time in which an activity can be completed. Reality is needed. For example, if concrete has to be transported by a truck for a distance of 2 miles through heavy traffic, it would not be reasonable to say the most optimistic time would be two minutes, or 60 miles per hour, with a loaded truck in heavy traffic. Such a time estimate would be unrealistic rather than optimistic. The most pessimistic time (b) must also be estimated, but again judgment must be used. Some pessimists might predict the concrete truck would never show up at the building site. While such an eventuality is possible and could occur, another truck would be brought into service, and the "never" estimate would be cut short. To arrive at sound time estimates, a knowledgeable person should be asked to help in arriving at the best possible estimates for most likely, optimistic, and pessimistic times. Time estimates for activities that have been done repeatedly will be more accurate than for activities that are unique or new to the persons involved in the planning process. The range of time estimates from most optimistic to most pessimistic will be narrower for familiar activities, while the range generally will be wider for unique or new activities.

When time estimates are made, the following assumptions exist:

1. Prime resources will available.
2. Time estimates are based on a five-day workweek; thus, a half day is equal to one-tenth of a week or 0.1.
3. Calendar dates are not used and have no effect on initial time estimates; once a PERT network is completed, it can be started at any desired calendar date.

The computation of the most likely time involves the beta curve, which, according to mathematicians, is a mathematically established cousin to the normal curve of distribution and contains, as a normal characteristic, a skew. A formula, derived from the beta curve, has been established to determine the time estimate for completing an activity. To compute t_e (expected elapsed time), the estimate of time for completing an activity, the following formula is used:

$$t_e = a + 4m + b$$

The estimate of t_e can be computed in various ways. Rather than calculating each estimate by hand or with a hand calculator, one can put the data [(a), (m), and (b)] into a spreadsheet, and the expected elapsed time estimates can be generated as fast as the numbers are inputted. The values for t_e can then be entered into the PERT program on a computer as the network is generated (see

Figure 10.21
PERT Computations of Expected Times

PERT: COMPUTATION OF EXPECTED ELAPSED TIMES						
Acitivity	Event Numbers	Optimistic Time (a) a+	Most Likely Time (m) 4*m+	Pessimistic Time (b) b/6=	Total Elapsed Time	Days & Weeks
Determine Need	2 to 3	2	4	6	4	0,4
Determine WHAT to Ask	3 to 4	1	1	1	1	0,1
Generate List of Questions	4 to 5	1	2	7	3	0,3
Edit/Revise Questions	5 to 6	1	1	5	2	0,2
Prepare/Print Pilot	6 to 7	1	1	4	2	0,2
Identify Pilot	4 to 9	1	1	1	1	0,1
Contact Pilot Sample	9 to 10	1	3	10	4	0,4
Conduct Pilot	7 to 8	8	10	24	12	2,2
Tabulate/Review Pilot	8 to 11	1	2	7	3	0,3
Revise Questionnaire	11 to 12	2	5	20	7	1,2
Prepare Quest. to Print	12 to 13	1	3	10	4	0,4
Print Questionnaire	13 to 14	6	12	27	14	2,4
Determine HOW to Ask	3 to 19	1	1	1	1	0,1
Plan Data Collection Schedule	19 to 20	1	1	1	1	0,1
Identify Data Collection Team	19 to 21	5	7	18	9	1,4
Train Team	21 to 22	1	1	5	2	0,2
Determine WHO to Ask	3 to 15	1	1	1	1	0,1
Identify Population	15 to 16	2	3	10	4	0,4
Select Sample	16 to 17	1	1	1	1	0,1
Prepare Sample List	17 to 18	1	1	1	1	0,1
Collect Data	23 to 24	5	17	18	15	3,0
Tabulate Data	24 to 25	2	8	10	7	1,2
Analyze Data	25 to 26	5	10	15	10	2,0
Prepare Report	26 to 27	5	10	25	12	2,2

Note: The spreadsheet formula for computing expected elapsed time = (C10 + (4*D10) + E10)/6.

Figure 10.21). The variability of time estimates can also be determined from a spreadsheet if that information is desired. The range of time is simply the standard deviation of the activity times. The formula for the standard deviation of t_e is $\sigma = b - a/6$

By employing the concept of a normal distribution curve, one can use the standard deviation coefficients to estimate the probability that an activity will be completed within the range of estimated times. An approximate 68 percent chance exists that a given activity will be completed within the range covered by a plus or minus one standard deviation from the mean. Following the normal curve, there would be a 95 percent chance that the activity will be completed within two standard deviations from the mean and a 99 percent chance that it will be completed within three standard deviations.

Figure 10.22
PERT Computing T_E Values for a PERT Network

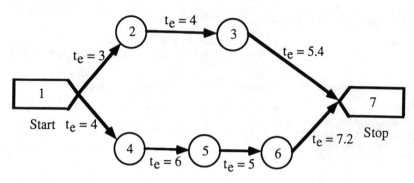

T_E of path 1,2,3 and 7 = 12.4

T_E of path 1,4,5,6 and 7 = 22.2

When the expected elapsed time (t_e) for all activities in the network is computed, the total time for the combined t_e estimates is the *earliest expected time,* or T_E. The *latest allowable time* is the latest time by which an event must occur without causing a delay in the network. The latest allowable time is represented by T_L. The latest allowable time for each event can be computed

Figure 10.23
PERT Computing Slack Time

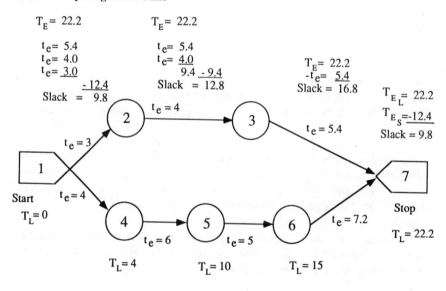

by examining the final event of a network and subtracting the t_es of preceding activities (see Figure 10.22).

Once the value for T_E and T_L have been computed, the *slack time* can be determined. Slack time is figured by subtracting T_E from T_L, as shown in Figure 10.23.

Quite possibly once the total time estimates have been determined for a network, the planner is faced with the realization that there is not enough time available to complete the tasks as shown on the PERT network diagram. Due to a fixed time constraint, a decision may be made to shorten the process and absorb some of the slack time in shorter paths of the network. Consequently, it will be necessary for the planner to consider reallocating resources or changing processes to shorten the longest path to fit into the prescribed or imposed time limit. The longest path of the network, in a case where an imposed reduction of time is involved, will have a *negative slack*. If a project was planned for 12 weeks and a determination was made that there was a time limit of 10 weeks, a 2-week negative slack would be experienced in the longest path in the 12-week network.

Planners using PERT frequently assign a scheduled date (T_S) to significant events anticipated in the network. Any scheduled date assigned to an event must of necessity be the same as, or earlier than, the anticipated completion date. At times, a completion date may be dictated by an outside authority, and the local planners have no control of the date. In such cases, the imposed or externally mandated date is referred to as a directed date (T_D). The scheduled date for the final event is identified as T_L. For significant or special events such as T_S or T_D, the planner may note the significance by using a key or milestone event box in place of the usual event circle.

By contrast to negative slack, a slack condition exists when the available time for a subnetwork is greater than the estimated time for the total network. In such cases the slack is referred to as *positive slack*. As shown in Figure 10.23, the positive slack for the network involving events 2, 3, and 7 is 9.8. The longest path is 22.2, and the shorter path is 12.4; the difference of 9.8 in the shorter path is the positive slack.

The *critical path* is the longest path through the total network. As can be seen in Figure 10.23, the longest path contains 22.2 weeks. A double or heavy arrow is used to display the critical path on a PERT network.

When constructing a network, one should remember that each event is unique and can occur only once. If there are several occasions when a scheduled meeting of the school board is contained in the network, each meeting is considered unique in the network. There are no feedback loops in PERT. A network path cannot return to a completed event or cycle through that event a second time. In this respect, PERT is different from LOGOS. The critical path is the longest path in terms of time requirements; however, it may not be the path with the most activities and events. The length of activity arrows in a PERT network has no relation with the actual expected elapsed time (t_e). Commonly, an arrow connecting two events extends for a very long distance and has a t_e that is very small; of course, the reverse can be true. PERT is a particularly applicable tool for projects in which there are thousands of activities to complete. For projects with a relatively small number of activities and, consequently, fewer parallel paths involved, the value of a PERT network is diminished. As a general rule of thumb, the use of PERT is not necessary, nor will it be of maximum benefit, until the number of activities exceeds several hundred. An example of a computer-generated PERT network is given in Appendix E-1. Although the characteristics of the product are shown in the example, the small number of activities in the illustration would not warrant using PERT.

At one time, PERT charts were constructed with neat circles and arrows, and expected elapsed times were carefully penned in by appropriate activity arrows. The critical path was denoted with a double arrow that was often highlighted with a colored marker. Time calculations were noted on separate data sheets, and documentation or descriptions of each activity were included in an accompanying manual. Quite often, a project manager would have a PERT chart circling the walls of his or her office. With the use of computer software to develop a PERT chart, a professionally done network chart can be presented that just about any person can read and understand.

Persons using computers to construct PERT networks have an additional advantage; built-in budgeting components can be a part of the computer program. The budgeting process of PERT projects is much easier when the computer is used. A budget amount can be allotted to each activity; thus, a budget for each path and ultimately the total project is generated.

A busy mind is required to schedule the activities in a PERT chart. The planner should develop an outline for each major path in the proposed chart. Each path must then be broken into individual activities to complete. The points where paths divide or merge should be conceptualized by the person devising the PERT chart. When using the computer, the planner uses software to lay out the tasks in the sequence in which they are entered, place them in the diagram, and assign a number to each event at the end of an activity arrow. The computer cannot build the chart for the planner because, at this time, most computers and especially personal computers do not have conceptual skills, nor can they make judgments in terms of building the network. Therefore, the planner needs to (1) identify and sketch the primary paths that will be included in the PERT network; (2) list each activity envisioned for each path in the total PERT network; and (3) input the paths and activities in the general sequence desired. With this much prescheduling of the PERT network, the computer can be used to make the network and assign all the needed event numbers.

The PERT networks will have dependencies. A dependency that is built into the network exists when one activity or event cannot be scheduled until preceding activities and events have been completed. The construction of a building would be an obvious illustration; the contractor cannot start building the walls until the footings and foundation are poured. A constraint, which is an event or activity that has a relationship with other events and activities, can be planned in which the completion of certain activities is seen as desirable but not essential or mandated. Dummy activities may be used to signify the desired relationship between two events as a matter of convenience or preference on the part of the planner.

As a planning and management tool, PERT affords the opportunity to allocate prime resources and at the same time monitor performance. Whether developing a PERT network with mainframe computer support, using a personal computer, or doing it the "old-fashioned way," the intent to be accomplished is the same. The PERT/COST system is used to aid in developing realistic cost estimates in the planning stage, make forecasts of cost estimates, and compare estimated and actual costs throughout the implementation of the program.

Cost estimates inputted into a PERT system follow the breakdown of the total project into mission functions, functions and subfunctions, and tasks. Where appropriate, cost estimates for prime resources are determined for each activity listed on a PERT network. Judgment calls are essential in this process. For example, an activity may be to "Get Approval of Staffing at Board Meeting." Although board meetings actually have associated costs, a determination may be made that there would not need to be a cost factor attached to the activity involving approval from the board of education in the project budget. Phone calls are another illustration of an activity that may consume resources but would not be included as an expense on a PERT breakdown of activities. There might well be an activity that required "Calling All Members of the Task Force," which might consist of 12 persons. The personnel and the phone costs could be absorbed in the normal operation of a school district and not charged out to the project. By contrast, if a major activity in a project was to "Conduct Telephone Survey" and such a survey would require trained telephone interviewers and be designed to reach over 1,000 persons, cost estimates, which would ultimately be a part of the project budget, would be essential. When all cost factors are placed with each activity, the total becomes the project budget.

Some terms used by Cook[2] and revised over the years are listed below. The use of computer software for developing PERT charts has resulted in modifications in terms and design.

Activity. The work that requires the use of prime resources.

Activity slack is the difference in time between the earliest completion date (S_E) and latest completion date (S_L) for any activity.

Activity time estimate. The computed time estimate for completion of an activity. Time estimates are generally specified in weeks and tenths of weeks. Some computer programs automatically insert time estimates (t_e) in which two weeks and three days are presented as follows: 2,3.

Constraint. When one activity may not be started until a preceding event is completed, a constraint has occurred.

Critical path. The sequence of events and activities that consumes the greatest amount of time or has the longest path through the PERT network is the critical path. When computer printouts of networks are made, most software programs are written so the critical path is automatically computed and denoted with a heavier path of arrows than other paths. Handmade PERT charts are generally constructed so the critical path is represented by a double arrow or a color-highlighted arrow or path.

Directed date. There are instances when those persons in charge of a project may, for various reasons, need to establish certain dates when a project or a portion of a project is to be completed. A date established outside the PERT process is a directed date and will be used to specify when certain events will be finished or when selected events can start. The network must be designed to accommodate the directed date.

Dummy activity. There are instances in a network when paths or events need to be merged or fanned out or may be running in parallel and so require a relationship or coordination in timing to be depicted. The dummy event is demonstrated by a broken-line arrow in place of the solid arrow, and unlike normal activities that use prime resources, dummy events do not use any resources. Dummy activities can be used to depict interface ties in a network.

Earliest completion date (S_E). The earliest time when an event can be completed.

Earliest expected date (T_E). The earliest date when an event may be expected to occur, which is the sum of all of the expected elapsed times (t_e) in a path of the PERT network.

Event. A specific event that has been accomplished. Events do not take up time; they occur instantaneously.

Event slack. The difference between the earliest expected date (T_E) and the latest allowable date (T_L) for a given event.

Expected elapsed time (t_e). The expected elapsed time is computed from three time estimates by planners. The estimates, as described previously, are computed from the most likely time (m), the optimistic time (a), and the pessimistic time (b).

Latest completion date (S_L). The latest calendar date on which a network can be scheduled for completion without causing a delay in some other network or the total network.

Milestones. Key events that must occur in some networks, which are depicted by a rectangular event symbol in place of the circle used for normal events.

Most likely time (m). When computing expected elapsed time (t_e), the person knowledgeable about the work to be accomplished will make an estimate or judgment about the most likely time that will be required to complete the task.

Negative slack. The amount of time in excess of the available time on a given slack path computed to be required to reach a specified event.

Optimistic time (a). The estimate of a person knowledgeable about the task to be performed that is, in that person's best judgment, the earliest time an activity could be completed. It is important that such estimates are as accurate and realistic as possible.

Pathway. A sequence of events and activities that may run parallel to other pathways in a network. A major pathway is the equivalent of a mission function in other forms of diagramming.

Pessimistic time (b). When one makes the three time estimates that will be computed to arrive at (t_e), the longest time estimate is referred to as the pessimistic time.

Positive slack. The amount of extra time available in a network to perform a series of activities.

Scheduled completion date (T_S). The date that has been "assigned" by officials for project completion. If no pre-assigned date of completion is determined for the PERT network development, the T_S is equal or one and the same as the S_E.

Slack. Slack is extra time in a network. It is figured by computing the difference between the latest allowable date and the earliest expected date (T_L-T_E). Slack may also be the difference between the latest completion date and the earliest completion date (S_L-T_E).

COMBINATIONS AND DERIVATIONS OF DIAGRAMS

Efforts have been made to choose the best elements in any charting or diagramming language by combining selected attributes from various approaches into one diagram. Capabilities and limitations exist in each charting and diagramming approach; if certain capabilities are needed and planners wish to avoid limitations, why not make combinations? An example of a diagram used for a funded project, in which the planners wished to communicate the timeline of the project, the process or steps involved in completing the project, the products generated at various stages of the project, and a review or monitoring scheme for the project, is included in Appendix E–2.

The timeline for the project, an idea derived from Gantt's work, is depicted as a bar across the top of the page (see Appendix E–2). The number representing the month is listed, and the bar is divided into segments, each segment representing one month. Unlike the time bars used in a Gantt chart, the length of the time bar in the combined diagram has no fixed distance to represent a month; however, by contrast, a bar across the top of a page can represent one or several months.

The process is presented in a manner similar to the way in which LOGOS diagrams are constructed. The process functions are shown below the timeline toward the top of a page, as a second tier in the diagram. Function boxes are used; each box has a caption and an identification number. Function boxes are connected with arrows. Since the combined diagram extends over a number of pages, an arrow from the last function box on a page is continued to a small circle, which indicates a connector to the ensuing page.

The product produced at any given time in the project is identified in a third tier of the chart as a diamond that contains a caption. The product or diamond is connected with the process chart appearing above it by a broken arrow.

The review or monitoring scheme is displayed by using ellipses in which captions are printed and connected to the process diagram with broken lines. By depicting the review process in the total effort, a built-in plan for monitoring is present that was designed in advance or before the project ends.

By use of the documentation or narrative that accompanies the combined diagram, some of the elements of the project are explained in detail, an explanation that is not possible in a diagram. Just like the diagram, the written narrative or documentation is an essential part of the communication process of a plan. The written documentation and the diagram, when juxtaposed, give the full picture of what is planned (see Appendix E–2).

SUMMARY

The diagrams and charting approaches depicted above are only a few of the diagramming schemes that may be encountered as various plans are explored. Careful selection of charts or diagrams on the part of the planner can enhance the communication of a plan to constituents. As is the case with any means of communication, the more knowledgeable and skilled the person preparing the communication, the greater the likelihood the message will be presented effectively. Diagrams should not look dazzling and complex. They should be used, when appropriate, to help communicate. Knowing the language of charting and diagramming can be a valuable communication tool and an aid in conceptualizing and developing phases of a project.

NOTES

1. Desmond L. Cook, *Program Evaluation and Review Technique Applications in Education,* U.S. Department of Health, Education, and Welfare, Office of Education (Washington, D.C.: U.S. Government Printing Office, 1966).

2. Ibid., 89–92.

11

Evaluation

An abundance of materials has been written about evaluation, and the level of sophistication demonstrated by specialists has grown enormously in the last quarter of this century. Despite advances in the area of evaluation, debate, confusion, haggling, and a lack or avoidance of involvement in evaluation efforts at the local level continue. "Evaluation is one of the most widely discussed but little used processes in today's educational systems."[1]

Evaluation, in one form or another, has been around for centuries. For example, Chinese civil service officials were reportedly conducting examinations in 2000 B.C.[2] Various references have been made to the trials and tribulations of testing experienced by young men preparing for the priesthood during the Renaissance. The first major testing effort in the United States took place just prior to the turn of the century, when Joseph Rice conducted a comparative study of the spelling performance of 33,000 students in a large city. During the 1930s, there was an in-depth study directed by Tyler and Smith, known as the Eight-Year Study. For many years, policy decisions were based on the Eight-Year Study throughout the nation. Not only were K–12 programs influenced by the Eight-Year Study, but it had a rather far-reaching effect on higher education. During the first half of the current century, the evaluation of local agencies became somewhat standardized as the accreditation procedures were developed and implemented.[3]

The testing movement in America is recognized as an essential ingredient in the educational establishment and in the political arena. The testing movement has been perceived, for the most part, as the administration of standardized achievement tests. Much credence has been placed on the results of standardized achievement tests. In some circles, a level of credence and an assumption of scope and infallibility have been displayed that are in excess of reasonable expectations for standardized tests. Standardized tests have been assumed by some to answer questions they were not intended to answer.

In-depth studies have been conducted by sociologists and educators in an effort to determine the answers to pressing questions in our educational system and society. The 1966 longitudinal studies of Colman have been widely referenced. More recently, numerous major reports were published on the conditions Goodlad found in education in the 1980s.

With increased federal intervention efforts in education during the Sputnik era, so many evaluations have been conducted it is difficult to catalog them. Evaluators in agencies such as the Rand Corporation have been bold enough to suggest broad generalizations drawn from numerous, specific evaluation efforts. Evaluation reports in dissertations and journals have increased at an exponential rate, as programs grow and students in doctorate-granting institutions strive to meet graduation dates. A process to keep order and retrievability in the growing number of evaluation reports has been undertaken by librarians and personnel in Educational Resources Information Center (ERIC) agencies across the nation. Perhaps the next major frontier to be developed will include the use of artificial intelligence to synthesize the vast amounts of material and distill the reports so that kernels of truth can be found among the chaff. As the capability to retrieve and synthesize the literature grows, the use of information will possibly be enhanced in such a way that educators will be better able to capitalize on the constantly expanding knowledge base.

DEFINITIONS OF EDUCATIONAL EVALUATION

A distinction has been made between evaluation and assessment. *Assessment* involves fact-finding—gathering data to describe a particular program or person. Planners should know what data to gather and how to gather them to determine the status or conditions present in a planning effort. Assessment may be focused on either summative or formative considerations. *Evaluation* extends into the realm of making judgments based on data. Assessments are used by planners to determine conditions, to describe the current status, and to see "what is." In evaluation, planners go beyond researching "what is" and probe the meanings and implications as judgments are made.

The various definitions of evaluation, as used in education, reflect the philosophy of the individuals who have presented the definitions. Some authorities emphasize accountability, while others place more attention on the concept of evaluation as a means of improving programs. Clearly, the authors of definitions do not suggest a strict dichotomy between program improvement on the one hand and accountability on the other, as it is evident that both concepts are important.

A broad range of functions and purposes is encompassed by evaluation. In a definition that is broadly conceived, evaluation may be defined as "the collection and use of information to make decisions about an educational program."[4]

A similar view of evaluation was given by Beeby when he suggested that evaluation was the systematic collection and interpretation of evidence, leading to a judgment of value intended to produce action. Unfortunately, achieving action has "not been conspicuously successful in most schools."[5] The position that decisions are to be made and actions taken on the basis of information rather than on personal preferences, hunches, or expediencies underlies the definition by Beeby. While it is suggested that information is to be gathered in a systematic way, data that are beyond the limits of the specific research questions specified for the evaluation effort should not be precluded. In some instances there are data other than officially generated data that may be as important or even more important than data gathered by design.

When reviewing various definitions of evaluation presented by authorities in the field, Worthen and Sanders[6] summarized several additional definitions. They interpreted Stake as defining evaluation as "describing and judging an educational program." From Scriven's definition, they presumed evaluation to be "gathering and combining performance data with weighted sets of goal scales." Provus defined evaluation as "comparing performance against standards"; Hammond, as "assessing effectiveness of current and innovative programs at the local level by comparing behavior data with objectives"; Alkin, as "the process of ascertaining the decision areas of concern, selecting appropriate information, and collecting and analyzing information"; and Tyler, as the comparison of "student performance with behaviorally stated objectives."

REASONS TO EVALUATE EDUCATIONAL PROGRAMS AND ADMINISTRATIVE PRACTICES

Just as there are numerous definitions of the process of evaluation, there are numerous pronouncements regarding the reasons for conducting evaluations. As suggested above, the reasons presented for conducting evaluations generally follow a continuum, ranging from a position of accountability to the stance taken by those who would emphasize program improvement. Political considerations, a third factor related to accountability, have become a fact of life. Thus, the continuum may be extended to include political considerations, with accountability toward one end of the continuum and program improvement toward the other end of the continuum.

Over two decades ago, Cronbach and Suppes prophesized: "There has been agreement, both within and without the ranks of educators, that systematic investigation has much to offer. Indeed, there is agreement that *massive, lasting changes in education cannot safely be made except on the basis of deep objective inquiry.*"[7]

When considering instructional programs, Bloom stated: "The main purpose of . . . [formative evaluation] is to determine the degree of mastery of a given learning task and to pinpoint the part of the task not mastered . . . [and] summative evaluation is directed toward a much more general assessment of the degree to which the larger outcomes have been attained."[8] Viewed in a slightly broader context, "evaluation must always be to provide the answer to an all-important question: Does the phenomenon under observation [which could be an educational program or an administrative or management function] have greater value than its competitors or sufficient value of itself that it should be maintained?"[9]

When evaluation is carried out in an effort to improve a course, an educational program, or a management function, the primary purpose is to determine the effect of the phenomenon, as reflected in changes in pupil behavior or the effectiveness or efficiency of the management function. When components of a phenomenon that can be improved are identified, the evaluation effort has been used to perform a valuable function. If, when identifying the effectiveness of a phenomenon, the capacity to answer questions related to accountability and the demand for political considerations is demonstrated in the evaluation process, educational leaders will have reaped maximum benefits. Decisions should be made based upon the information generated in an evaluation effort as contrasted to creating information based on personal impressions or expediencies.

THE EDUCATIONAL MISSION AND A CALL FOR ACCOUNTABILITY

For a number of decades, the Seven Cardinal Principles have been used as a primary guide in the educational enterprise. Local leaders have incorporated the essence of the Seven Cardinal Principles in local mission statements. Educators and some laypersons are familiar with the Seven Cardinal Principles, which were posed by the Commission on the Reorganization of Secondary Education in 1918.[10] The topics included in the Seven Cardinal Principles were (1) health, (2) command of fundamental processes, (3) worthy home membership, (4) vocation, (5) civic education, (6) worthy use of leisure, and (7) ethical character. Much of the educational policy of the nation was based on the foundation provided by the Seven Cardinal Principles.

Since the original work of the Commission on the Reorganization of Secondary Education, the principles have undergone numerous revisions, as new emphases on educational mission have been espoused. In most instances, those persons modifying the Seven Cardinal Principles have seen the need to keep the principles abreast of changing times, while holding fast to the principle of universal, public education. Interestingly, a different tone was reflected in the Six National Education Goals, which came from the deliberations of President George Bush and the nation's governors in 1990. The thinking of leaders in a time of social turbulence is shown in the six education goals, briefly summarized below. In considering the implications of the national goals generated by the president and the governors, Cuban has suggested that extended deliberations by policymakers will take place regarding the steady pressure on centralization. Cuban asked: "To what degree will these national goals and performance standards reverse, alleviate, or worsen the present conditions in big-city school systems?''[11]

Goal 1. Readiness for School: by the year 2000, all children in America will start school ready to learn.

Goal 2. High School Completion: by the year 2000, the high school graduation rate will increase to at least 90 percent.

Goal 3. Student Achievement and Citizenship: by the year 2000, American students will leave grades 4, 8, and 12 having demonstrated competency in challenging subject matter including English, mathematics, science, history, and geography, and every school in America will ensure that all students learn to use their minds well, so they may be prepared for responsible citizenship, further learning, and productive employment in our modern economy.

Goal 4. Science and Mathematics: by the year 2000, U.S. students will be first in the world in science and mathematics achievement.

Goal 5. Adult Literacy and Lifelong Learning: by the year 2000, every adult American will be literate and will possess the knowledge and skills necessary to compete in a global economy and exercise the rights and responsibilities of citizenship.

Goal 6. Safe, Disciplined, and Drug-Free Schools: by the year 2000, every school in America will be free of drugs and violence and will offer a disciplined environment conducive to learning.

Each of the Six National Goals was accompanied by more specific objectives to be achieved. Debate continues over the Six National Goals for education, as presented by the president of the United States and the governors from the 50 states. Two themes among the many themes found within the set of goals ring loud and clear: school personnel are charged with the well-being of citizens and the health of the economy. Thus, persons in the educational establishment are perceived to carry responsibilities of a broader scope than teaching the basic fundamentals of reading, writing, and computations to the students. The link between the Six National Goals and the issue of evaluation will become more prominent and continue to be the center of attention and debate as legislators at the state level struggle to translate the goals into state legislation and local school board members endeavor to blend the federal and state mandates into local initiatives. Evaluation will play an important function as planning takes place—both strategic and operational planning—as school officials face the demands of the citizens in a pluralistic society fraught with changing conditions and expectations.

TYPES OF EVALUATION

Many approaches and techniques are embodied in evaluation. The nature of what is to be assessed varies so much that many different tools and approaches are used in the area of evaluation. In most respects, evaluation draws upon the tools of the researcher; however, it has been pointed out that evaluation differs from research.

Research is generally considered to create new knowledge that is generalizable. Evaluation is intended to assess the worth of a phenomenon and is typically not considered for purposes of generalizability. While research may also draw upon historical perspectives or even be a historical study, evaluation seldom encompasses historical considerations other than as part of the background or to develop a rationale for conducting a given evaluation project. While a pure researcher may be interested in the findings achieved in a research effort and does not consider application, persons who conduct evaluations are very much interested in the applicability of their efforts. Worthen and Sanders pointed out, however, that "both research and evaluation are primarily dependent upon empirical techniques and methods." [12]

"Research is the activity aimed at obtaining generalizable knowledge by contriving and testing claims about relationships among variables or describing generalizable phenomena." [13]

"Evaluation is the determination of the worth of a thing. It includes obtaining information for use in judging the worth of a program, product, procedure, or objective, or the potential utility of alternative approaches designed to attain specified objectives." [14] There is an assumption that the results of evaluation efforts will be used in making decisions.

Development is a third area of consideration. As Worthen and Sanders noted, development in education is "the production and testing of curriculum materials (such as books, films, computer-assisted instruction programs), organizational or staffing plans (such as team teaching, differentiated staffing, modular scheduling), and other applied media or instruments of schooling." [15] Certain elements of development overlap with research and evaluation. Developmental workers call upon many of the same tools used in research and in evaluation.

When the three levels of searching for information or truth—research, evaluation, and development—are considered, clearly, the tools and procedures will be similar. Many of the skills required to accomplish one are required to accomplish the others.

Organized inquiry has been classified by Stufflebeam and Webster into 13 types of studies. Two types, by their own definitions, are "pseudo studies" involving "politically controlled studies" and "public relations–inspired studies." Five studies are classified as "question-oriented" studies, and 6 as "values-oriented" studies.

The politically controlled and public relations–inspired pseudo studies are, as the label implies, not studies in the true sense of the word. A political study is often a distortion of data to prove a point. The public relations–inspired effort is a potential distortion of reality simply to generate a favorable image. [16] The only classification that would be lower in ethical considerations would be the failure to conduct any evaluation of a project.

The five question-oriented types of evaluation include the objectives-based study in which the advance organizer for conducting the evaluation is provided with a statement of objectives. Objectives by which the study is focused may come from clients or staff members, as efforts are made to determine if the specified objectives have been achieved. The methods used in conducting the objectives-based evaluation involve the collection and analysis of performance data specifically identified to measure the specified outcomes. The data may be paper and pencil tests, interviews, or observations. One of the perceived limitations of objectives-based evaluations is that the results do not lend themselves to program improvements, since data are collected on end results.

Accountability studies emerged in the 1970s and have persisted as concerns continue to be expressed by constituent groups regarding the quality of education in the United States. Accountability studies have followed many of the federally funded efforts to improve the quality of education. The advance organizers for accountability studies are derived from staff members in educational institutions who are responsible for implementation of a funded project in an effort to improve education.[17] One of the concerns that accompanies such studies is the pressure to ensure that results will always be positive and show a "significant" difference. An added concern, especially where state or federal funding is involved, can grow from political expediencies and pressures that accompany accountability studies.

Experimental research is another form of question-oriented efforts. Experimental research designs are frequently employed when examining the worth of a new approach or product as contrasted to what has been employed. In experimental research, a control group and a treatment group are enlisted, data may be collected that are derived from pre- and post-treatments, and the results of the two groups are compared to test a hypothesis. The advance organizers, or the source of questions, typically come from the persons doing the research and not from clients.[18] One of the proverbial concerns of persons conducting an experimental study is the influence of the Hawthorne effect. Lest the results be meaningless, there is need for the findings of the studies to be reviewed to make sure the numbers were sufficient, the samples were comparable or controlled, and the treatment was realistic in terms of time and the control of variables.

Testing programs, in which all students at a given grade level are tested with the use of a standardized achievement test, are also categorized by Stufflebeam and Webster as question-oriented evaluations. The focus is on the school curriculum and how well students score on standardized tests. The questions are generated by personnel in the firm where the test is constructed, and in some instances selected teaching staff members have been called upon as consultants. The primary purpose of the testing program is to "compare the test performance of individual students and groups of students to that of selected norm groups."[19]

A final question-oriented evaluation approach is provided by management information systems. The management information system, which may be located at a state department of education or in a local education agency, is used to supply managers with information needed to conduct programs and make improvements. While managers may use management information systems to derive a political advantage, unlike the politically controlled pseudo study, if data are accurate and used judiciously, the persons who are responsible for making decisions can do so with a much firmer base of information when drawing upon a management information system.[20]

Of the six values-oriented types of studies, Stufflebeam and Webster identified the first as the accreditation/certification study.[21] Accreditation studies were developed during the first quarter of the current century, and outside experts were called upon to make value judgments regarding the quality of a given program. The practice has continued; although modifications have been made in accreditation studies, many characteristics of the early form of study persist. The advance organizers are derived from a set of standards or criteria for minimum levels regarding facilities, staff, and curriculum as specified by some accrediting agency. The purpose of such studies has been to determine "whether institutions, programs, or personnel should be approved to perform specified functions."[22] While the intent of accreditation studies has never been questioned, the results often fail to generate meaningful improvements. Not uncommonly, an accreditation study is carried out in which a primary effort of the first phase, or "self-study," is to fill out the forms in a manner that will pass inspection, regardless of what the actual nature of the existing program may be. A second criticism is that after the visitation team has made a report, a public relations effort or news release pointing to all the good things in the local educational agency is the greatest benefit derived from the study; no subsequent follow-up occurs. Fortunately, there are leaders in local school districts who demonstrate integrity and who capitalize on periodic accreditation studies to plan for improvements in a district. As a portion of the internal environmental scanning, the data from an accreditation study can be valuable in strategic planning.

Policy studies have been growing in importance in the eyes of educational leaders and constitute an important form of values-oriented evaluation in the field of education. Policy studies have been perceived to be growing in importance as educational leaders search for ways to communicate effectively with legislators and opinion leaders concerning the direction for education. At the beginning of the twentieth century, educational leaders, such as Eliot and Dewey, provided the thoughtful and insightful leadership that helped shape public and universal education in the United States. At the midpoint of the twentieth century, a major shift occurred in the development of policy in America. The policy leadership moved from the realm of the educator to the halls of legislative bodies and to the courtrooms of the land. The reins of leadership were picked up by judiciary and legislative bodies at the national and state levels to establish educational policy. Educators were forced into a responding mode as they struggled to carry out the policies—the judicial and legislative mandates—with which they were confronted. Consequently, in an effort to exert a more proactive influence on educational policy, various policy study centers have emerged.

The advance organizers for a policy study are derived from a given policy issue. Approaches for conducting policy studies are multiple; the focus is often on identifying current thinking by using such approaches as the Delphi technique, conducting polls, or synthesizing what is known and available in the existing data base of educational and cultural knowledge. Forecasting and projection techniques are also employed in efforts to determine what can be expected in the future.

One of the main concerns of policy studies is that they are often "corrupted or subverted by the political environment in which they must be conducted and reported."[23] The manner in which the information in a policy study is reported becomes a major consideration. Two steps that would precede a formal written report have been suggested: early reporting and oral reporting. When dealing with an issue that is politicized, the actors may have strong views, even biases, for which they are looking for support. If a formal written report is held back until early and oral reports can be given, all concerned may be afforded some time and elbow room before final commitments are made. Early reports can reduce the element of surprise, and those who must lobby are given time to consider their options.[24]

Policy researchers recognize that a study may be outstanding, but unless it is effectively communicated to the appropriate audiences, it becomes worthless. Consequently, those who are involved in policy studies must be willing to "invest a significant amount of their time and energy in communicating . . . [and] must be able to interact effectively with politicians, bureaucrats, housewives, and minority leaders."[25]

Educational planners are regularly involved in the need to conduct decision-oriented studies as they search for ways to improve a program, explore the best option for carrying out a plan, or determine how revisions should be made to enhance a program. The source of questions in a decision-oriented study is the decision makers themselves. The methods employed for conducting decision-oriented studies are numerous. Needs assessments, surveys, the use of data bases, discrepancy analysis, and even experimental studies are approaches that are often utilized. A recognized advantage of the decision-oriented study is that it encourages planners to use evaluation data for rational decision making.[26]

Consumer-oriented studies are still another form of evaluation identified by Stufflebeam and Webster.[27] The advance organizers are defined as societal values and perceived needs. The purpose of consumer-oriented studies "is to judge the relative merits of alternative educational goals and services and, thereby, to help taxpayers and practitioners make wise choices in their purchase of educational goods and services."[28] Here again, it can be seen that various evaluation techniques or methods may be called upon to gather and interpret the data for dissemination. As in several other types of evaluation studies, the consumer-oriented study can be subjected to the vagaries of political winds.

The client-centered study stands in contrast to the consumer-oriented study in that it is focused directly on questions derived from the client, not the consumer. While the consumer-oriented study is focused on broad issues that emerge from society, the client-centered study is focused on the pupils and their parents or guardians, and immediate questions about the education program at hand are addressed. The advance organizers are the questions or concerns that relate to the program at the local level.[29] The client-centered evaluation is intended to provide information so local persons can understand, assess, and make informed decisions. Through client-centered evaluation, local persons can become immediately involved, not only in generating advance organizers but in helping to conduct the collection of information; ownership is fostered. A weakness can grow from parochialism and a lack of external credibility, especially if local evaluators are not competent.

The final values-oriented type of evaluation suggested by Stufflebeam and Webster was the connoisseur-based study.[30] Put in a more common vernacular, such an evaluation is undertaken when it is deemed advisable to call in an "expert with a briefcase" from at least 50 miles away to conduct an in-depth analysis. The rationale for bringing in an expert is that such a person, if carefully chosen, is perceived to have the needed expertise and experience to perform a study more effectively than anyone on the local staff. In an unpublished survey involving eight states (Minnesota, North Dakota, South Dakota, Iowa, Missouri, Nebraska, Kansas, and Colorado), the author found that local school administrators most frequently called upon outside evaluators to conduct facilities studies, while the next two most often requested evaluation services were program evaluation and organizational assessments. The two most frequently identified criteria for choosing a consultant were reputation and experience. While consultants work with school boards and assist in the selection of new chief administrators or in policy development, and a larger number of consultants are being asked for assistance in strategic planning, such services are in a different category than evaluation consultation.[31]

JUST DO IT

The advertisement for a popular sports item of clothing reiterates "Just Do It." The slogan for a drug-free world was, at one time, "Just Say No." Both are, perhaps, gross oversimplifications of something that may be very complex if translated into evaluation considerations. When it comes to evaluation in the educational setting, that too is a highly complex process, but the admonishment to "just do it" may be very appropriate. A reverse view of the situation may be to suggest to educators to "just say no" to the temptation to avoid evaluation.

While many educators have demonstrated an avoidance of evaluation efforts, there is a natural tendency for some, when planning for evaluation, to become enthralled with the potential and be carried away with the whole idea. Thus, while the call is loud and clear that evaluation is essential, it is also important to keep it in balance. As long as the evaluation effort is planned and carried out appropriately, keeping it simple to the extent that is possible has some real value. A balance between what is ideal and what is possible in the realm of evaluation will evolve. The balance between the ideal and the real is the crux of the matter.

As alluded to previously, local expertise may not be available to conduct an evaluation in some situations. In such instances, an evaluation specialist should be contacted. There is, however, an appropriate middle ground in some situations. An evaluation plan may be well within the capabilities of local personnel; however, it may also be appropriate to have the plan reviewed by an outside specialist to assure that the chosen design, techniques, and plan for data analysis are appropriate. With the identification of some improvements in the design by the evaluation specialist, the local personnel may be able to conduct an evaluation with credible results.

USE OF THE STATE-OF-THE-ART TOOLS

Judgment, hard work, and technology are requisites for conducting evaluation studies. Another key requisite is a knowledge base regarding evaluation or research tools. To make appropriate assessments, the planner or evaluator will need a list of key requisites and tools. There is also an assumption that planners have an attitude or understanding of the importance of assessment; that is, planners need to demonstrate an evaluation state of mind.

One of the tools that is often taken for granted is a data base. A data base can encompass libraries and current periodicals. Note that the term *periodicals* was used in place of *educational periodicals*. Planners, especially strategic planners, need to draw from a wide data base in which disciplines other than education are taken into account. Planners should also become familiar with computerized data bases. Since networks are becoming so widespread, any local school district can have access to major data bases. Such data bases can be identified in any given area by contacting state departments of education, state library commission offices, institutions of higher education, and intermediate educational agencies or personnel in neighboring school districts. The kinds of data frequently sought include census figures, test results, demographic information, economic indicators at the national, state, and local levels, sociological trends, and technological developments.

The use of computer technology is a well-established means of supporting evaluation efforts. Mainframe computers have been an integral part of research efforts and instruction in colleges and universities since the 1950s. With the emergence and sophistication of microcomputers in approximately 1980, computer capabilities have been vastly enhanced. An evaluator has several options available because of computer technology. A microcomputer can, with appropriate software and a modem, become a major research tool. An evaluator can input data and crunch some numbers with statistical software on a microcomputer, or the data may be inputted, using a microcomputer as a terminal, and transmitted to a mainframe for number crunching. As computer software has become more accessible, more sophisticated, and more user friendly, the options available to the evaluator have been enhanced almost beyond the wildest dreams of some old-timers.

Computers at the local level are being used with increased frequency to develop local data bases. Staff understanding of how to implement an integrated data base and use it to gather information and support data-based decision making is growing steadily. As previously mentioned, there are methods to conduct and record interviews with computer assistance that add still another dimension to the list of tools for planners. Inventory management has been greatly improved with computers. At one time, inventories were seldom taken; if they were taken, they had limited applicability because it would be another year before another inventory would be taken. With the advent of the computer, not only can an inventory be taken and the data inputted effectively, but the inventory information can also be kept current. Current inventory data are very usable in decision making, while stale inventories are about as valuable as a bumper sticker supporting a political candidate who failed to get elected at the previous general election.

If the planner-evaluator uses the personal and contemporary tools that are available, adequate evaluation efforts may lead to better results. Much is known about evaluation and the tools needed. What is needed is evaluation-minded planners who apply the knowledge base regarding evaluation to their trade.

APPROACHES TO EVALUATION OF EDUCATIONAL PROGRAMS

Planners, over an extended period of time, will be involved in planning educational efforts that encompass classes, courses, or total educational programs. Much has been written by numerous specialists about how to evaluate educational programs. Models for evaluation are presented in textbooks with varying degrees of complexity. Some of the major concepts recommended by evaluation specialists can be found in several of the evaluation models, as similarities and differences are posed by authors. Specified objectives are contained in some models; in contrast, goal-free assessment is offered in others.

The CIPP model, developed by Stufflebeam, draws upon systems theory. The acronym CIPP was derived from Context Evaluation (C), Input (I), Process Evaluation (P), and Product Evaluation (P). "The CIPP approach is based on the view that the most important purpose of evaluation is not to prove but to improve."[32] The CIPP model has an essential dimension for assessing educational programs because it includes both process and product evaluation. But the model, as conceptualized by Stufflebeam, has an additional ingredient or component that further enhances its capability, and that is the inclusion of context evaluation.

Context evaluation is designed to identify the strengths and the weaknesses in an educational setting as related to the instructional program. By determining the context, goals become more meaningful and the discrepancy between desired outcomes and the reality in which the educational program is taking place can be observed. If a program is being conducted in an area with full family support, conditions will be much different than for the same program offered in a setting in which there is a high level of broken homes and limited family support. The contextual difference can be a major factor. "Finally, context evaluation records are an excellent means by which to defend the efficiency of one's goals and priorities."[33]

Input evaluation was designed to provide assistance in the consideration of various alternatives in the context. Needs and environmental circumstances have a relationship to the selection of alternatives, which can better be understood with the support of input evaluation.

Process evaluation can provide an ongoing check to help managers determine if the plan is being followed. It is, in this respect, a management function. The process evaluation should be designed to provide feedback so that managers will know if the project is progressing according to schedule and, if not, why. If a schedule is not being maintained, a manager can possibly allocate additional resources and make related schedule adjustments, as suggested through the process evaluation.

The product evaluation is, as the term implies, an assessment to determine if the objectives specified for a class, course, or educational program have been reached. The focus can be on an individual student or group of students in product evaluation. Product evaluation can be viewed as short-term, exit measures or as follow-up studies.

A flowchart, as shown in Figure 11.1, can be reviewed to gain a gestalt of the CIPP model and to examine the progression of events or functions conceptualized by its originators.

If the concepts, or evaluation components, described by Hammond were placed by the Stufflebeam model, an extension or expansion can be seen. Hammond presented a three-dimensional model depicting the structure of evaluation. Behavior categories, including the cognitive domain, the affective domain, and the psychomotor domain, were included in one axis. The instructional-related categories of organization, content, method, facilities, and cost were contained in the second dimension or axis. Finally, the institutional dimensions of students, teachers, administrators, educational specialists, family, and community were incorporated in the third axis.[34] The dimensions proposed by Hammond are of such a nature that they can, if incorporated in an evaluation process, contribute to a comprehensive effort and meaningful results.

The structure of educational program evaluation can be further extended to incorporate performance measures as well as an assessment of outcomes or competencies. The various factors in an evaluation scheme, in which behavioral measures, performance outcomes, and competencies or results are considered, are shown in Figure 11.2. Pretest measures, process or formative evaluation, outcomes or summative measures, and follow-up are also encompassed in the structure. A determination of the context in which the evaluation is located and a clear definition of goals or desired outcomes are requisite to the model for program evaluation presented in Figure 11.2.

Behavioral measures are typically paper and pencil tests in the area of cognition and the affective domain. Psychomotor measures are frequently observed and measured by counting and measuring physical performance in most instances. For example, how many words can a pupil input into a keyboard in a given time frame? How many errors did the student commit? In physical education, psychomotor skills are typically determined by observing and recording frequencies and repetitions. The behavioral measures typically deal with single items or measures rather than with the gestalt.

In *performance measures,* a student is asked to perform a number of behaviors. For example, if students' ability to perform an operational planning process was to be assessed, they might be expected to demonstrate that they could carry out the entire process, from A to Z, according to specified criteria. Their performance would be measured, but their competence would probably not be measured. The determination of students' ability to demonstrate competence in planning or their ability to perform in a competent manner and demonstrate desirable results on the job would require a setting in which they could demonstrate their competence and be observed and evaluated in terms of the results they achieved. The level between being able to perform specified procedures and being able to show satisfactory results, or to demonstrate competence, is sometimes a major step. When performing in the real world, with the myriad of variables and crosscurrents of reality, competence or result measures are much more complex than performance or outcome measures.

As suggested, behavioral measures can involve cognitive outcomes, affective measures, and psychomotor measurements. Pretests could be employed as a primary area of emphasis in behavioral measures. Pretest measures could also be applied to performance outcomes in some selected situations, but not in most cases. Pretests would not be considered, as a general rule, in the area of competencies. Pretests could be focused on any pupil or learner (a pupil, a teacher, an administrator, a parent, or an adult learner from the community).

Process measures, or formative evaluation, can be employed as described previously in the CIPP model developed by Stufflebeam.[35] To gather process evaluation information, evaluators can solicit data not only from the learner but from the instructors and the supervisors. Additional process information may be gathered from specialists and patrons from within the agency or from outside the agency. Process data gathered from specialists and patrons should be col-

Figure 11.1
A Flowchart Depicting the Role of CIPP Evaluation in Effecting System Improvement

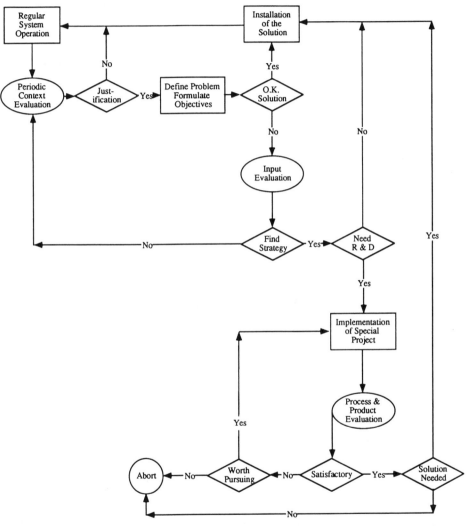

Source: Daniel L. Stufflebeam, "The CIPP Model for Program Evaluation," *Evaluation Models,* ed. George F. Madaus, Michael S. Scrivens, and Daniel L. Stufflebeam (Boston: Kluwer-Nijhoff Publishers, 1983). Used by permission.

Figure 11.2
Evaluation of Educational Classes, Courses, and Programs

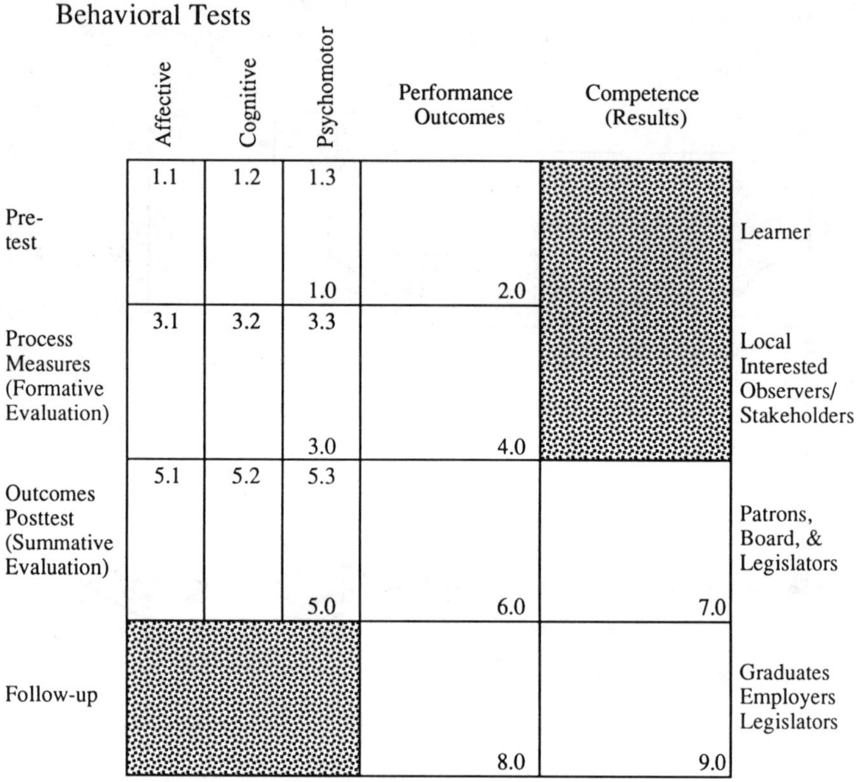

Behavioral Tests

	Affective	Cognitive	Psychomotor	Performance Outcomes	Competence (Results)	
Pre-test	1.1	1.2	1.3			Learner
			1.0	2.0		
Process Measures (Formative Evaluation)	3.1	3.2	3.3			Local Interested Observers/ Stakeholders
			3.0	4.0		
Outcomes Posttest (Summative Evaluation)	5.1	5.2	5.3			Patrons, Board, & Legislators
			5.0	6.0	7.0	
Follow-up						Graduates Employers Legislators
				8.0	9.0	

Organizational costs and Developmental and Operating Costs (Time, Facilities, Space, Equipment, Information, Overhead)

lected in a systematic way as a general rule; however, there may be some "data from behind the data" that appear unexpectedly and are of value. There may also be some unexpected sources of data that may be of value; thus, the evaluator needs to be alert to such fugitive sources of information and review them with judgment.

Outcomes, or summative evaluations, are often viewed as the "bottom line." Outcomes, related to instructional objectives, are often solicited with the greatest amount of vigor; yet, they tell only a partial story of program effectiveness. The data regarding achievement of goals or outcomes are derived from the learner, whether that learner is a pupil in a K–12 setting, a staff member in an in-service program, or a parent or patron in an adult education program. The measures for cognitive and affective behaviors are typically collected by paper and pencil tests, while the psychomotor skills are generally considered to be observable activities.

Follow-up measures are much less frequently incorporated in evaluation efforts than are pretests or formative and summative measures. Follow-up measures are generally not conducted on behavioral dimensions. Follow-up measures come into consideration when reviewing performance measures and are the main focus of competence measures. Follow-up studies are often loosely associated with goals of an educational program. For example, there are very specific goals for academic courses in a secondary school that may be measured in behavioral terms. As important as such behavioral or achievement measures may be, it could be even more important to determine if a graduate, as reflected in an academic follow-up study, is competent as a college student. A different set of questions from those used to measure behavioral dimensions or the pupil's ability to perform certain functions is required to determine the competence of a graduate who goes on to college. The follow-up evaluation, while focused on the learners or graduates, also can be expanded by collecting information from patrons, employers, legislators, and board members.

It is important to recognize that data in educational program evaluation should be gathered from multiple sources. Data of differing kinds are required for behavioral tests as contrasted to performance measures or measures of competence.

The issue of cost-effectiveness is a final consideration when viewing the comprehensive structure for educational program evaluation. The allocation of prime resources (time, staff, space, information, materials) may be viewed from a number of perspectives and with various levels of intensity. Actually, in many situations, little or no consideration is given to the determination of cost-effectiveness of a class, course, or educational program. There are ways, just as in budget allocation procedures in planning, to consider the cost of a program. One approach to determine cost-effectiveness is the use of a discrepancy model. For example, how does a new program compare to the old program in terms of time, staffing costs, including supervisory costs, space requirements, information costs, and operating costs and materials? While some financial auditors, such as in institutions of higher education, claim that overhead costs in an institution may range from 36 percent to 62 percent, such overhead costs are generally not taken into full account in local K–12 agencies. Overhead costs, however, are real costs, and evaluators are well advised to take them into account when considering cost-effectiveness questions.

Staffing costs generally are not too difficult to identify. A complex issue frequently surfaces when a staff member spends only a part of his or her time in a given effort. A determination must then be made concerning what percentage of a full-time equivalent (FTE) is involved. Based on that estimate of the percentage of FTE involved, a figure for salary and benefits can be determined.

Organizational considerations can enter into costing out a program. If an existing organizational structure will suffice and no changes are required, an assumption may be made that no added cost is involved. If, however, an organizational change is involved, the cost determination may become complex and difficult to define. To illustrate, if a secretary was working with one administrator and was, as a result of organizational changes, assigned to work with two administrators, what does the change in the organization and operation of the new structure mean in terms of costs? As a general suggestion, a cost estimate should be made for an educational program. The determination can, however, be made in rather general and direct or immediate costs without including sophisticated overhead computations designed to count every paper clip and the cost of turning on every light switch.

The entire procedure of collecting data in an evaluation effort provides the grist for the mill—the numbers to be computed and the observations to be synthesized, that is, the data to be analyzed. It is important to have a definite plan for analysis before the data are collected. There should be an orderly format for "coding, storing and retrieving the information."[36] At this point, particularly if data are to be subjected to statistical analysis, a specialist should be contacted for consultation. Untold difficulties can be avoided and clearer results obtained if the analysis is properly planned in advance.

The final phase of the evaluation process includes preparing a written report and communicating the results to appropriate audiences. Evaluation reports can become bulky documents in many instances. When an evaluation report becomes too long, an abstract should be prepared. School board members, parents, and patrons generally are not interested in examining every item and number that may appear in an appendix. Preliminary reports or oral presentations given for political reasons do not cancel out the need for an appropriately prepared, final, written report. The final report, like any form of communication, should be prepared in such a way that the intended audience is given full consideration.

If the needed information has been communicated in a way that the intended audience read and understood it, the final report has been well prepared. The foregoing is such a broad generalization, however, that it may be somewhat meaningless. If a report is to stand the scrutiny of evaluators and be recognized as credible, certain criteria should be used. Worthen and Sanders suggested that the following 11 points should be used when evaluating reports.[37]

1. "Internal validity. Does the design provide the information it is intended to provide?"

2. "External validity. To what extent are the results of the study generalizable?" In many studies focusing on a specific or narrow issue, generalizability does not become an issue as it does in a study designated as a "research" study.

3. "Reliability. How accurate and consistent is the information?"

4. "Objectivity. [Has there been a legitimate effort] to strive to collect information

and make judgments in such a way that the same interpretations and judgments would be made by any intelligent, rational person?''

5. ''Relevance.''
6. ''Importance.''
7. ''Scope. How comprehensive is the design?''
8. ''Credibility.''
9. ''Timeliness.''
10. ''Persuasiveness.'' Have the results been presented in such a manner that the information will be made available to all individuals and interested groups?
11. ''Efficiency.''

When evaluating projects in an educational agency that are not in the instructional realm, Management by Objectives (MBO) has proven to be a most satisfactory approach. Through the use of the operational planning model and consideration of the measurable outcomes that have been identified, the next step—the identification of preliminary criteria for evaluation—can be reached. Each specified outcome should be accompanied by one or more criteria to assess when that outcome is reached and to make a determination about the effectiveness of the results.

Evaluation procedures and concepts can be adopted and modified to measure the effectiveness of a building project as contrasted to a new reading program implemented in the primary grades of a school. The degree of emphasis on measuring satisfactory results for accountability purposes may be different for a building project than the emphasis on improving the process of constructing a building. In other words, an instructional program evaluation effort may be directed primarily at program improvement, while in some management efforts, such as a building project, an effort to demonstrate accountability may receive more emphasis. There are, however, noninstructional plans in which management processes are involved that can also draw heavily upon formative measures to improve an effort. For example, as new computer capabilities are introduced and upgraded in school systems, a considerable amount of attention should be directed toward how staff are adapting, what works smoothly, where the bugs are, and what time and cost factors are visible.

As is true in the case of assessing educational programs, management efforts need to be evaluated in terms of costs. Prime resources that go into a noncurricular program need to be determined and estimates made for planning and developmental costs, implementation costs, and ongoing operational costs.[38] The general means of determining personnel costs, time, information, use of space and facilities, and overhead costs should be analyzed. Actually, cost-effectiveness measures are initiated at the time the project budget is developed. Project budget systems or cost estimates accompanying Program Evaluation and Review Techniques (PERT) can provide planners and managers with the means of projecting and managing allocated resources in conjunction with a project.

One approach to planning or measuring costs is simply to list the direct resources needed for a particular program. Until overhead and indirect costs are considered, however, the list of needed resources may provide only a partial picture. When various alternatives are considered in the operational planning stage of a program, it may be necessary for the planners to list the costs associated with each option considered so comparisons can be made. The process of making comparisons between options or alternatives becomes more complex if the "potential value to be derived" is taken into consideration. There are no simple answers or mathematical formulas to take into account all the variables and value considerations that may come into play when comparing costs associated with various alternatives. Values associated with various alternatives may involve, in addition to actual costs, identifiable advantages as well as limitations that will call for judgments. There are procedures for weighing and comparing each advantage and disadvantage proposed for a project; however, at some point, a chief executive officer may be called upon to make a judgment.

To determine all project costs or benefits in advance is not always possible. Due to the uncertainties that may accompany a project, the chief executive officer may be placed in the position of making a decision based on limited or sparse information. The leaders who are early adapters emerge at one end of a continuum, and the late adapters and laggards maintain the status quo, low-risk position at the opposite end of the continuum. Officials in a school district of approximately 6,500 K–12 students were observed to make a decision based on partial information. A minicomputer facility was installed with the capability to provide a local area network (LAN), among other enhanced computer capabilities. After approximately 18 months, the superintendent commented on an unexpected benefit derived from the LAN; personnel had observed that the level and quality of human interaction and communication had moved to a higher, more positive, and more productive level. The superintendent of schools expressed the view that no one had anticipated such results. An unplanned and unexpected outcome had been achieved.

In operational planning, human factors that are not easily predicted or weighed can enter into cost considerations. The impact of an innovation upon staff morale can be measured in a speculative way, but not always determined with precision in advance. Questions about relocating or assigning staff, working climate, job security, and self-esteem may be major considerations when planning some management projects; however, such considerations do not yield to precise premeasures.

Cost considerations, while constituting a major factor with respect to implementation, have not typically been a major influence in evaluation efforts.[39] While an exhaustive and precise analysis of costs may not be possible, nor always practical, such a limitation cannot be used as a rationale for avoiding making any cost analysis.

EVALUATION AND DECISION MAKING

The entire intent of conducting evaluations is embodied in the fact that decisions need to be made. Evaluation will enable decision makers to work from a data base, even if that data base is not complete, and make more judicious, informed decisions. The results from an evaluation effort do not, however, negate the need for decision makers to use judgment; nor will evaluation remove all risks. Judgments need to be made about the worth or value of a project; from that judgment a projection should be made about future actions.

Suggestions have been made that conducting evaluations of programs and projects is a complex and elusive undertaking. Perhaps the point of interpreting and making judgments is one part of the total process that makes evaluation so difficult—the process of making decisions based on the findings, which may ultimately provide only partial information. Perhaps in an oversimplified approach to making judgments, the suggestion can be made that the decision-making process begins with the findings and the extent to which the intended objectives have been reached as identified in the findings. The decision makers, however, need to direct their attention beyond the limits of a set of findings. Findings may show that a program is liked by stakeholders, but the results or the end product may not be improved. A judgment will be needed to determine if the project is to be continued. Or a staff development program may be very successful in training library personnel in the use of a computer-managed library system, while a decline in student use of library materials is shown through the library circulation figures. In such a case, there may be a call for more information, and further evaluation efforts may be needed. "The determination of the worth of a program involves considerably more than achieving its [specific] objectives."[40]

Decision making in educational agencies, whether educational considerations with regard to curriculum and instruction issues or management functions are considered, is never done without the potential of political influences. Judgments made in ignorance or the avoidance of political considerations can be ill-advised or downright stupid. Various ways of dealing with political pressures have been recognized. Officials should recognize, in a realistic way, that there are pressures and that some individuals, often elected officials, in their zest for achieving their personal interests, are willing to set aside evaluation results. Unfortunately, there are employees in the educational enterprise, as well as elected officials, whose motives and practices have been justifiably questioned as they push, intimidate, politicize, and try to manipulate results. To pretend that such politically motivated persons do not exist is naive.

The approach to deal with negative political influences has been considered for decades by Machiavellian advocates on up to modern political scientists. Truthfully, there are no easy answers. Perhaps the first approach for coping and confronting negative political behavior is to know where you stand and what you stand for. The second suggestion is to be open and honest and not to succumb to fighting fire with fire. Know the law and abide by it. A suggestion can also be made to refrain from avoidance techniques. Pretending a politicized problem will go away is worse than futile; the problem is compounded. Know the art of compromise and the strategy of "win-win" in place of "win-lose." Be expert in the realm of conflict resolution. Know the power structure. Develop open communication skills with all segments of the culture in which a politicized problem may exist. Use data and make information available to all stakeholders. Finally, listen—listen carefully.

One of the hardest decisions to make in educational institutions and one that is typically politicized is a reduction of some body or subagency within a bureaucracy. Bureaucracies are agencies of survival and resistant to change. Decision makers can use evaluation results, including cost-effectiveness figures, and still face insurmountable political pressures against the proposed cuts. In spite of the political expediencies and the traditions that cause resistance to cutting a subagency, clearly it is much better to enter a political struggle or an evaluation armed with data than it is to try to fly by the seat of one's pants. Information can be an important force with which to confront political resistance, even if that information may fall short of achieving desired decisions.

SUMMARY

Within the space of one chapter, no more than a brief overview of some selected elements of the evaluation process can be presented. A brief summary of some elements of the chapter follows.

1. Evaluation is essential to provide information for improvement efforts and for accountability. Through evaluation people within and outside of an educational institution learn about that institution.

2. The greatest sin in evaluation may be the sin of omission.

3. The complexity of evaluation leads to two suggestions: (a) when appropriate, seek expert advice and (b) in many instances "quick and dirty" assessments may suffice. Whether simple or complex evaluation efforts are involved, the analysis requires more than "conventional wisdom" of laypersons.

4. Because of political entanglements, evaluation is often inexorably encumbered by political pressures. Consequently, to derive benefits from the findings, the planner may be led into the political arena in numerous instances.

5. Decisions cannot be dictated or judgment supplanted by the findings of an evaluation. Judgments may remain difficult and demanding even with evaluation results in hand; however, a difficult decision is better faced with some knowledge rather than

in total ignorance. Evaluations will not provide all the answers. Decision makers must still reach judgments with only partial information.

6. Credibility of the findings in an evaluation report can be enhanced if an outside, unbiased evaluator is involved.

7. The following should be avoided in evaluation efforts: (a) choosing the wrong test, one that does not measure the right things; (b) assuming cause and effect simply because a statistical relationship can be identified; (c) selecting a biased or inadequate sample; (d) using one measure when multiple dimensions need to be assessed; (e) hiding behind "grounded theory" as the only approach when statistics are feared; (f) proposing casual or shoddy methodology; (g) selecting the design or method first and then choosing the program to be evaluated; (h) using an inadequate "treatment" in experimental studies; (i) using "test-driven" evaluation programs rather than choosing the appropriate test for the program being evaluated; (j) waiting too long to determine measurement criteria and thus beginning the data collection "after the horse is out of the barn"; (k) succumbing to the temptation not to review the literature and embarking on a monumental effort to rediscover the wheel; (l) yielding to the temptation not to organize and plan for coding and retrieving the data; (m) selecting too few variables and making wrong assumptions about the findings; and (n) reaching conclusions before the evaluation has begun.

NOTES

1. Blaine R. Worthen and James R. Sanders, *Educational Evaluation: Theory and Practice* (Worthington, Ohio: Charles A. Jones, 1973), 1.

2. P. H. DuBois, *A History of Psychological Testing* (Boston: Allyn and Bacon, 1970), 3.

3. Worthen and Sanders, *Educational Evaluation,* 3.

4. Lee J. Cronbach, "Course Improvement Through Evaluation," in *Evaluation Models,* ed. George F. Madaus, Michael S. Scriven, and Daniel L. Stufflebeam (Boston: Kluwer-Nijhoff, 1983), 105.

5. C. E. Beeby, *Assessment of Indonesian Education: A Guide to Planning* (Wellington, England: Oxford University Press, 1979), 138.

6. Worthen and Sanders, *Educational Evaluation,* 110–111.

7. Lee J. Cronbach and P. Suppes, *Research for Tomorrow's School: Disciplined Inquiry for Education* (New York: Macmillan, 1969), 12.

8. Benjamin S. Bloom, Thomas J. Hastings, and George J. Madaus, *Handbook on Formative and Summative Evaluation of Student Learning* (New York: McGraw-Hill, 1971), 61.

9. Worthen and Sanders, *Educational Evaluation,* 26.

10. Commission on the Reorganization of Secondary Education, *Cardinal Principles of Secondary Education,* Bulletin 1918, no. 35 (Washington, D.C.: U.S. Government Printing Office, 1918), 9.

11. Larry Cuban, "Four Stories About National Goals for American Education," *Phi Delta Kappan* 72, no. 4 (December 1990), 270.

12. Worthen and Sanders, *Educational Evaluation,* 12.

13. Ibid., 19.

14. Ibid., 19.

15. Ibid., 19.

16. Daniel L. Stufflebeam and William J. Webster, "An Analysis of Alternative Approaches to Evaluation," in *Evaluation Models*, ed. George F. Madaus, Michael S. Scriven, and Daniel L. Stufflebeam (Boston: Kluwer-Nijhoff, 1983), 25–26.

17. Ibid., 28.

18. Ibid., 28–29.

19. Ibid., 29.

20. Ibid., 30.

21. Ibid., 31.

22. Ibid., 31.

23. Ibid., 32.

24. Richard M. Wolf, *Evaluation in Education* (New York: Praeger, 1984), 197.

25. N. Castleman and P. Poty, *Center for Policy Research: The First Five Years, 1968–1973* (New York: Center for Policy Research, 1974).

26. Stufflebeam and Webster, "An Analysis of Alternative Approaches to Evaluation," 33.

27. Ibid., 33–34.

28. Ibid., 33.

29. Ibid., 34–35.

30. Ibid., 35.

31. Ward Sybouts, "Consultation Services Used in Local Schools" (University of Nebraska-Lincoln, 1986).

32. Daniel L. Stufflebeam, "The CIPP Model for Program Evaluation," in *Evaluation Models*, ed. George F. Madaus, Michael S. Scrivens, and Daniel L. Stufflebeam (Boston: Kluwer-Nijhoff, 1983), 118.

33. Ibid., 130.

34. R. Hammond, "Context Evaluation of Instruction in Local School Districts," *Educational Technologies* 9, no. 1 (1969), 13–18.

35. Stufflebeam, "The CIPP Model for Program Evaluation," 132.

36. Worthen and Sanders, *Educational Evaluation*, 147.

37. Ibid., 219–220.

38. Wolf, *Evaluation in Education*, 96.

39. Ibid., 91.

40. Ibid., 188.

12

The Management of Change: A Look at Change Models

An individual or team of planners may have the most ingenious plan in a 500-mile radius, with slick paper and multicolored presentations, but if the plan is not implemented, all the resourcefulness is for naught. Plans have to be implemented. Consequently, planners become involved in the change process or the management of change.

Most plans, even those not designed to be innovative, have the implied intent of being achieved to the best of the planner's ability or succeeding better than previous plans. Plans developed to involve the adoption or development of an innovation universally involve change. Plans will almost always change, whether they are conceived to change a business procedure, improve a personnel function, expand a technological management process, conduct a conference, build a facility, or improve an instructional program. Strategic planning is, by its very nature, designed to create the future in the image perceived by planners. Operational planning that is a direct outgrowth of strategic planning is the extension of some priority from a strategic plan; thus, operational planning is intended to implement a portion of the strategic plan to bring about intended improvements or meet perceived needs. Operational planning that is not a direct outgrowth of strategic planning can be structured by planners to bring about changes of various dimensions to improve some facet of an educational agency. Planning means changing, and often the changes are innovative in nature. Planning is conducted to improve various kinds of programs, and implementation is the stage where the intent of the plan is realized.

In approximately 500 B.C., Heracleitus said, ''Nothing endures but change''; his words were spoken at a time modern observers often reference as stable and unchanging. With the almost incomprehensible acceleration of change in the last half of the twentieth century, various observers have suggested that the only form of stability comes from knowing how to cope with change. To accomplish stability amidst change and turmoil, those involved must find a delicate balance. "The truly difficult challenge is to find and keep the balance—or perhaps, a better phrase would be the *dynamic imbalance.*"[1] Waterman suggested, "To change is to risk something. That makes us insecure. Not to change is a bigger risk, but it seldom feels that way."[2]

Toffler wrote about the powershift in violence, wealth, and knowledge from a global outlook. When considering change from Toffler's perspective, one could argue that such broad powershifts are somewhat removed from a local educational agency. Actually, any local educational agency is riding on the current of a society that literally precludes such immunity to powershifts. Schools are, or should be, at the heart of the information age. The quality of education becomes a crucial consideration when it is recognized that "quality is power . . . [and] those who understand 'quality' will gain a strategic edge."[3]

Whether viewing change from a global perspective or the confines of a local educational agency, continual and even accelerated rates of change are suggested by changing environments, demands on educational agencies, and major shifts in worldwide competition as well as the competitive environment in which a single individual must survive. Resistance results from every substantive innovation or change. Resistance has even been experienced due to minor modifications or cosmetic changes in the educational enterprise. As citizens demand ever greater "reforms" in schools, the degree of resistance from significant segments of the educational establishment that accompanies such demands will be in direct proportion to the scope and intensity associated with the proposed changes. Whether proposed changes are in an international, national, or educational agency, transfers of power from one entity, group, or individual to another is a source of concern and conflict.

Various observers have suggested that educators have shown little enthusiasm about changing the basic structure of the educational establishment. While legislative efforts to encourage reform have abounded and leaders in schools across the nation have embarked upon efforts to improve the outcomes of their schools, the results have often been disappointing to many critics. When considering the lack of positive results, Shanker wrote that one reason was that school officials have not "really carried out the reforms."[4] He concluded by noting, "Unless an institution has the capacity for change, it will not succeed for long."[5]

Even if the educational establishment in the United States would be assured of continued public and legislative support indefinitely, various additional motives still persist for bringing about change in local schools. Some individuals feel compelled, even driven, to compete internationally in selected academic areas; thus, there are calls for greater efficiency as well as effectiveness. Some industrial leaders have compared their manufactured electronic devices with children and youth and hold expectations for schools based on that perspective. In states where parents have been given the opportunity through legislation to choose the school that their children will attend, a surge in competition to improve programs was predicted. The motivations for planning and changing various aspects of an educational institution are varied, reaching from global considerations and extending into a given school site or classroom in which educators, as groups and as individuals, strive for excellence. Planning can become a means of keeping abreast of developments and trends and searching for quality; within that search for quality, educators hope to achieve a strategic advantage. To plan for educational excellence and implement the plans for an improved educational system, educators and people from outside the establishment should be involved in more effective shared responsibilities.

Individuals within the educational establishment and from other segments of society have expressed a need to improve education. Expectations for education, as expressed by some legitimate stakeholders, are often in conflict, and responsive educators are torn by the differing demands they confront. Of the many concerns expressed about the perceived shortcomings of education, one theme is ever present and often ignored: schools are charged with solving the ills of society, and educators are blamed for societal circumstances over which they have no control. A classic illustration of the theme of unrealistic and conflicting demands can be seen in the claimed "failure of schools" to curb the use of drugs in a society in which there is actually a rather high level of acceptance of the use of drugs. When persons in the society outside the school are using drugs, citizens who assume that there will be no drugs in schools or that the use of illegal drugs can be curbed in the schools are extremely naive.

Expressions about the failure of American students to measure up to Japanese students in mathematics achievement test scores constitute another illustration of the unrealistic expectations placed upon schools. Is it realistic for American students, who spend much less time in school (for example, about 30 hours a week in school contrasted to approximately 48 hours in school per week in Japan) and who have numerous school cocurricular activities and part-time jobs, to learn as much content in an area such as mathematics as students in Japan? Would American parents tolerate the demands seen in some foreign schools and insist that the majority of American students give up cocurricular activities and evening television? How can teachers impact students who listen to hard rock music for more hours than they attend school each day? How can educators deal with a student who is pregnant, has no positive home environment or parental support, and is not impressed with the "American work ethic?" When the school remains either unchanged or isolated from the broader environment from which its pupils come, expectations for a staff to countermand the influences in that conflicting culture are not realistic.

Another method of examining the motives for planning and changing leads the observer to study ways to avoid some of the inadequacies and abuses that have occurred in efforts to bring about change in local educational agencies. Numerous reasons have been suggested for failures in the management of change. Of course, what constitutes failure is akin to the reverse side of beauty; failure may often be in the eyes of the beholder. It has been suggested that ''an alarmingly high failure rate has characterized the past efforts of executives in industry, government, the military and education.''[6] Probably one of the most colossal examples of failure in this century has been the collapse of the Communist form of government and economy, as witnessed in the late 1980s and early 1990s. In spite of the mandates and severe controls, multiple bureaucracies and masses of people were not motivated or led to the achievement of excellence for the national or collective welfare of the people in Communist nations. Perhaps the greatest achievements were in the area of competitive athletics at the international level, as pampered athletes were nurtured and motivated to excel. The frustration brought about by the ''failure'' in schools to achieve expected results has been the reason for much of the legislation passed in various state legislative bodies. Often, however, people are not ''motivated'' by legislated programs, whether in the United States or other nations. While legislation aimed at education is valuable, experience does suggest that proponents of many bills to improve education have been, and may well continue to be, somewhat disappointed with results achieved from legislative mandates.

The question has been pondered and debated, mostly by noneducators, concerning the unproductivity of many educational innovations. The human factor has been identified most frequently as the cause for the failure of educational innovations, with the accusing finger often pointed toward those persons charged with the responsibility to administer and teach in educational institutions. Such critics often fail to comprehend the difficult position faced by most school superintendents, who are expected to improve an educational program that is defined by different pressure groups whose members have very different expectations. Superintendents work with a school board that is confronted with the necessity of interpreting needs and expectations; at the same time they administer to staff members who may have still different needs and expectations. More significantly, school officials are expected, even demanded, to do something about math scores, drugs, teenage pregnancy, sex and race equity, and spelling—all in a society in which multiple demands are made on students' time and the airways of the media vibrate with conflicting values. The restructuring of the American home, in which there are uncontrolled levels of dissonance and chaos, is not the least of the compounding influences, and the impact has not yet been fully comprehended.

Errors in definition have been acclaimed to have contributed to the perceived failures in educational planning.[7] Leaders in industry have, with little or no understanding about some societal and human factors, suggested that achievement scores for ''all American'' youth need to be competitive or superior to achievement scores of youth in different cultures. ''There is only the faintest suggestion in these neat, logical, and antiseptic definitions of the messy, disorderly affairs of people!''[8] From still other observations, suggestions have been made that planning has been relatively well done in educational institutions for such factors as budgeting, scheduling for transportation, and the construction of facilities. The human dimensions of education and the disastrous impact of "antiplanning" are the two greatest areas of failure. Some observers have suggested that people are disposed to resist change, particularly change imposed by others, and some persons may tend to be absorbed, day by day, doing the routine things that require no planning and no change. The various views regarding the effectiveness of innovation in education and the adaptability of educators to changing demands underscore the point that there is no single or simplistic solution to bringing about change in the educational enterprise. Consequently, educational leaders will need to explore the knowledge base at their disposal regarding the management of change.

LEARNING FROM PAST ABUSES OF INNOVATIVE EFFORTS

Like the athletes and coaching staff who review films to see the mistakes made in a game and to discover how to improve the quality of play, educators may be able to profit from examining some past innovative efforts in which outcomes were less than desirable. Unfortunately, detailed explanations of educational failures are seldom found in reports to funding agencies and in literature in educational periodicals. One might believe that all efforts to improve education and all educational innovations and modifications in instructional programs have been great successes. The "failures" in the educational enterprise are typically reported by noneducational writers. It would seem that educational writers generally point to the achievements and successes in specific education programs, and the noneducational writers expound upon the dismal record of educators in general terms. In one sense, such a dichotomy in reports and research articles may pose a problem for those who wish to improve education, as they seek to find where the truth may be found between the two extremes.

Actually, several educational innovations have been introduced in local schools, have been carried on for a few years, and then have faded from the scene. The inevitable reaction has been to point to the isolated innovation as another failure. An interesting phenomenon often took place when such innovative efforts were in the period of decline. For example, as some educators viewed the open classroom concept and determined it was an abominable way to run a school, they reached the conclusion that two things were in order. First, walls should be built to negate the open classroom arrangement. Second, without any data to support the decision, the alternative to the open classroom was to revert to the traditional organizational and instructional arrangement. Suggestions have been made, with fairly sound substantiation, that the open classroom had some clear limitations. The determination, however, that the seemingly singular option to the abandonment of an innovation was to revert to the traditional patterns is an interesting and telling pattern of behavior. Such behavior has supported the contentions of some observers that in many instances educators have been oblivious to a data base and that a much stronger influence may derive from tradition than is often recognized. Shanker has written, "Looked at in this light, the disappointing results of the education reform movement thus far are not surprising. The initial tendency of most reform efforts is to tighten rules and do more of the same."[9]

Several major efforts to restructure educational institutions have been observed, in which the innovation may have been well planned and conceptually sound but the manner in which the implementation was undertaken led to failure. Many well-intentioned people have caused the failure of some innovations when they jumped on the proverbial bandwagon in an effort to keep up with the current trend; in so doing, they have subscribed to an ill-advised and misguided effort. Second, efforts have failed because those responsible for implementing an innovative program have not employed what is known about the management of change. Many abortive efforts to change education have come about, in part, from "a most superficial conception of how complicated settings are organized, their structure . . . dynamics . . . power relationships, and their underlying values and axioms."[10]

Change for the sake of change has been a cause of frustrating and fruitless efforts in some schools. While it may be possible for something worthwhile to be derived from change for the sake of change, such a strategy must be seriously questioned. First of all, considering all the issues and conditions in education for which improvements are needed, why not select a need and target that need? Deer hunters will tell tales about the city slicker, inexperienced and perhaps a bit intoxicated, who hears a sound in the thicket and fires several shots in that general direction without knowing what he is shooting at. The likelihood of bagging a trophy buck by taking such "brush shots" is about as great as the success of the educator who embarks upon a plan to change education based on the idea that change for the sake of change is good. Change should be purposeful and directed to the accomplishment of a predetermined need.

Conventional wisdom has also been the bane, and ultimately the downfall, of some innovative efforts. Common errors in this domain are perpetrated by those persons in positions of responsibility who are impatient and who see no need to take the time to involve others. In so doing, they fail to acknowledge that two heads are better than one. Conventional wisdom has also been exhibited by those persons who forge ahead without understanding such concepts as internal consistency, do not consider any form of evaluation, and seem to demonstrate that they, as individuals, are the singular and most viable source of information, as they ignore the discipline and data base at their disposal. The dependence upon conventional wisdom and rejection of the knowledge base are often reflected in unmotivated behavior, undeveloped staff, and the presumption that dictating what professional staff will do is efficient and the best way to accomplish any major undertaking.

Some "pop" change agents have found their way to the educational establishment and maintain their personal income through effective promotional efforts. Educational consumers can be blinded by their "glitter," and the lack of substance in their product is quickly obscured. Quick fixes and absolute answers can be proposed by charismatic promoters and used as substitutes for well-designed and conceptualized plans and implementation efforts. Unfortunately, education is much too complex to be reformed with simple contrivances.

Efforts to reform education by legislative laws and edicts from state departments of education have been less than encouraging. Bluntly stated, it may not be possible to legislate behavior effectively. The control of detrimental behaviors on the part of citizens in our society has not accomplished desired results, as witnessed in the war on drugs. As the number of laws to limit the use of illegal substances has increased, even greater growth has occurred in the use of the illegal drugs targeted by the legislation. While legislation has been passed to enhance the test scores of students in the United States, the trends have been contrary to the intentions of those who passed the laws. The same phenomenon can be observed in local policies and rules. In some locales, there have been mandates to increase the amount of homework assigned to students. Such well-intentioned mandates often fall short of intended results, especially for students who live in broken or disruptive homes. All too often laws and mandates, well intentioned as they may be, prove to be less than effective when the environment that surrounds the targeted population and institutions is not taken into consideration or those who mandate programs or results fail to keep in mind that it is not likely that human behavior can be legislated.[11]

An unfortunate practice has taken place in some school districts in which innovations have failed because insufficient attention was given to the allocation of prime resources. Some failures have been the result of allocating insufficient prime resources to a project or individuals' not comprehending what constitutes prime resources. If staff members are not given sufficient time, they cannot be expected to plan and implement meaningful changes in education. If sufficient information is not made available, a project can be suffocated by ignorance—or conventional wisdom. Innovation cannot be achieved if prime resources are not allocated judiciously.

The widespread failure to plan and employ appropriate evaluation efforts has been an Achilles' heel to the approaches used by some educators to improve education. Although many stories of poorly planned evaluation efforts can be exposed, the limitations of some evaluation efforts are much less significant than the situations in which no evaluation of an educational innovation took place.

The structure of education, in which teacher isolation is fostered, has been recognized as an inhibitor to change in schools.[12] Traditions in school structure, as well as routines perpetrated by administrative practices in which the continuation of teacher isolation is fostered, contribute to a pattern that resists change. Vision has been claimed to be the antidote to tradition. With the help of vision, administrators can break the shackles of educational rites by demonstrating values and a commitment to the achievement of goals. A sense of common purpose and direction among the staff can be undergirded by vision and by organizational innovators who constantly focus on the future.[13]

Clues can be gathered to help avoid some of the pitfalls of the past. An honest appraisal, without hasty searches for excuses, may be valuable for future innovators or change facilitators. Educational leaders have demonstrated the ability to plan and to plan effectively. If attention is directed to better ways of implementing plans or managing change, greater benefits for pupils through educational planning will be the result.

AN HISTORICAL PERSPECTIVE OF MANAGING CHANGE IN EDUCATION

Change, as an area of study or an academic discipline, came to educational personnel from anthropological and sociological sources. Anthropologists studied cultural change by examining the clashes of "modern and primitive" societies in several settings. Barnett was one of the pioneers in the study of cultural change; a large amount of his information is relevant to educators.[14] The contributions made by Barnett included the clarification of definitions of what constitutes an innovation and the identification of antecedents or prior conditions necessary for cultural change to take place. As Barnett studied various Indian cultures, he was attracted to the concept of selective borrowing of innovations or the transfer and adaptations of innovations from one locale to another. Early work in the area of cultural change was the forerunner to sociological studies of change in agriculture and medicine.[15]

As sociologists attempted to develop a greater understanding of how change came about, their quest led them to observations and investigations about the rate of adoption, or how long it took a change to be implemented. As a result of the work of a number of the researchers in the sociological tradition, the S-shaped curve was affirmed. Trade has described the S-shaped curve as a growth curve with a "slow advance in the beginning, followed by rapid and uniformly accelerated progress, followed again by progress that continues to slacken until it finally stops."[16] The work of sociologists was built upon by educators, such as Mort and Carlson, who became interested in the length of time it took to adopt selected innovations in education and what factors seemed to influence the time of adoption.[17] While Trade emphasized the importance of opinion leaders in the rate of adoption, Carlson explored and confirmed the impact of superintendents of schools who were recognized as opinion leaders among their peers. Carlson concluded that superintendents who were recognized as opinion leaders actually exerted an influence on the rate of adoption in schools other than their own.

Community size has been studied by sociologists who have analyzed innovations; sociologists have confirmed that innovations tend to take place in population centers and then spread to less populated areas.[18] Bowers also found that more mass communication channels were utilized for diffusion in metropolitan communities, while people in smaller communities were influenced through personal communications.

A Change Model for Agriculture

The classical area of study about innovation in agriculture concerned the adoption and use of hybrid corn seed. During the 1930s, agriculture extension agents gave information to corn farmers that impelled the business of growing corn from a crop planted and tended with some well-established practices to one with advanced yields.[19] The spread of knowledge about hybrid corn and the conviction regarding its advantages were achieved through clearly identified channels. The farmer was contacted by a county farm agent who possessed manuals and promotional literature explaining the advantages of hybrid corn over conventional corn seed. Other researchers found that information traveled to the ultimate user or adopter first from other farmers, then from agricultural extension agents, and finally from mass media, which in the 1930s consisted largely of radio, newspapers, and farm journals.[20] When communication channels are examined, it can be seen that the county agent possessed materials and oral instructions prepared by farm extension specialists who worked in agricultural departments in universities. Prior to the development of dissemination materials and information by extension specialists, university staff members performed laboratory tests on hybrid seeds, and university experimental farm plots were used for field-testing. The knowledge base used by agriculture department staff members had come from researchers in natural science departments who had conducted experiments to provide the information upon which an application was made. The agricultural change model can be used to trace the development of hybrid corn from scientists who added to the knowledge base, to applied research specialists in schools of agriculture, who were supported by the dissemination of information through mass media, through the hands of dissemination specialists or local opinion leaders, and eventually to the user.

In the case of hybrid corn, other factors came into the scope of consideration. Through the use of hybrid corn, farmers were not required to change their practices significantly. Such use did not change their value system, and there was basically no added investment in equipment or time. The results were only one growing season away from being observable. Farmers who were not risk takers were able to plant one plot and do their own field-testing, or they could look across the fence at the results of their neighbor. In the adoption of hybrid corn, the process was definable and relatively easy, and the results were gratifying and observable. What more could a student of innovation ask?

Rogers and Beal probed even further into the change process by examining the length of time needed to complete an adoption. The S curve was applied as it related to agriculture, and change models were refined.[21]

Students of agriculture change revised their model to agree with the suggested five stages of adoption: awareness, interest, evaluation, trial, and adoption.[22] The stages of adoption were explained, and the source of information documented as it related to each stage. Suggestions were made that a person became *aware* of a product through the mass media, meetings, conferences, newsletters, or audiovisual materials. *Interest* grew as an individual gained more information through classes, demonstrations, reading, and traveling. Interest was fanned by the behavior of the potential user of a proposed innovation as that person took the responsibility to seek out more information. *Evaluation,* in the context used by Beal and associates, was actually a more in-depth investigation on the part of the potential user through individual and small group conferences, telephone contacts, review of abstracts and programmed information, and correspondence study. In the evaluation phase a potential user had to make the decision to try the product or to walk away. *Trial* consisted of individual consultation with specialists, simulations, and the use of case studies, models, or mock-ups. The trial was a form of a dress rehearsal of the real thing and was, if the decision was confirmed to try the new product, the prelude to the actual *adoption.*

The Model of Adoption, with five phases spanning from awareness to adoption, was a popular model and was applied to education after its proposal as an appropriate explanation or model in the field of agriculture. Actually the Model of Adoption, as it was referred to, was a fairly sound model if the innovation being considered had already been developed and was ready for adoption. The model was functional if the innovation under consideration was in existence and simply had to be adopted, was fairly simple, and did not impose on the values of the adopter. Consequently, the Model of Adoption became known for not only its usefulness but also its limitations.

The results of Rogers's efforts to categorize people into levels of innovativeness also found their way into the field of education. He concluded there was a small percentage (2 to 3 percent) of truly innovative individuals. He identified approximately 13 percent as early adopters; 34 percent were classified as early majority; and a corresponding group of 34 percent were categorized as late majority. The remaining 15 or 16 percent were identified as laggards.[23] As the transfer has taken place from agriculture to the field of education, educators have also agreed with the concept developed by Rogers.

The Medicine Model

A series of change and adoptions studies was conducted by the medical profession that was somewhat similar to the studies conducted in the field of agriculture. The definition of client-user in the medical profession studies was somewhat different than in the agriculture studies. Studies of adoption in the area of medicine focused on the level of acceptance demonstrated first, by the physician and second, by the patients. At the conclusion of several sociological studies related to adoption, in the medical field, a model was produced with distinct similarities to the model of adoption in the field of agriculture. The patient was seen as the ultimate client, who went to the provider for services. The provider could include a hospital, a medical clinic, or a physician. The provider of medical services received information about innovations from professional journals or from attending meetings sponsored by medical associations. The authors of articles in medical journals and the presenters at association meetings derived their information from medical schools and research hospitals or from pharmaceutical companies. There was also a person referred to as a "detail man," from whom providers received information regarding selected innovations. Medical school personnel and scientists in pharmaceutical companies received their information and the data base with which they worked from the natural scientists who worked in their laboratories between classes at universities and wrote articles for journals and textbooks. So, as was the case in the agricultural model for adoption, the medical model can be traced from the basic research scientist who generated knowledge through the specialists who translated basic knowledge into applications; the applications were then extended and communicated to providers of medical services.

While the medical and agricultural models for innovation were clearly appropriate for the field and profession for which they were developed and had some elements of applicability for education, they were not quite the fit needed to explain how change took place in the educational enterprise. The interest of educational research and developmental people was peaking as they drew upon the previous findings of anthropologists and sociologists who had laid the foundation and knowledge base for studying change in education. An assumption that accompanied the work of the developmental people was that if a better understanding of change could be documented, leaders in education could initiate and manage the change process to the advantage of children and youth in the nation's schools.

Educational Change Models

Each of several models developed for education, which followed work in agriculture and medicine, was used to depict how change or innovations were carried to the stage of adoption or implementation in education; the models had varying degrees of applicability. Different models can be identified to use in one of three situations: (1) when some object or process has been developed and tested at a location other than the local educational agency and is then chosen for local adoption; (2) when planners are confronted with a need to develop a new approach or to innovate, test, and adopt their own innovation; and (3) a combination of one and two, in which a complex or highly technical innovation developed in a noneducational setting is adopted in a local school and major changes are required within the educational agency in terms of the processes and procedures in which staff are to be involved.

A new textbook and set of instructional materials would be an example of the first type of adoption process. Such materials are typically developed and tested and then selected by staff members from a local district. Once the selection decision is made, the new text is adopted. The linear adoption model, in which the stages of awareness, interest, evaluation, trial, and adoption are identified, fits such a situation well. In the second type of situation, in which staff members are confronted with a need and must design new or different structures for accomplishing outcomes to fulfill that need, a much more complex set of conditions has been generated. The problem-solving and social interaction models are much more adequate to explain how innovation and adoption take place. In the third type of situation, in which there is the need to adopt some complex tool, such as the videodisc, and at the same time develop innovative ways to employ the new technological devices, the change facilitator comes face-to-face with demands that are highly complex. The second and third patterns of adoption and innovation will be the locus in which major educational renewal or reform programs will function.

The operational planning process described earlier in this book can provide a framework and set of concepts that serve not only for planning but as a change and management system. If the main concepts of problem solving and the social interaction models for managing change are used and the key concepts from the change literature and the various models that have been developed are incorporated, they can be applied to a fully integrated planning and change management structure.

The components of the Model of Adoption and the Lippit Problem Solving Model, as they can be related to the operational planning model, are shown in Figure 12.1. In like manner, the external and internal factors studied by Haney and Brandt, as well as the point of impact for such concepts as Stages of Concern, Levels of Use, and Innovation Configuration derived from the Concerns-Based Adoption Model (CBAM), are depicted in Figure 12.2.

As planners progress through a planning effort, employing the concepts built into the planning process presented in earlier chapters, the concepts in change management can be addressed at the same time. Planning and managing change are not two separate and distinct functions done at different times and places; as planning is accomplished, the management of change should progress simultaneously under the direction of the planner. As indicated at the outset of this chapter, planners must be managers of change, lest they find they have developed an impressive plan but are impotent in the realm of implementation. The management of change starts with the decision to plan. Change is not something that follows once a plan has been devised.

To illustrate how the management of change is integrated with planning and starts at the same time, review the first step in planning, in which all relevant

Figure 12.1
Relationship of Components from the Model of Adoption and the Problem-Solving Change Model to the Systems Planning Model

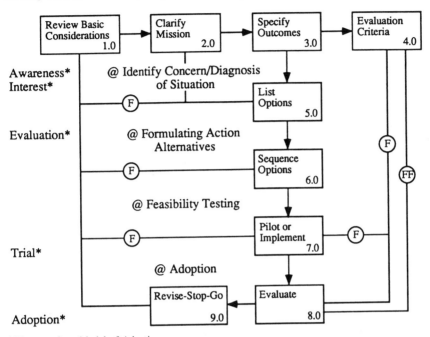

*Elements from Model of Adoption
@ Elements from the Problem-Solving Change Model

influences that could have an impact on what is planned are considered. The collection and use of information derived from internal and external environment assessments are emphasized in the first step; data bases of various kinds, needs assessments, legal considerations, and policy reviews are studied, and other relevant sources of information are examined. As the review of basic considerations takes place and staff members are involved in that process, a base of agreement and understanding is built that will help sustain the planned project to fruition. The understanding generated in the planning process should also be addressed in elements of a change model, as people should have a base of agreement from which to work if they are to be led in a productive pattern of change. Consequently, when staff members are engaged in the planning step of an environmental assessment, they are also involved in the change process.

All elements of the Problem Solving Change Model are incorporated in the Systems Planning Model. The first phase of the Systems Planning Model (review basic considerations, 1.0) consists of the identification of concerns or needs and the diagnosis of the situation, which is a part of the Problem Solving

Figure 12.2
Relationship of Components from the CBAM and the Knowledge Utilization Model to the Systems Planning Model

* Scientific Knowledge
* Knowledge of Setting
* Research
* Resources

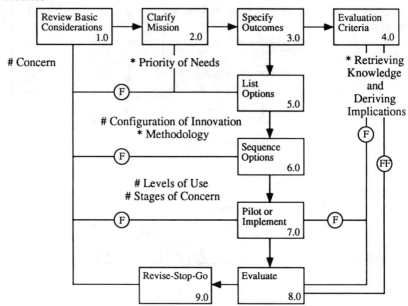

\# Elements from Concerns—Based Adaption Model
* Elements from Knowledge Utilization Model

Change Model. The second portion of the Problem Solving Change Model is formulating action alternatives, which is parallel to listing options (phase 5.0) and sequencing options (phase 6.0) in the Systems Planning Model. In the Problem Solving Change Model, feasibility testing is similar to the pilot or implementation phase (phase 7.0) in the Systems Planning Model, while the adoption phase of the Problem Solving Model is comparable to phase 9.0, revise-stop-go, of the Systems Planning Model.

When the elements contained in the Model of Adoption and Systems Planning Model are compared, it can be seen that considerably more scope is incorporated in the Systems Planning Model than in the Model of Adoption. In one interpretation, all steps in the Model of Adoption, with the exception of the last, which is adoption, could be carried on at level 5.0, which is the listing of options in the Systems Planning Model. In the Model of Adoption, no items are identified for consideration in a review of basic considerations. No major attention is given to mission, since it is assumed that some need will be met by the innovation under consideration at the levels of awareness, interest, evaluation, and trial. There is a parallel at the point of adoption in both the Model of Adoption and the Systems Planning Model. At this point, however, the similarities in the two models end; there are no actual pilot or field-testing, no determination of evaluation criteria, and no evaluation to collect formative or summative data for analysis in the Model of Adoption.

The elements of the Concerns-Based Adoption Model (CBAM) and the Systems Planning Model have rather straightforward linkages. In the early phases of the Systems Planning Model, attention is directed to determining needs or concerns, which are carried on into mission and goals (phase 2.0) and eventually into outcomes (phase 3.0). In the CBAM, attention is directed at the configuration of the innovation, which is found in phase 5.0 (list options) of the Systems Planning Model. A major contribution of the CBAM can be found in the parallel between the measures of levels of use (LoU) and stages of concern (SoC) and phase 7.0 (pilot or implement) in the Systems Planning Model.

Elements from the Knowledge Utilization Model are also found in the Systems Planning Model, as seen in the relationship or congruence between review of basic considerations (phase 1.0) in the Systems Planning Model and the consideration given to the use of scientific knowledge, knowledge of the setting, research, and a review of resources listed in the Knowledge Utilization Model. Developers of the Knowledge Utilization Model suggested a phase dealing with setting a priority of needs; the Systems Planning Model includes phases 2.0 and 3.0, clarify mission and specify outcomes. The methodology phase of the Knowledge Utilization Model parallels the sequencing of options (phase 6.0) in the Systems Planning Model. One of the final elements contained in the Knowledge Utilization Model is the inclusion of the component, new scientific knowledge. While the Systems Planning Model calls for a decision with respect to the future of an innovation or a program, generalizable or scientific knowledge is not expected to be generated from such a system. Use of the Systems Planning Model does not, however, prevent or discourage findings that could be generalizable, although such findings are not the primary intent of the combined elements of the system.

SUMMARY

If planners utilize a planning model, such as the Systems Planning Model for operational planning, take into consideration what is known about the change process, and make a direct application of that knowledge, an automatic linkage between what is known about planning and the knowledge base about change can take place. The vast quantity of information about how change takes place should not be ignored. In a culture that is rampant with changes, knowledge of the process becomes increasingly more important, if for no other reason than to exert some control over the management of what changes will be fostered as educators learn to cope with a fast moving environment.

NOTES

1. Robert H. Waterman, Jr., *The Renewal Factor* (New York: Bantam Books, 1987), 233.

2. Ibid.

3. Alvin Toffler, *Powershift, Knowledge, Wealth, and Violence at the Edge of the 21st Century* (New York: Bantam Books, 1990), 15.

4. Albert Shanker, "The End of the Traditional Model of Schooling—and a Proposal for Using Incentives to Restructure Our Public Schools," *Kappan* 71 (January 1990), 345.

5. Ibid., 356.

6. David W. Ewing, *The Human Side of Planning* (London: Macmillan, 1969), 16.

7. Ibid., 38.

8. Ibid.

9. Shanker, "The End of the Traditional Model of Schooling," 356.

10. Seymour B. Sarason, *The Predictable Failure of Educational Reform* (San Francisco: Jossey-Bass, 1990), 4.

11. Myron Lieberman, "Why Reform Was 'Dead on Arrival,' " *Education Week* 5 (January 29, 1986), 20.

12. Susan J. Rosenholtz, "Political Myths About Education Reform: Lessons from Research on Teaching," *Kappan* 66 (January 1985), 350.

13. Edward W. Chance and Marilyn L. Grady, "Creating and Implementing a Vision for the School," *NASSP Bulletin* 74 (November 1990), 13–14.

14. Homer G. Barnett, *Innovation: The Basis of Cultural Change* (New York: McGraw-Hill, 1953).

15. For a review of information about cultural change and how a base for further exploration into the field of change and innovation came from that information, see Donald H. Ross, *Administration of Adaptability: A Sourcebook Drawing Together the Results of More than 150 Individual Studies Related to the Question of Why and How Schools Improve* (New York: Metropolitan School Study Council, 1958); Elihu Katz, Martin L. Levin, and Herbert Hamilton, "Traditions of Research on the Diffusion of Innovation," *American Sociological Review* 28 (April 1963), 237–253; Herbert F. Lionberger, *Adoption of New Ideas and Practices: A Summary of the Research Dealing with the Acceptance of Technological Change in Agriculture, with Implications for Action in Facilitating Social Change* (Ames, Iowa: Iowa State University Press, 1960); M. Everett and Floyd Shoemaker, *Communication of Innovation* (New York: Free Press, 1971); and Ronald G. Havelock and Alan Guskin, *Planning for Innovation Through the Dissemination and Utilization of Knowledge* (Ann Arbor, Michigan: Center for Research on the Utilization of Scientific Knowledge, University of Michigan, 1973).

16. Gabriel Trade, *The Laws of Imitation* (New York: Holt, Rinehart, and Winston, 1903), 382.

17. Paul R. Mort, "Educational Adaptability," *School Executive* 69 (November 1951),

46–47; and Richard O. Carlson, *Adoption of Educational Innovations* (Eugene, Oregon: Center for the Advanced Study of Educational Administration, 1965), 14–28.

18. Raymond A. Bowers, "The Direction of Intra-Societal Diffusion," *American Sociological Review* 2 (1937), 829.

19. Bryce Ryan and Neal Gross, "The Diffusion of Hybrid Seed Corn in Two Iowa Communities," *Rural Sociology* 8 (March 1943), 15–24.

20. Eugene Wilkening, *Acceptance of Improved Farm Practices in Three Coastal Plain Counties,* Technical Bulletin 98 (Raleigh, North Carolina: North Carolina Agricultural Experiment Station, May 1952), 60–62.

21. Everett M. Rogers and George M. Beal, "The Importance of Personal Influence in the Adoption of Technological Change," *Social Forces* 36 (May 1958), 331; and Everett M. Rogers, *Diffusion of Innovations* (New York: Free Press of Glencoe, 1962), 152–159.

22. G. M. Beal, E. M. Rogers, and J. M. Bohlen, "Validity of the Concept of Stages in the Adoption Process," *Rural Sociology* 22 (June 1957), 167.

23. Rogers, *Diffusion of Innovation,* 217–247.

13

Guidelines for Managing Change

INTRODUCTION

A considerable amount of information that can be used by educational planners to plan change can be found in literature from the various disciplines and information contained in several change models. Planners no longer need to rely on conventional "wisdom" for managing change. A knowledge base exists for the management of change by which planners and change facilitators can achieve a level of sophistication that far outdistances the efforts of their uninformed peers. Planners who try to initiate change and lead staff members through the development and adoption of innovations without possessing knowledge about change can prove to be a detriment to the process.[1]

LEADERSHIP AND THE MANAGEMENT OF CHANGE

Leaders create change. Planning is often seen as a top-down process, in which the leadership is found, for the most part, in top and middle management. Not all leadership, however, will reside in the hands of the administrative staff; teachers, parents, patrons, and board members also possess leadership qualities, which should be given consideration. The significance of leadership has been recognized in business,[2] as well as in education.[3] The literature on site- or school-based management contains many references about the importance of building principals. Principals occupy a key role in the management of change.

Leaders who would be builders are persons with vision and insight. "Insight . . . enables [an administrator] to create successful strategies. Insightful executives mull over all facets of problems, situations, and information . . . [and]

discover opportunities, advantages, and strengths others ignore or never see."[4] While insight may be considered one end of a continuum, vision is the other end. Vision can be observed in people who have strong personal values and intense commitment, who are able to develop a sense of common purpose and direction among staff, and who "consistently focus on a future that represents something better."[5] Planners who do more than maintain the status quo need to gain understanding and vision to look beyond the immediate and see how a better educational enterprise can become a reality.

Leaders who would be change facilitators must also extend their vision into the realm of commitment. Leaders must be involved and committed if they expect people to accept the challenge and to pursue improvements that may change their behavior.[6] Leaders who are highly involved with an innovative project will ultimately generate more cooperation from their staff members than if they delegate and fail to accept personal involvement.

Effective leaders communicate vision and clarity of the mission to the staff and constituents. Staff members work more effectively when they know the vision of the leader and understand what is expected of them. Even if staff members disagree with their leader, they are more satisfied than if they do not know the thinking of the person in charge. Leaders who project ambiguity, confusion, or lack of direction are locking the door on possible program improvements.

The management of change is accomplished best by persons who have high levels of skill in sensitivity. Planning and change, as has been noted repeatedly, are a human endeavor. People respond to a positive climate, in which significant others are sensitive to their needs. Coercion, fear, disrespect, and disregard for others do not go far when working with productive staff members who are capable of planning and changing. Along with sensitivity, planners and those who would foster change must know how to work with small groups and to enlist and involve people in a meaningful way so that each individual understands the contribution she or he can make. People need to know that they are involved in something of value and that what they do counts and can make a difference. Sensitivity is a base for building a sense of self-worth in every person. During the first phase of strategic planning, in which an environmental assessment is made, followed by mission clarification, much of the groundwork for involving key people can take place, and the superintendent of schools can communicate to staff members their importance to the organization and to the well-being of children and youth.

Sensitivity, if genuine, will be reflected in sustained behavior. The planner should not indicate that planning is important at the beginning stages of an effort and then abandon sensitivity as other pressing demands emerge. When staff members indicate that they made a personal investment and commitment but that their work had been ignored or distorted since the start of the planning project, the effects of such perceptions are devastating to planning. Leaders have to be genuinely interested in people; they must acknowledge the worth of each individual and have the personal security to capitalize on the capabilities of others. There are many illustrations in which a successful superintendent has been identified as one who was able to attract top-quality support staff. The same is true in planning. Those leaders who believe they personally hold the key and know all the answers and what should be done and how to do it lack the capacity to capitalize on the human potential of their staff members or the leadership in their communities. Self-centeredness is not compatible with sensitivity.

Coercive managers can still be found in some settings. They represent a hangover or cultural lag from an era in which management was "bossing." The traditions of coercive management inhibit, even destroy, virtually all efforts to be innovative. Glasser pointed out that "magnet schools and other structurally innovative schools can also fail if traditional coercive management prevails."[7] In place of coercion, modern leaders involve or engage staff in meaningful discussions regarding the mission of their school. Modern leaders ask questions and elicit the expertise of the staff; they support staff members not only with resources but with their confidence.

Leaders who would be change facilitators set an example; they lead by actions and model behavior. Actions often speak much louder than words. At the building level, the "lead-management and the concepts of quality will not flourish in our classrooms unless they are implemented at the building level. The principal is the crucial element in education reform."[8]

MOTIVATION OF STAFF TO FACILITATE CHANGE

Motivation of staff members is often a major challenge faced by change facilitators. Several theories of motivation are applicable to the educational arena, such as the hierarchy of needs developed by Abraham Maslow and others who followed him and built upon the identified needs of physiological, security, social, esteem, and self-actualization. Unmet needs serve as motivators. In the work regarding the study and application of "needs" by Porter, the force of a given need was acclaimed to be directly proportionate to its lack of satisfaction.[9]

If change facilitators wish to practice motivation theories, they should understand the level at which most educators are perceived to function. The crucial level of personal needs, which is basic because self-concepts are involved, is in the area of self-esteem, which is often lacking in teachers.[10] Since higher levels of need, such as autonomy and self-actualization, cannot be addressed until other basic needs are met, including self-esteem, the person who motivates others should understand the hierarchy of needs. Once lower-level needs are addressed, focus can be placed on higher-level needs, which will motivate staff members to confront substantive change. Upper-level motivators lead directly to work accomplishment. Motivators that lead to increased responsibility, independent decision making, pleasure in the work itself, recognition, advancement, and challenge are perceived by staff members to be exciting and satisfying conditions that result in self-actualization. By contrast, the lack of hygiene factors may bother, annoy, or distract people, but their presence does not necessarily motivate staff members. Good hygiene factors may result in the maintenance of an environmental condition that allows people to function on the job; however, staff members will not be motivated to perform well if they are dissatisfied with low-level maintenance needs.[11] Change facilitators are challenged to strike a very delicate balance when trying to motivate staff. Lower-level needs represented by such issues as salary, tenure, and formal and informal group work must be satisfied to allow staff members to focus on higher-level needs, such as personal and professional recognition and the feelings reflected at the level of self-actualization. At the same time, opportunities to achieve the satisfaction of higher-level needs must be guaranteed so motivation seekers will not regress. Staff members achieve best when a wide range of their needs has been met as they work simultaneously toward achieving personal goals and institutional goals. Obviously, when personal goals are congruent with institutional goals, the probability of staff members' working at higher levels of need satisfaction is enhanced.

Motivation is fostered by repeated successes. A history of successes empowers staff members to take risks and believe they can meet the demands of new challenges. The opportunity to demonstrate competence and assume responsibility is, in and of itself, a motivating force.

The power of expectations is also a motivator that can be employed to foster staff involvement in an adoption or change process. The power of expectations was identified by Barnett[12] and built upon in more recent efforts to gain greater insight into what encourages or compels people to change.[13] High expectations motivate staff to achieve at high levels; low expectations can greatly diminish productivity.

STAFF INVOLVEMENT AND EMPOWERMENT

Staff involvement has been equated to the loss of power in the eyes of some administrators. The fear of losing power is expressed repeatedly in actions and seldom in oral communications. The reasons that some persons in positions of responsibility are motivated are not always easy to ascertain. Certainly, some individuals seek power and self-aggrandizement. Becoming involved in a politically popular reorganization effort has been perceived as one way to gain power.[14] The idea that the way to wield and build power is to keep it in one person's hands is fallacious. Power is generated by sharing it with others; when a leader shares power, it grows. The expertise of staff members will emerge and flourish when leaders call upon them to share power. Consequently, the leader who would bring about change in a school is one who understands how to share power and, in so doing, build a power base that is more potent and influential than in settings where power is not shared. Sharing power generates commitment from staff.

The empowerment of staff, which is required of all leaders and planners who would foster change, is a complex process. Power, because of its very nature and potential, must be directed, nurtured, developed, and invested wisely. "In theory the people are sovereign, in practice, in most so-called democracies, they are at best semi-sovereign, since their power is circumscribed by the positions of other actors in the policy-making and decision-making process."[15] Whether the semisovereign state of humans is viewed from the words of a songwriter who proclaims that "no man is an island" or whether it is viewed from a systems theory perspective, people in any given setting are influenced by the other people and their work structure; as individuals they have, or can have, an impact on that setting in which they work.

One effort to structure education in such a way that staff and parents are empowered to accomplish school improvements is site-based management. When, however, structures and procedures designed to achieve staff empowerment are used, an adequate mix of structure and leadership forces should be present to make up that development and investment of power. The development and investment of empowerment are involved in strategic planning as "stakeholders are involved in arriving at consensus beliefs, developing a vision, creating a mission . . . [and in the operational planning efforts as] . . . stakeholders are involved in the development of yearly action plans which are designed to arrive at the desired outcomes . . . [specified] in the mission and vision statements."[16] Suggestions for empowering staff that have come from noneducational settings have applicability for educators. Some of the points made by Waterman seem particularly relevant, such as: "Start by examining your own attitudes about your role as boss. Treat all your people as the main creative engine for your organization. . . . Ask, explain, communicate. Stop worrying about looking dumb, out of control, and 'not really in charge' to those reporting to you. Expect that backing away from tight control is a frightening experience. . . . Recognize how unique each individual is."[17]

The delegation of power is also a skill needed by leaders and planners who would improve schools. Delegation is first established on a base in which high expectations from and confidence in people are demonstrated. It does little or no good to delegate responsibility to a person and fail to give the person the opportunity to carry out that commitment. Delegation can, if properly carried out within an appropriate structure, be a major means of facilitating work and avoiding a bottleneck in the institution. To delegate successfully, a leader must make expectations clear, define what is delegated in such a way as to avoid ambiguity, monitor the results of the delegation, provide support to the person to whom the function was delegated, and, finally, follow up to see the job was completed and what spin-offs or side effects may have occurred.

CHANGE FACILITATORS AND THE POWER STRUCTURE

Effective leaders of change are persons who can walk on both sides of the cultural tracks in a community. As expressed in *The Music Man,* "You Gotta

Know the Territory." Leaders who can communicate effectively and generate confidence among the civic and opinion leaders in a community possess an important skill; however, leaders with the interest, understanding, and ability to communicate with the "powerless" will find they can enlist and benefit from the political strength derived from working with the lower socioeconomic segments of a community. All people are of worth—those who have been elected to public office, those who are opinion leaders, those who are power brokers, those who are in the silent majority, and those who do not have the "power resources" within their grasp but who nevertheless have a major stake in the improvement of schools. The leader who is able to work effectively with all segments of a community will have an advantage over leaders who are politically motivated only by persons perceived to be in power positions.

School change facilitators work in a political arena and must be sensitive to the politics of the community and possibly the region or state. Politics is a reality; as soon as people are confronted with change, politics becomes involved. People resist change in bureaucracies by politicizing issues, just as others strive to accomplish change through the use of political influence. Like it or not, leaders and planners for the improvement of education—those who would bring about change—must know how to face and, if possible, harness political pressure. Those who espouse the need for change will confront almost insurmountable odds in their quest to make changes for the improvement of education. First, the need must be demonstrated; the opposition is usually only required to raise a question and prove nothing regarding the lack of a need. Second, the advocates of change must lead others through planning efforts and decision making; the opponents need only sit back and do nothing to cause the effort to collapse. But even if the first two levels—selling the need and completing a plan—are accomplished, the tremendous and often intractable forces of a bureaucracy are still left, which can simply smother an effort to change.[18] A colossal example of the lack of bureaucratic compliance has been seen in the U.S.S.R., as efforts to reform have become impotent as a massive bureaucracy simply does not accept what was "mandated." As a bureaucracy fails to perceive power shifts, however, the path is prepared for even greater change, which may come in the form of revolution at the national level or at the local level in educational agencies.

The alert and effective change facilitator or leader is one who can decipher the intricacies of a power structure and the political milieu. Once the political structure, within both a bureaucracy and a community, are understood, the forces contained in such political power structures can be harnessed. If an administrator views a political power structure from a systems perspective, he or she can gain valuable insights into that structure. By developing a more indepth understanding of political systems, those systems can be employed to accomplish desired outcomes. "Political behavior in organizations is perfectly natural and legitimate. Sometimes it is the *only* way to get things done."[19] Some educational leaders seemingly thrive in the political arena; others abhor it. Regardless of what taste politics leaves in the mouth of an educational leader, politics must often be digested and capitalized upon to bring about change.

BUREAUCRACY AND CHANGE MANAGEMENT

When recognizing the influence of an intractable bureaucracy, those who would facilitate change will eventually need to face the issue of the reallocation of prime resources. The natural pattern of people working in a bureaucracy is to do in the future what has been done in the past. While the pattern of continuation has been addressed by "reorganizing" the structure of an organization, such efforts are generally less than significant. Most organizational changes are changes in administrative procedures; little, if any, change occurs in the quality of education. If changes are to occur in the learning environment of children and youth and if no great infusion of revenue is to be found, meaningful and substantive change will be possible only by reallocation of resources. If every person in a bureaucracy continues to do what was done in the past, how will change be achieved? The message is clear. People cannot continue to do what they did in the past; therefore, if more than superficial change is to occur, resources cannot continue to be allocated as they were in the past. Thus, the leader who is dedicated to bringing about change in education must accept the responsibility of reallocation of prime resources. Even if additional financial resources were available to support a change, it could be counterproductive to approach an innovation as another add-on. People in the existing organization would be given the opportunity to continue just as they had in the past, and a select project staff involved in an innovative program could become a part of the status quo.

Leaders, planners, or change facilitators would do well to examine their personal perceptions of what an organization is and why and how it functions. The reinforcement of the status quo—maintaining the organization for the sake of the organization—seems to be an integral part of the bureaucratic environment. Individuals who are on the payroll often seem to be transcended by bureaucratic organizations. To use organizational structures in ways that will permit and foster change, leaders must view organizations as establishments that serve the needs of people. "Organizations—which after all, are merely collections of people—exist for only one purpose: to help people reach ends together that they could not achieve individually. Most leaders in renewing organizations share a belief that the organization stands in service to the individual. When the organization starts getting in the way, they change it."[20] Symbolic changes in the educational enterprise, however, "are the most we can expect unless the present bureaucracy is changed."[21] Changes in an organization may help manage change; however, changes in people and what they do in schools must also be fostered.

VIEWING CHANGE AS STAFF DEVELOPMENT

If leaders expect major changes in education, an understanding must be developed that change comes primarily when people, not organizations or tools, change. People need to be led to understand the need, to be involved with focusing on a vision, and to clarify the direction they and the organization will be moving. As change facilitators lead and nourish people to change as individuals, they must be supported in every possible way. If a systematic view of change is taken and if staff are seen as a pivotal element of the total system, until staff members are given support in changing their behavior, major changes will not occur. Again referring to systems theory, until staff changes occur, there will be no substantive changes in a school, since one of the key elements of the system, the staff, has not gone through a change. To foster growth or change in staff members requires many things: understanding and managing change, the investment of major prime resources, creating a productive climate, providing continued reinforcement and support; in short, changing staff is a major investment and requisite to changing a school.

As leaders foster change in educational systems, they will inevitably be confronted with the necessity to resolve conflict. A sound planning system is the best strategy to deal with conflict; all significant individuals should be involved and understand the needs addressed and the strategies for meeting those needs. If the planner builds cohesiveness and ownership, people can work together on a common cause that is built upon a solid base of agreement and reflected in such documents as "we agree" statements. Even after building a solid conceptual base, however, interpersonal and intergroup conflicts will emerge. When conflicts do emerge, they should not be avoided. Conflict must be dealt with when it is present. Problem analysis and interpersonal skills, along with negotiations, may be necessary. Ideally, the leader who can come up with a "win-win" resolution will be far ahead of an outcome in which one part wins and another loses. Effective leaders and change facilitators are skillful at conflict resolution.

Some individuals perceive that change can be brought about only by provoking such a high level of dissonance that staff members become so uncomfortable they cannot tolerate the problem and will seek solutions. While it is imperative for staff members to be able to recognize and articulate a need, creating dissonance to achieve sufficient discomfort so that people will be motivated to respond is questionable. Creating such a high level of discomfort that people want to make corrections can be a form of subterfuge and coercion. Planners will be more successful if they use facts and open communication to point to a need and build from a rational perception of a need rather than fear or discomfort. There is an old saying that contented cows give sweet milk and aggravated oysters produce pearls; however, changes in institutions based on aggravation have not proven to be an effective means to reform education. Rational people want to be involved and informed, not aggravated, but a staff is not to be left unchallenged to continue to do what has always been done; in the changing culture in the last portion of the twentieth century, the status quo may be seen as stale milk, not sweet milk. Staff members who are to be involved in change must be given sufficient security; they should be given freedom to experiment and know that if they fail to reach a given goal, they will not be penalized. Staff security, not complacency, is needed to foster change.

Staff security does not come from a fixed platform amidst a current of change. Security for staff members will grow when they know they have the freedom to explore and to reach for something better. One practice should be addressed by educational leaders of change. Presently, every effort in education, especially those efforts labeled as innovative, must be effective and generate positive results that can be shown to yield significant differences by a statistical test. We, as educators, may have placed an unrealistic or even misdirected set of expectations on our efforts by harboring expectations that will be attained by statistically significant differences. Not all change will be successful. Staff members should know they are permitted the luxury of failure if there is an honest effort to achieve, clients have been considered and protected, and a lesson was learned in the experiment. Educators should be willing to learn from mistakes. Mistakes can provide a great learning experience.

Innovators, or those who would foster change in education, must address the issue of quality. Effective school proponents have agreed that students should have high expectations held up before them. The same has been suggested regarding teachers. Staff members must be challenged and expected to achieve high levels of accomplishment. Society members expect a quality product, whether that product comes from automobile manufacturers or from schools. While it seems at times to be a national pastime for individuals or special interest groups to point accusing fingers at various targets, schools not being the least of such targets, accusation contests are not much of an answer. Quality, by whatever standard and in whatever field, is desired, and in the realm of education it is essential. In most instances, educational leaders undertake planning efforts in an effort to achieve quality. If quality becomes recognized and associated with education, the educational enterprise will survive and flourish. If quality, in the eyes of the citizens of the United States, is missing in the public schools of the nation, a sure and definite move to replace public schools with "something of value" will surface. Educators must be committed to improving education. Planning and the management of change are interrelated processes that can be employed to foster improvements in the educational enterprise.

SUMMARY

The management of change is perhaps the most complex, difficult, and demanding task for leaders who would foster change in education. Plans to improve education are valuable only if they can be implemented; in many situations changes are implied—some minor and nonthreatening changes and some that encompass major behavioral adjustments in what people do and how they do it. Some changes reach to the very core of the value systems and traditions embedded in the educational enterprise. In such cases, change does not come easily. Only those leaders who are students of the change process and who demonstrate skills in the area of human considerations, as well as a thorough understanding of how change is fostered, can be expected to have a measurable impact on education. It will do educational leaders little good, and it will not serve the children and youth of America, to make major pronouncements of organizational or structural changes in the educational workplace if those changes have not reached into the behavior of teachers, pupils, and parents in ways that can influence what is learned and how it is learned.

NOTES

1. Terrance L. Walker and Judith E. Vogt, "The Social Administrator as Change Agent: Skills for the Future," *NASSP Bulletin* 72 (November 1987), 44–48.

2. Robert H. Waterman, *The Renewal Factor* (New York: Bantam Books, 1987), 47.

3. Gene E. Hall and Shirley M. Hord, *Change in Schools: Facilitating the Process* (Albany, New York: State University of New York Press, 1984), 1–2.

4. Craig R. Hickman and Silva A. Michael, *Creating Excellence: Managing Corporate Culture, Strategy, and Change in the New Age* (New York: New American Library, 1984), 125.

5. Edward W. Chance and Marilyn L. Grady, "Creating and Implementing a Vision for the School," *NASSP Bulletin* 74 (November 1990), 13–14.

6. Eugene Huddel, "All That Glitters Isn't Gold—Four Steps to School Improvement," *NASSP Bulletin* 71 (May 1987), 80–86.

7. William Glasser, "The Quality School," *Kappan,* 71 (February 1990), 427.

8. Ibid., 431.

9. Lyman Porter, "Job Attitudes in Management: Perceived Need Deficiencies in Need Fulfillment as a Function of Job Level," *Journal of Applied Psychology* 47 (December 1963), 386–390.

10. Thomas J. Sergiovanni and Fred D. Carver, *The New School Executive* (New York: Dodd, Mead, 1974), 57.

11. Frederick Herzberg, *Work and Nature of Man* (New York: Wiley, 1966), 24.

12. Homer G. Barnett, *Innovation: The Basis of Cultural Change* (New York: McGraw-Hill, 1953).

13. J. Sterling Livingston, "Pygmalion in Management," *Harvard Business Review* 47 (July–August 1969), 82.

14. David W. Ewing, *The Human Side of Planning* (London: Macmillan, 1969), 9.

15. Peter Hall, *Great Planning Disasters* (London: Weidenfeld and Nicolson, 1980), 199.

16. Jerry J. Herman, "A Decision-Making Model: Site-Based Communications/Governance Committees," *NASSP Bulletin* 73 (December 1989), 61.

17. Waterman, *The Renewal Factor,* 107–110.

18. Hall, *Great Planning Disasters*, 203.

19. Waterman, *The Renewal Factor*, 218.

20. Ibid., 339.

21. Robert V. Carlson and Gary Akerman, *Educational Planning Concepts Strategies, and Practices* (New York: Longman, 1991), 105.

APPENDIX A-1

Staff Development Strategic Plan

INTRODUCTION

In March 1988, a 15-member planning team, comprised of teachers from all levels, building administrators, and central office administrators, was established to determine the thrust of staff development focus for the Westside Community Schools. The focus of strategic planning is on the future rather than the present, on proactive leadership rather than reactive response, and on stretching one's thoughts for the ideal conditions rather than limiting one's vision to the easily obtainable everyday goals. With this charge, the 15-member group, over the course of time, developed draft statements regarding the mission, beliefs, policies, objectives, and strategies.

In June 1988, strategic planning action teams were formed. The 50 members of these teams were teachers of all levels, building administrators, and central office administrators. The teams were charged with the development of action plans that outlined the specific activities, resources, and timelines necessary to accomplish the assigned strategy.

The 15-member planning team met again in the fall of 1988 to discuss the action plans and make revisions where necessary.

In November 1988, the draft of the Staff Development Strategic Plan was presented to Superintendent James Tangdall for his review and editing.

The following information is a summary of the Staff Development Strategic Planning Team's work.

BELIEFS

(A statement of the organization's fundamental convictions, its values, and its character.)

We believe that staff development

- Is a vehicle to move the district toward its strategic objectives.
- Is built upon the emerging needs of students, teachers, classified staff, and administrators.
- Is an ongoing, job-related process to enrich, maintain, and refine an individual's skills.
- Is a process that increases student achievement.
- Is directly linked to the evaluation process.
- Is the responsibility of each staff member at the district, building, and individual levels.

MISSION

(A broad statement of the unique purpose for which the organization exists and performs its specific functions.)

The mission of staff development in the Westside Community Schools is to improve learning for all students by increasing staff effectiveness through on-going, research-based opportunities for growth and renewal.

STRATEGIC POLICIES

(Management pronouncements that establish the parameters with which the organization will accomplish its mission.)

- All staff members will participate in an approved staff development program.
- Participation in all staff development activities will be verified through the evaluation process.
- All staff development must be job-related.
- Staff development programs required at the district level will not be restricted or compromised because of limitation of funds or staff.
- Staff members will be paid or given release time for district staff development programs.
- All staff development programs required at the district level will provide evidence of the following competencies: research, objectives, follow-up, and evaluation.

OBJECTIVES

(An expression of the desired, measurable end results for the organization.)

- By October 15, 100 percent of the buildings in Westside Community Schools will have a staff development plan for the school year.

- By September 1989, 100 percent of district's certificated staff will implement, within the framework of the evaluation process, an annual staff development growth plan.
- 100 percent of the evaluators in the Westside Community Schools will be trained in basic instructional supervision by September 1, 1990.
- 100 percent of Staff Development Council members will be active participants in the staff development communication network by October 1, 1989.
- By December 31, 1990, all certificated staff will have completed 30 hours in Essential Elements of Instruction. New teachers will have three years from the date of employment to complete this requirement.

STRATEGIES

(The broadly stated means of deploying resources to achieve the organization's mission and objective.)

- We will implement a comprehensive staff development program.
- We will develop a communication network for the staff development program.
- We will develop a program to coordinate evaluation and staff development.

ACTION PLANS

(A step-by-step outline telling how the strategy will be accomplished. Action plans include designating those who will be responsible for the plan, timelines, and a benefit analysis.)

- Strategy: Implement a comprehensive staff development program.
    Action plans: A new staff development program will consist of three levels: district, building, and individual. The program will consist of continued work in Essential Elements of Instruction with optional training in Classroom Management and Organization and Phase II: Elements with Peer Coaching. Other items included are new teacher mentor program, sessions for classified staff, and continued work on instructional supervision with department heads and administrators.
- Strategy: Develop a communication network for the staff development program.
    Action plans: The Staff Development Council, comprised of representatives of professional educators of the Westside Community Schools, will serve as a communication link between the building staff or represented groups. A job description explicating the roles and responsibilities of the Staff Development Council will be developed. Periodic sessions will be held to explain the what, why, and importance of staff development to all professional staff. Consistency when communicating staff development procedures will occur through the use of videos, as well as a designated bulletin board in each building.
- Strategy: Develop a program to coordinate evaluation and staff development.
    Action plans: Evaluation will be an ongoing process with growth plans developed in October and implemented throughout the school year. Staff development will be an

integral part of the evaluation process—reflected in the growth plan. Staff development progress will be monitored by the evaluator and the superintendent's office.

IMPLEMENTATION

The district-level component includes

1. Training as determined by the district's strategic plan and the staff development's strategic plan, such as Essential Elements of Instruction.
2. Staff development days, implementation of new curriculum adoptions and emerging needs such as technology, communications skills, and classroom management.

The building-level and/or department component includes each building's own staff development program as designed by the building principal and staff. The building plan must be consistent with, but not limited to, the district-level component. The building plan will be developed annually and submitted to the director of staff development by October 15 and reviewed by the director of elementary education and the associate superintendent.

The individual-level component consists of one's growth plan incorporated in the evaluation process. Examples at the individual level may include the following:

1. The staff development book of offerings, follow-up strategies (such as peer coaching), conferences, workshops, seminars, and specific convention sessions that are job-related.
2. Any other areas listed under the district-level component.
3. College courses.

EXPECTATION OF EACH STAFF MEMBER

Each certificated staff member is expected to participate annually at the district, building, and individual levels.

RECOGNITION AND VERIFICATION

The annual evaluation is the key component that will bring together both the verification and the recognition of each person's staff development participation. In addition, an individual's records will be kept by the person, the person's evaluator, and the staff development office. The records will be jointly reviewed by the building administrator and the superintendent's office annually.

EXPECTATIONS OF THE STAFF DEVELOPMENT PROGRAM

It is expected that results of this staff development program will be (1) an increase in each person's skills and knowledge associated with his or her job assignment; (2) an application by each person of the research and information obtained from the staff development programs; and (3) an increase in morale, enthusiasm, and respect among the professional staff. Assessment of the expectations will be accomplished by (1) a survey taken in the spring of 1989 to establish baseline data; (2) related questions on the annual reports to the superintendent; and (3) a survey taken in the spring of 1993.

Source: *Staff Development Strategic Plan.* Omaha: Westside Community Schools, May 1989.

APPENDIX B-1

Futures School Facility Study

The Delphi technique has been used in a variety of ways. Two examples of Delphi instruments are contained in Appendices B-1 and B-2.

This example of a Delphi instrument is taken from a study in which experts from education and architecture were asked about possible future developments and needs to be addressed in future construction of school facilities. The responding experts were given the first instrument, a portion of which is contained here, and asked to read a brief statement that gave background material about a topic. They were asked to examine each prediction and indicate on a modified Likert scale their judgment about the likelihood of the prediction's occurring; they were then to indicate on a timeline when they felt the prediction would occur. Finally, they were asked to make any comments or give any explanations they felt appropriate.

The second round of data collection was done in a standard Delphi approach, with the exception that respondents were given the actual frequencies of responses for each answer, along with the means and standard deviations. (In the traditional Delphi approach medians and quartiles above and below the median are usually reported.) The experts were asked to study the pattern of responses from the first round and read a summary of comments; after reevaluating their first response, they were to react a second time to each prediction. In the second round, experts were also asked for comments.

In the third round, the experts were again given feedback in the form of frequencies of responses, means, standard deviations, and comments from peer experts in the second round. Experts were asked once more to study the feedback and reenter their ratings for each prediction after considering all the input.

Two items, number 6 and 7, have been selected from the Futures School Facility Study to illustrate the nature of the questions and the format in which they are presented. Questions are presented in various ways for Delphi studies as can be seen by comparing the items chosen from the Futures School Facility Study and the Year-Round School Study.

(6) Distance learning, the live, two-way interaction of teachers and students at different locations via satellites, television, computer or cable, will increase dramatically in the future. Technology currently exists that makes distance learning a viable educational instruction tool. In the future, distance learning will encompass not only the rural school, but will be used to bring a wide variety of experts and information into all classrooms, rural or urban.

Prediction: In the future, distance learning will be utilized more extensively and creatively to bring learning experiences to all students.

Probability of future prediction becoming widespread:
☐ Highly probable. Will unquestionably occur.
☐ Probable. A strong possibility that it will occur.
☐ Somewhat probable. A weak possibility that it will occur.
☐ Somewhat improbable. A weak possibility that it will not occur.
☐ Improbable. A strong possibility that it will not occur.
☐ Highly improbable. Will unquestionably not occur.

Time:
The above future prediction will become widespread in how many years?

TODAY	5	10	15	20	25	30	35	40	45	50	NEVER
☐	☐	☐	☐	☐	☐	☐	☐	☐	☐	☐	☐

Based upon this future prediction, what characteristics (educational specifications) must the school facilities of the future have in order to optimally house the educational program?

_____
_____
_____
_____
_____
_____
_____
_____
_____
_____
_____
_____
_____
_____
_____
_____
_____
_____
_____
_____

(7) Children's educational television is a cost-effective technology that is currently being under-utilized. In 1987 the U.S. spent about $713 per capita on elementary and secondary schools, in contrast to 12 cents per capita on programming for children's public television. Ten years of TV learning at the rate of one hour each weekday equals two full school years, a considerable amount of learning time which could enrich a child's formative years. By bringing education into the homes, via television, parents can become partners in enhancement of their children's education.

Prediction: Children's television programming will be expanded, including programs targeting disadvantaged children and older students (junior and senior high age).

Probability of future prediction becoming widespread:
☐ Highly probable. Will unquestionably occur.
☐ Probable. A strong possibility that it will occur.
☐ Somewhat probable. A weak possibility that it will occur.
☐ Somewhat improbable. A weak possibility that it will not occur.
☐ Improbable. A strong possibility that it will not occur.
☐ Highly improbable. Will unquestionably not occur.

Time:
The above future prediction will become widespread in how many years?
TODAY   5   10   15   20   25   30   35   40   45   50   NEVER
☐   ☐   ☐   ☐   ☐   ☐   ☐   ☐   ☐   ☐   ☐   ☐

Based upon this future prediction, what characteristics (educational specifications) must the school facilities of the future have in order to optimally house the educational program?

_____
_____
_____
_____
_____
_____
_____
_____
_____
_____
_____
_____
_____
_____
_____
_____
_____
_____

APPENDIX B-2

Year-Round School Study Involving School Patrons

In the second example of a Delphi instrument, patrons (not experts) were asked to respond to a list of items related to the year-round school. In this example, the Delphi was used not to study the possible future but to determine the degree of acceptance and interest in the year-round school by patrons in a school district. Three items from the study are given, in which the traditional means of showing medians and quartile deviations to reflect the respondents' answers for each item is present. Comments were also given from one round of the instrument to the next. Patrons in the school district were asked, when considering the second round of responses, to look at their first-round response, study the pattern of other persons' responses, and read the summary of comments. After reviewing the feedback, each patron was asked to reconsider the answer given in the previous round. The process went through three rounds, as is illustrated in the second set of Delphi instruments.

Delphi Survey Instrument No. 1

[Note: Questions soliciting demographic information would be asked at this point of the instrument, especially if the participants in the survey were opinion leaders and not individuals recognized as "experts" in the field.]

We would be most grateful if you would provide an answer for EACH item. Responses will be treated in complete confidence. As explained to you in earlier correspondence, the second opinionnaire will be mailed to you on approximately ___(date)___ and the final opinionnaire is expected to be mailed approximately ___(date)___.

Please enter your judgment (X) as to the DESIRABILITY of the year-round school in connection with each item. A +3 represents "highly desirable," a 0 is "neutral," and -3 represents "very undesirable."

-3	-2	-1	0	+1	+2	+3

Please enter your judgment (X) as to the IMPACT the adoption of the year-round school would have with respect to each item. A +3 would be a "very positive impact," a 0 is "neutral," and a -3 represents a "very negative impact."

-3	-2	-1	0	+1	+2	+3

ITEM

1. Prevention of much of the loss of retained knowledge which occurs over the summer.

Comments:

Delphi Survey Instrument No. 1 (continued)

Please enter your judgment (X) as to the DESIRABILITY of the year-round school in connection with each item. A +3 represents "highly desirable," a 0 is "neutral," and -3 represents "very undesirable."

Please enter your judgment (X) as to the IMPACT the adoption of the year-round school would have with respect to each item. A +3 would be a "very positive impact," a 0 is "neutral," and a -3 represents a "very negative impact."

ITEM

2. Will allow students to graduate earlier by taking courses during the summer.

-3	-2	-1	0	+1	+2	+3

-3	-2	-1	0	+1	+2	+3

Comments:

3. Will provide families the opportunity to take vacations at different times of the year.

-3	-2	-1	0	+1	+2	+3

-3	-2	-1	0	+1	+2	+3

Comments:

281

Delphi Survey Instrument No. 2

We would be most grateful if you would provide an answer for EACH item. Responses will be treated in complete confidence. As explained to you in earlier correspondence, the final opinionnaire is expected to be mailed approximately ___date___. Please read the comments made by other respondents, reconsider your previous response and respond in the new space provided below the summary of first-round responses. Please add any comments you may wish to make.

Please enter your judgment (X) as to the DESIRABILITY of the year-round school in connection with each item. A +3 represents "highly desirable," a 0 is "neutral," and -3 represents "very undesirable."

Please enter your judgment (X) as to the IMPACT the adoption of the year-round school would have with respect to each item. A +3 would be a "very positive impact," a 0 is "neutral," and a -3 represents a "very negative impact."

ITEM

(Quartiles on either side of the median are shown in the shaded areas and your response is shown by the large X.)

1. Prevention of much of the loss of retained knowledge which occurs over the summer.

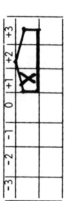

Summary of Comments:

The loss of cognitive retention during summer vacations puts American youth at a disadvantage, and summer shool would avoid this disadvantage. [This comment was made by five respondents.]

Research shows that children-at-risk can gain by being involved in summer school programs.

Kids and their parents need to realize the importance of education, and summer school should be a clear signal to support and foster more support for education.

282

Delphi Survey Instrument No. 2 (continued)

Summary of
Comments
(continued)

A much better use of facilities could be made. [This comment was made by seven respondents.]

There could be a cost benefit derived from year-round programs. [This comment was made by four respondents.]

Kids need to be kids and have time off in the summer.

Parents are not in favor of year-round school.

Comments:

Please enter your judgment (X) as to the DESIRABILITY of the year-round school in connection with each item. A +3 represents "highly desirable," a 0 is "neutral," and a -3 represents "very undesirable."

Please enter your judgment (X) as to the IMPACT the adoption of the year round school would have with respect to each item. A +3 would be a "very positive impact," a 0 is "neutral," and a -3 represents a "very negative impact."

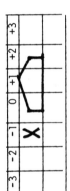

ITEM

2. Will allow students to graduate earlier by taking courses during the summer.

Summary of Comments: Early graduation and advanced placement would help students with their college programs and movement on into graduate school.

Comments: Enrichment is more significant than early graduation. School officials should avoid efforts to push youth through school too fast. Youth may be able to learn factual knowledge at an early time, but maturation (developmental tasks) take time. Youth should not be advanced too fast.

Please enter your judgment (X) as to the DESIRABILITY of the year-round school in connection with each item. A +3 represents "highly desirable," a 0 is "neutral," and a -3 represents "very undesirable."

-3	-2	-1	0	+1	+2	+3

Please enter your judgment (X) as to the IMPACT the adoption of the year-round school would have with respect to each item. A +3 would be a "very positive impact," a 0 is "neutral," and a -3 represents a "very negative impact."

-3	-2	-1	0	+1	+2	+3

ITEM

3. Will provide families the opportunity to take vacations at different times of the year.

Delphi Survey Instrument No. 2 (continued)

Summary of
Comments:

The question of vacations is not of sufficient consideration to be a factor in the overall issue.

Obviously, those who like winter sports would appreciate a winter vacation time.

The impact on the tourist industry would be major, especially in states where tourism is the leading economic factor.

Young people have to learn the value of work, and much work is available in the summer, so it would be to the disadvantage of many concerned if summer employment for youth were lost.

Comments:

Delphi Survey Instrument No. 3

We would be most grateful if you would provide an answer for EACH item. Responses will be treated in complete confidence. As explained to you in earlier correspondence, this is the final instrument you are being asked to complete. Please review the summary of responses from the second round of instruments. You will note your second response is shown with a heavy X. As you review the pattern of responses and the comments, please mark your final response in the space provided.

Please enter your judgment (X) as to the DESIRABILITY of the year-round school in connection with each item. A +3 represents "highly desirable," a 0 is "netural," and -3 represents "very undesirable."

Please enter your judgment (X) as to the IMPACT the adoption of the year-round school would have with respect to each item. A +3 would be a "very positive impact," a 0 is "neutral," and a -3 represents a "very negative impact."

ITEM

1. Prevention of much of the loss of retained knowledge which occurs over the summer.

-3	-2	-1	0	+1	+2	+3
				X		

-3	-2	-1	0	+1	+2	+3
					X	

Summary of Comments: In reviewing the research on the impact of summer school on the loss of cognitive knowledge, there is no clear evidence, as suggested earlier. [This comment was made by three respondents.]

There is not good research on how summer school might affect students-at-risk.

286

Delphi Survey Instrument No. 3 (continued)

Please enter your judgment (X) as to the DESIRABILITY of the year-round school in connection with each item. A +3 represents "highly desirable," a 0 is "neutral," and -3 represents "very undesirable."

Please enter your judgment (X) as to the IMPACT the adoption of the year-round school would have with respect to each item. A +3 would be a "very positive impact," a 0 is "neutral," and a -3 represents a "very negative impact."

ITEM

2. Will allow students to graduate earlier by taking courses during the summer.

-3	-2	-1	0	+1	+2	+3
	X					

-3	-2	-1	0	+1	+2	+3
	X					

Summary of Comments:

Enrichment is, according to some of the literature I have been able to get my hands on, going to do young people more good than early graduation.

The person who suggested enrichment is, I think, on the right track.

Wouldn't a college graduate of 19 years of age have a hard time getting appropriate employment?

287

Delphi Survey Instrument No. 3 (continued)

Please enter your judgment (X) as to the DESIRABILITY of the year-round school in connection with each item. A +3 represents "highly desirable," a 0 is "neutral," and -3 represents "very undesirable."

Please enter your judgment (X) as to the IMPACT the adoption of the year-round school would have with respect to each item. A +3 would be a "very positive impact," a 0 is "neutral," and a -3 represents a "very negative impact."

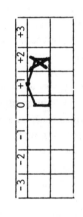

ITEM

3. Will provide families the opportunity to take vacations at different times of the year.

Summary of Comments:

While educators may not feel the issue of when people take a vacation is important, most patrons do consider it important.

When youth return to school each fall, the tourist business goes through a major staffing problem in many instances. By having a year-round school, a more even supply of young labor would be available throughout the year.

APPENDIX C-1

Fremont Enrollment History and Projections

	A	B	C	D	E	F	G	H	I	J	K	L	M	N	O	P
1	ENROLLMENT HISTORY															
2																
3	Fremont Public School			1												
4																
5																
6	YEAR	1Yr.		2 Yr.		3 Yr.		4 Yr.		5 Yr.		Kinder.		1st Gr.		2nd Gr.
7	1979-80	165		334		368		345		357		328		361		370
8			1.55		0.95		0.95		0.94		1.07		1.02		0.98	
9	1980-81	127		256		316		351		326		382		336		354
10			2.05		1.01		1.01		0.99		1.03		1.03		0.97	
11	1981-82	107		260		258		318		347		337		392		326
12			2.63		1.13		1.18		0.96		1.08		0.92		0.99	
13	1982-83	126		281		294		304		306		376		311		390
14			1.98		1.08		1.07		1.00		1.28		0.94		1.05	
15	1983-84	134		250		303		316		305		391		355		325
16			2.24		1.16		1.08		1.15		1.24		0.94		0.91	
17	1984-85	142		300		289		327		363		377		368		324
18			1.83		1.03		0.98		0.98		1.17		0.94		0.96	
19	1985-86	155		260		309		282		319		425		353		354
20			1.90		1.16		1.09		1.08		1.23		0.92		1.03	
21	1986-87	174		294		302		338		304		393		391		362
22			1.71		1.08		1.07		1.11		1.33		0.98		0.97	
23	1987-88	160		297		318		323		374		403		384		381
24			1.63		1.02		1.04		0.99		1.16		0.95		1.00	
25	1988-89	136		260		303		331		319		433		381		384

	Q	R	S	T	U	V	W	X	Y	Z	AA	AB	AC	AD	AE	AF
1																
2																
3																
4																
5		3rd Gr.		4th Gr.		5th Gr.		6th Gr.	Total K-6		7th Gr.		8th Gr.		9th Gr.	
6		397		411		376		360	2603		300		319		355	
7	0.97		1.02		0.97		0.98			0.88		1.02		1.09		1.14
8		359		403		400		370	2604		318		305		347	
9	0.96		0.99		0.99		0.98			0.87		1.05		1.12		1.13
10		341		355		397		393	2541		323		335		343	
11	0.94		0.95		0.97		0.98			0.88		1.00		1.01		1.07
12		307		325		346		390	2445		345		324		339	
13	0.92		0.98		1.02		1.07			0.92		1.07		1.10		1.04
14		358		300		333		370	2432		358		369		355	
15	0.98		0.96		0.95		0.97			0.85		1.01		1.05		0.94
16		319		344		286		322	2340		315		362		386	
17	0.97		1.01		0.97		0.98			0.88		0.99		1.05		1.01
18		313		321		332		279	2377		282		311		381	
19	0.95		0.99		0.96		0.97			1.03		1.05		1.06		1.03
20		336		311		309		321	2423		287		296		331	
21	0.97		0.99		0.96		1.03			0.98		0.97		1.02		1.03
22		352		334		298		317	2469		316		278		302	
23	1.01		0.96		1.06		1.01			0.94		0.97		1.12		0.97
24		384		338		354		300	2574		298		306		312	
25																

	AG	AH	AI	AJ	AK	AL	AM	AN	AO
1									
2									
3									
4									
5									
6	10th Gr.		11th Gr.		12th Gr.	Total K-6	Total 7-12	Total K-12	Year
7	430		417		408	2603	2229	4832	79-80
8		0.84		0.99					
9	403		360		411	2604	2144	4748	80-81
10		0.84		1.08					
11	392		339		388	2541	2120	4661	82-82
12		0.85		1.00					
13	368		333		338	2445	2047	4492	82-83
14		0.87		0.96					
15	351		319		319	2432	2071	4503	83-84
16		0.88		1.00					
17	335		308		319	2340	2025	4365	84-85
18		0.96		0.99					
19	391		322		305	2377	1992	4369	85-86
20		0.92		0.97					
21	393		360		312	2423	1979	4402	86-87
22		0.96		0.95					
23	341		376		343	2469	1956	4425	87-88
24		0.91		0.93					
25	294		312		350	2574	1872	4446	88-89

	A	B	C	D	E	F	G	H	I	J	K	L	M	N	O	P
26	ENROLLMENT PROJECTIONS															
27	YEAR	1Yr.		2 Yr.		3 Yr.		4 Yr.		5 Yr.		Kinder.		1st Gr.		2nd Gr.
28	Mean SR		1.95	265	1.07		1.05		1.02		1.18		0.96		0.99	
29	89-90	136		265		278		319		338		375		416		375
30			1.95		1.07		1.05		1.02		1.18		0.96		0.99	
31	90-91	136		265		283		292		326		398		360		409
32			1.95		1.07		1.05		1.02		1.18		0.96		0.99	
33	91-92	136		265		283		297		299		383		382		355
34			1.95		1.07		1.05		1.02		1.18		0.96		0.99	
35	92-93	136		265		283		297		304		351		368		376
36			1.95		1.07		1.05		1.02		1.18		0.96		0.99	
37	93-94	136		265		283		297		304		357		337		362
38			1.95		1.07		1.05		1.02		1.18		0.96		0.99	
39	94-95	136		265		283		297		304		357		343		332
40			1.95		1.07		1.05		1.02		1.18		0.96		0.99	
41	95-96	136		265		283		297		304		357		343		338
42			1.95		1.07		1.05		1.02		1.18		0.96		0.99	
43	96-97	136		265		283		297		304		357		343		338
44			1.95		1.07		1.05		1.02		1.18		0.96		0.99	
45	97-98	136		265		283		297		304		357		343		338
46			1.95		1.07		1.05		1.02		1.18		0.96		0.99	
47	98-99	136		265		283		297		304		357		343		338
48			1.95		1.07		1.05		1.02		1.18		0.96		0.99	

	Q	R	S	T	U	V	W	X	Y	Z	AA	AB	AC	AD	AE	AF
26																
27	0.96	3rd Gr.	0.98	4th Gr.	0.98	5th Gr.	1.00	6th Gr.	Total K-6	0.91	7th Gr.	1.01	8th Gr.	1.07	9th Gr.	1.04
28		370		378		333		352	2599		274		302		327	
29	0.96		0.98		0.98		1.00			0.91		1.01		1.07		1.04
30		362		364		372		331	2595		322		278		323	
31	0.96		0.98		0.98		1.00			0.91		1.01		1.07		1.04
32		394		355		358		370	2598		303		327		298	
33	0.96		0.98		0.98		1.00			0.91		1.01		1.07		1.04
34		342		388		350		356	2531		338		307		350	
35	0.96		0.98		0.98		1.00			0.91		1.01		1.07		1.04
36		362		336		382		348	2485		326		343		329	
37	0.96		0.98		0.98		1.00			0.91		1.01		1.07		1.04
38		349		356		331		380	2449		319		331		367	
39	0.96		0.98		0.98		1.00			0.91		1.01		1.07		1.04
40		320		343		351		329	2381		347		323		354	
41	0.96		0.98		0.98		1.00			0.91		1.01		1.07		1.04
42		326		315		338		349	2365		301		352		346	
43	0.96		0.98		0.98		1.00			0.91		1.01		0.98		1.01
44		326		320		310		336	2330		319		305		345	
45	0.96		0.98		0.98		1.00			0.91		1.01		0.98		1.01
46		326		320		315		308	2307		308		324		299	
47	0.96		0.98		0.98		1.00			0.91		1.01		0.98		1.01
48																

	AG	AH	AI	AJ	AK	AL	AM	AN	AO
26									
27	10th Gr.		11th Gr.		12th Gr.	Total K-6	Total 7-12	Total K-12	
28		0.89		0.98					
29	325	0.89	262	0.98	307	2599	1798	4397	89-90
30	341	0.89	290	0.98	258	2595	1812	4407	90-91
31	341	0.89	290	0.98	258	2595	1812	4407	90-91
32		0.89		0.98					
33	336	0.89	304	0.98	285	2598	1853	4450	91-92
34		0.89		0.98					
35	310	0.89	300	0.98	299	2531	1904	4435	92-93
36		0.89		0.98					
37	364	0.89	276	0.98	295	2485	1933	4418	93-94
38		0.89		0.98					
39	342	0.89	324	0.98	272	2449	1955	4403	94-95
40		0.89		0.98					
41	382	0.89	305	0.98	319	2381	2030	4412	95-96
42		0.89		0.98					
43	368	0.89	341	0.98	300	2365	2008	4373	96-97
44		0.89		0.98					
45	349	0.89	328	0.98	335	2330	1983	4312	97-98
46		0.89		0.98					
47	349	0.89	311	0.98	323	2307	1914	4221	98-99
48		0.89		0.98					

APPENDIX C-2

Major Formulas

Major Formulas

$Y = T \times C \times S \times I$ or $Y = T \times S \times CI$	Classical Time Series Model
$Y_T = a + b x$	Linear Trend Equation
$b = \dfrac{\Sigma XY - n \overline{X}\,\overline{Y}}{\Sigma X^2 - n\overline{X}^{\,2}}$	Value of b for the linear trend equation, which is the slope of the trend line.
$a = \overline{Y} - b \overline{X}$	The value of a for the linear trend equation.
$Y_T = ab^{\,x}$	Exponential Trend Equation

APPENDIX D-1

School Survey of Perceptions of Community Leadership and Expectations of Citizens

In one school district, the superintendent and members of the school board expressed a growing concern about the expectations of patrons in the community and also indicated that there was a need to determine who the opinion leaders (individuals) and agencies or organizations were that influenced education and community life. Persons were aware that the power structure of the community had been in transition, and some individuals perceived a vacuum in the power structure and were of the opinion that competition was emerging as forces tried to fill that vacuum. Consequently, it was concluded that a community survey was needed to determine the nature of the power structure and the perceptions and expectations that citizens in the community had regarding the school system.

The questions upon which the survey was focused included the following items:

1. Who are the perceived opinion leaders in the community to whom the citizens look for leadership?

2. What are the agencies in the community that serve the population and to which people look for support and leadership?

3. How do patrons in the school district view the management and the program offered in the schools?

4. What are the expectations of the patrons in the school district?

Answers to the above questions could provide the school board with information upon which they could move forward with their planning effort with a data base in hand, rather than simply acting based on personal perceptions.

CRETE SCHOOL-COMMUNITY SURVEY

This survey is being conducted for the Crete Public Schools. Selected residents of Crete are being asked to complete the following information to assist officials of the Crete Public Schools as they plan to meet the needs of the people in the community. You will note that there is no place for you to sign the questionnaire. This is done to assure you that there is no way to link any of your answers to you or to reveal any of your responses. You are assured of complete confidentiality. This is done so that you can feel completely free to answer any and all questions. Your answers are important to the success of this survey. Not all citizens have been asked to answer these questions, but a sample of persons has been selected, like samples used in national polls, that will provide a representative response from the community. Since a sample is being used rather than asking every person in Crete to fill out the questionnaire, it becomes very important for the success of this survey to have your answers. Please fill out the questionnaire, which will only take you a few minutes, and return it in the enclosed envelope. No postage is needed. Your immediate response will be appreciated very much.

Please check the appropriate spaces or fill in the needed answer to the questions listed below.

1. Your age _____   Sex: ❑ male   ❑ female

2. Number of children you have_____, and their ages? _____

3. If your children are attending school, where do they go?

    ❑ Public Schools   ❑ Crete Christian   ❑ Other_____

4. What is the highest grade or level of education that you personally completed? (Check the appropriate answer.)

    ❑ 6   ❑ 7   ❑ 8   ❑ 9   ❑ 10   ❑ 11   ❑ 12 or high school

    ❑ 13   ❑ 14   ❑ 15   ❑ 16 or college graduate

    ❑ Masters degree   ❑ Professional degree

300

5. What are the occupations of you and your spouse? List job title or description. If you work at two jobs, list them both with the one that is your major source of income listed first.

Your job _____

Your spouse _____

6. Which best describes your present conditions of employment?

You	Your Spouse	
❑	❑	Self employed
❑	❑	Employed full time
❑	❑	Employed part time
❑	❑	Homemaker
❑	❑	Student
❑	❑	Unemployed
❑	❑	Retired
❑	❑	Other _____

THIS QUESTION IS OPTIONAL. YOU DO NOT HAVE TO COMPLETE IT.

7. This information will be helpful but is not required. If you do choose to answer, please be assured that there is no way of linking your answer to you. You are assured of complete confidentiality.

If you are employed at an hourly wage, what is it? $_____

If you are employed at a salary, or if you generate your income through self employment, what is the approximate monthly amount?
                         $_____

_____

8. Do you own or rent your home? ....❑ own   ❑ rent

9. Is your residence located in:...............❑ town
                                              ❑ rural farm
                                              ❑ rural non-farm

10. What is your type of residence? ....□ apartment
□ duplex
□ mobile home
□ condominium
□ single dwelling
□ retirement
center or home

11. Approximately how many years have you lived at your present address? _____

12. Do you subscribe to a newspaper?   □ Yes.
.......□ local □ other
□ No

13. Do you belong to any of the following?

□ Service club   □ Church
□ Social or fraternal organization   □ Labor union

14. Did you attend school in the Crete Public Schools at any time?

□ Yes. . . . . .How many years? _____
□ No

15. Are you a registered voter? □ Yes   □ No

16. If you were interested in seeing some community project
completed or some problem resolved in the community of
Crete, who would you recommend from the community who
would be able to get things done, or to get some problem
resolved? [You may name as many persons as you like.]

_____

_____

_____

17. When major decisions affecting the citizens of Crete are made, who influences those decisions most? [Name as many as you like.]

    _____

    _____

    _____

18. What are the agencies (such as civic groups, governmental agencies, unions, schools, churches) in Crete that contribute the most to the betterment of the community? [Name as many as you like.]

    _____

    _____

    _____

19. Citizens who speak up on issues and vote are a major form of influence in the decision making process in Crete.

    ❏ Strongly disagree
    ❏ Disagree
    ❏ Uncertain
    ❏ Agree
    ❏ Strongly agree

20. There are only a few people that make most of the important decisions in Crete.

    ❏ Strongly disagree
    ❏ Disagree
    ❏ Uncertain
    ❏ Agree
    ❏ Strongly agree

21. If you checked "strongly agree" or "agree," name the people that make the decisions. [List as many as you wish.]

_____

_____

_____

22. There are certain agencies or institutions (such as civic groups, governmental agencies, unions, schools, churches or other agencies) in which membership plays a major role in influencing public opinion and making decisions in Crete.

       ❑ Strongly disagree
       ❑ Disagree
       ❑ Uncertain
       ❑ Agree
       ❑ Strongly agree

23. If you checked "strongly agree" or "agree," name which agencies or institutions are the ones that influence decisions? [You may name as many as you like.]

_____

_____

_____

24. There is a number of small school districts that border the Crete School District. Assuming it would be possible for such districts to join the Crete School District without any additional tax burden, should such a merger or reorganization be encouraged?

       ❑ Strongly discourage
       ❑ Discourage
       ❑ Uncertain
       ❑ Encourage
       ❑ Strongly encourage

25. How would you grade the Crete Public Schools?

    ❑ A   ❑ B   ❑ C   ❑ D   ❑ F

26. Would you say, in the last five years, the Crete Public Schools have:

    ❑ Improved   ❑ Stayed about the same   ❑ Gotten worse

27. Do you feel the school board members listen to parents and citizens:

    ❑ Too much   ❑ About right   ❑ Not enough

28. How would you view student achievement in Crete Public Schools?

    ❑ Too low   ❑ I am uncertain   ❑ Very satisfactory

29. What are some of the biggest problems with which the board and the staff from the Crete Public Schools must deal?

    _____

    _____

30. Make any comments you wish about how you view the Crete Public Schools and what you think could or should be done for the staff to better serve the needs of the people in Crete.

    _____
    _____
    _____
    _____

Source: "Crete School-Community Survey" (Lincoln, Nebraska: Bureau of Educational Research and Field Service, Department of Educational Administration, University of Nebraska, March, 1988).

APPENDIX E-1

Example of PERT Chart

PERT Chart: How to Conduct a Survey

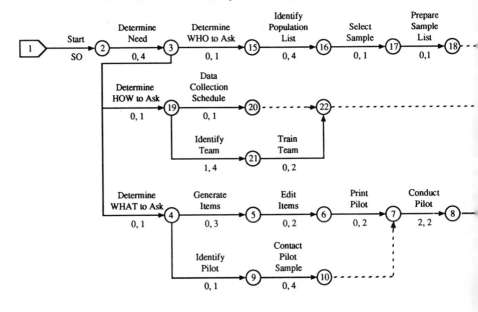

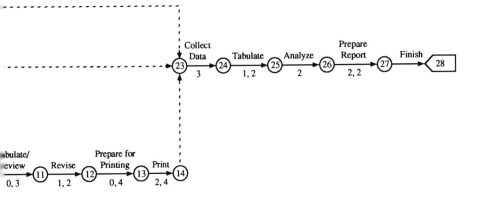

APPENDIX E-2

Developmental Plan and Technical Approach: Combination Diagram

The project plan will be executed in four major phases: (1) planning phase, (2) design phase, (3) production and teacher training, and (4) implementation, evaluation, and final production.

Two chemistry and two physics science videodiscs, computer programs, and print materials will be developed in this project to make them suitable for secondary school use; provide training to science/math teacher education students and selected secondary science teachers on the use of interactive videodisc technology; provide opportunities to implement new educational technology in classroom settings; and evaluate instructional improvement. In other words, all three of the discretionary program's goals are addressed:

1. The use of relevant teacher training for the utilization of videodiscs and computers through in-service activities for practicing teachers and preservice activities for students in teacher education programs will be demonstrated.
2. The effective use of educational technology (videodiscs combined with microcomputer-based instruction) in secondary school improvement will be demonstrated.
3. Ways for students to increase their competence in science through the use of technology in the classroom will be demonstrated.

OBJECTIVES

With the purpose of improving the quality of science instruction at the high school level, the accomplishment of the following overall objectives is proposed.

1. To adapt a series of existing interactive microcomputer-videodisc programs in chemistry and physics for use by high school pupils. These materials were prepared orig-

inally for use at the college level with a large grant from the Corporation for Public Broadcasting. Further development of the lessons was completed under a grant from the U.S. Agency for International Development.

2. To train teacher education and practicing mathematics and science teachers to use videodisc-computers as an instructional tool. Training of this nature will have a strong influence on curriculum decisions and will improve the quality of science and mathematics instruction. The objective of upgrading science instruction in high schools will be indirectly enhanced by teachers' being trained to use advanced technology in classrooms.

3. To conduct the necessary in-service teacher education activities to ensure the appropriate use of these materials.

4. To enhance the computer literacy of classroom teachers and students.

5. To demonstrate the effectiveness of this enhanced technology at the secondary level.

6. To test these materials in a variety of private and public school settings with emphasis on rural and inner-city schools.

7. To evaluate the effectiveness of these materials in teaching science concepts and enhancing problem-solving skills.

8. To provide a process for dissemination of the microcomputer-videodisc programs through the auspices of the Great Plains Instructional Television Library, a nationally recognized library of television materials.

APPROACH

Phase I (two months): Planning Phase

1.1 Establish priorities
1.2 Finalize selection of advisory board
   —add members to cover specific areas
   —mail detailed plans to members
   —confirm meeting dates
1.3 Orientation meeting for project staff and prepare for first advisory board meeting
   —set timelines for the project
   —define staff and advisers' specific areas of responsibility
   —establish procedures for both internal and external reporting
   —plan for initial revisions to adapt college-level science videodisc to meet the learning needs of high school students
1.4 First advisory board meeting
   —respond to preliminary drafts of revisions for science lessons
   —contribute to refinement of lesson outlines in terms of current thinking, research, and national emphasis
1.5 Submit initial report to the National Science Foundation
   —hands-on experience with videodisc simulator to review segments or all of the videodisc science materials
   —select criteria and respond to the formative evaluation plan
1.6 Submit initial report

Phase II (three months): Design Phase

2.1 Prepare four science interactive lessons: chemistry (two) and physics (two)
2.2 Design/revise branching schemata
2.3 Design print materials
2.4 Finalize evaluation plan
2.5 Revise videodisc and print materials based on input from AB members and related staff

Phase III (three months): Production and Teacher Training

3.1 Produce four videodiscs and computer software
3.2 Produce students' workbooks and instructor's manual
3.3 Conduct teacher training
   —train science and mathematics teacher education students
   —train selected science teachers and related staff
   —pilot materials during the training process
   —plan instructional strategies to integrate videodisc into curriculum
   —review evaluation procedures
3.4 Develop logistics and implement procedures
   —modify general plan to meet the unique needs of each school (time, space, materials, and staff)
   —simulate the total implementation plan and evaluation procedures for all involved personnel
   —organize additional staff development at each site by training teacher education students to serve as on-site instructional aides
3.5 Revise materials based on pilot feedback and teacher training information

Phase IV (two months): Implementation, Evaluation, and Final Production

4.1 Place equipment and materials at sites as determined by 3.4
4.2 Collect baseline evaluation data
4.3 Implement instructional materials
   —students
   —all interested faculty and related staff
4.4 Evaluate achievement, attitudes, and process
4.5 Debrief faculty and related personnel
4.6 Prepare final revision of materials based on evaluation data
4.7 Write and present preliminary report to AB members for review
4.7.1 Write final report and distribute to appropriate personnel
4.8 Final production
   —produce master videodiscs
   —copy printed material and computer software
4.9 Dissemination of materials
   —place materials in the Great Plains National Library for loan to schools
   —prepare articles for national journals
   —present papers to national and regional professional organizations
   —contract licensing agreements that would make materials accessible to schools at a reasonable cost

Phase I - Planning

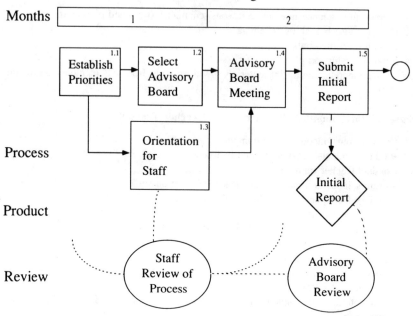

Phase II - Design

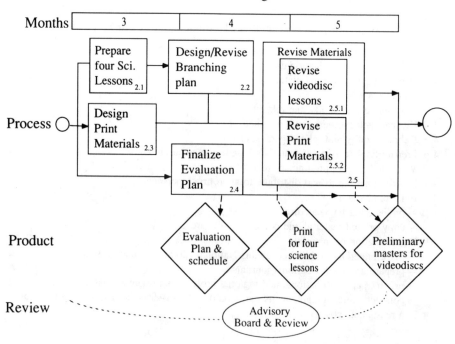

Phase III - Production and Teacher Training

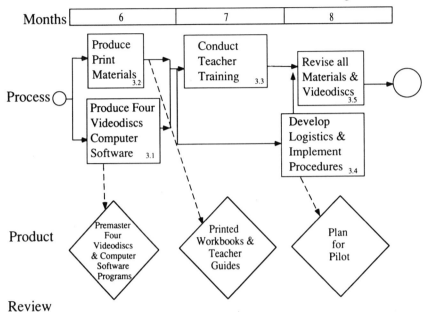

Months | 6 | 7 | 8

Process

Produce Print Materials 3.2

Conduct Teacher Training 3.3

Revise all Materials & Videodiscs 3.5

Produce Four Videodiscs Computer Software 3.1

Develop Logistics & Implement Procedures 3.4

Product

Premaster Four Videodiscs & Computer Software Programs

Printed Workbooks & Teacher Guides

Plan for Pilot

Review

APPENDIX E-3

Flowchart Symbols

Terminus. The terminus is used to indicate the beginning or ending point of a flowchart.

Task or Process Box. The task or process box is used to indicate any task or process other than an input/output operation or a decision.

Decision Diamond. The decision diamond is used to indicate a a decision or branching point.

Document. The document symbol is used to indicate input or output using the medium of paper, usually a report or form.

Display. The display symbol is used to indicate information output on a terminal or other online display device.

Online Storage. The online storage symbol is used to indicate input/output using online storage devices such as disk drives.

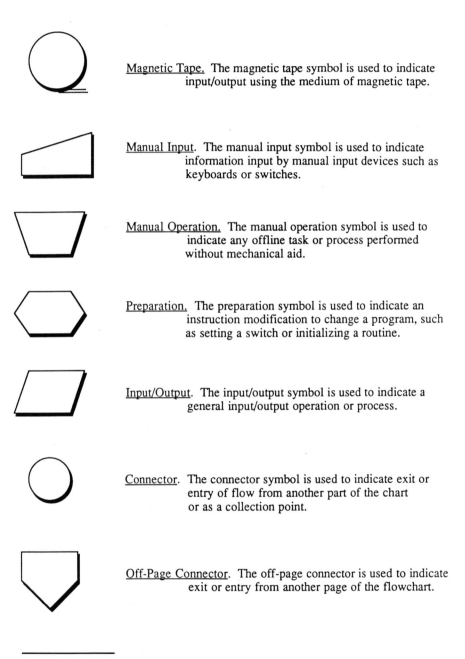

Magnetic Tape. The magnetic tape symbol is used to indicate input/output using the medium of magnetic tape.

Manual Input. The manual input symbol is used to indicate information input by manual input devices such as keyboards or switches.

Manual Operation. The manual operation symbol is used to indicate any offline task or process performed without mechanical aid.

Preparation. The preparation symbol is used to indicate an instruction modification to change a program, such as setting a switch or initializing a routine.

Input/Output. The input/output symbol is used to indicate a general input/output operation or process.

Connector. The connector symbol is used to indicate exit or entry of flow from another part of the chart or as a collection point.

Off-Page Connector. The off-page connector is used to indicate exit or entry from another page of the flowchart.

Source: MacFlow, Mainstay, 5311-B Derry Avenue, Agoura Hills, California 91301

Bibliography

Ansoff, H. Igor. *Corporate Strategy*. New York: Wiley, 1988.

Anthony, William P. *Practical Strategic Planning: A Guide and Manual for Line Managers*. Westport, Connecticut: Quorum Books, 1985.

Babbie, Earl R. *Survey Research Methods*. Belmont, California: Wadsworth, 1973.

Banathy, Bela H. *Instructional Systems*. Belmont, California: Fearon, 1968.

Barnett, Homer G. *Innovation: The Basis of Cultural Change*. New York: McGraw-Hill, 1953.

Beal, G. M., E. M. Rogers, and J. M. Bohlen. "Validity of the Concept of Stages in the Adoption Process," *Rural Sociology*, 22 (June 1957): 166–170.

Beeby, Clarence E. *Assessment of Indonesian Education: A Guide to Planning*, Wellington: England: Oxford University Press, 1979.

Begley, Sharon, and Mary Hager. "A Fantastic Voyage to Neptune," *Newsweek*, September 4, 1989, 52.

Below, Patrick J., George L. Morrisey, and Betty L. Acomb. *The Executive Guide to Strategic Planning*. San Francisco: Jossey-Bass, 1988.

Bennis, Warren G., and Burt Nanus. *Leaders: The Strategies for Taking Charge*. New York: Harper and Row, 1985.

Benveniste, Guy. *The Politics of Expertise*, 2nd ed. San Francisco: Boyd and Fraser, 1977.

Birnbaum, Robert. *How Colleges Work: The Cybernetics of Academic Organizations and Leadership*. San Francisco: Jossey-Bass, 1988.

Bloom, Benjamin S., Thomas J. Hastings, and George J. Madaus. *Handbook on Formative and Summative Evaluation of Student Learning*. New York: McGraw-Hill, 1971.

Borg, Walter R., and Meredith Damien Gall. *Educational Research*. 5th ed. New York: Longman, 1989.

Bowers, Raymond A. "The Direction of Intra-Societal Diffusion," *American Sociological Review* 2 (1937): 827–831.

Bowman, Cliff, and David Asch. *Strategic Management*. London: Macmillan, 1987.

Brightman, Harvey J. *Group Problem Solving: An Improved Managerial Approach.* Atlanta, Georgia: Business Publishing Division, Georgia State University, 1988.

Bryson, John M. *Strategic Planning for Public and Non-Profit Organizations: A Guide to Strengthening and Sustaining Organizational Achievement.* San Francisco: Jossey-Bass, 1988.

Bugher, Wilmer. "Sampling," *Polling Attitudes of Community on Education Manual.* Bloomington, Indiana: Phi Delta Kappa, 1980.

Byars, Lloyd L. *Strategic Management: Planning and Implementation.* New York: Harper and Row, 1987.

Carlson, Richard O. *Adoption of Educational Innovations.* Eugene, Oregon: Center for the Advanced Study of Educational Administration, 1965.

Carlson, Robert V., and Gary Akerman. *Educational Planning Concepts, Strategies, and Practices.* New York: Longman, 1991.

Castaldi, Basil. *Educational Facilities Planning, Modernization, and Management,* 2nd ed. Boston: Allyn and Bacon, 1982.

Castleman, N., and P. Poty. *Center for Policy Research: The First Five Years. 1968–1973.* New York: Center for Policy Research, 1974.

Chaffee, E. E. "The Concept of Strategy: From Business to Higher Education." In *Higher Education: Handbook of Theory and Research,* ed. J. C. Smart. New York: Agathon Press, 1985.

Chance, Edward W., and Marilyn L. Grady. "Creating and Implementing a Vision for the School," *NASSP Bulletin* 74 (November 1990): 10–14.

Checkoway, Barry. *Strategic Perspectives on Planning Practice.* Lexington, Massachusetts: D. C. Heath, 1986.

Commission on the Reorganization of Secondary Education. *Cardinal Principles of Secondary Education.* Bulletin 1918, no. 35. Washington, D.C.: U. S. Government Printing Office, 1918.

Cook, Desmond L. *Program Evaluation and Review Technique Applications in Education.* U.S. Department of Health, Education, and Welfare, Office of Education. Washington, D.C.: U.S. Government Printing Office, 1966.

Cook, William J., Jr. *Strategic Planning,* rev. ed. Arlington, Virginia: American Association of School Administrators, 1990.

Cope, Robert G. *Strategic Policy Planning: A Guide for College and University Administrators.* Littleton, Colorado: Ireland Educational Corporation, 1978.

Cronbach, Lee J. "Course Improvement Through Evaluation." In *Evaluation Models,* ed. George F. Madaus, Michael S. Scriven, and Daniel L. Stufflebeam. Boston: Kluwer-Nijhoff, 1983.

Cronbach, Lee J., and P. Suppes. *Research for Tomorrow's Schools: Disciplined Inquiry for Education.* New York: Macmillan, 1969.

Cuban, Larry. "Four Stories About National Goals for American Education," *Phi Delta Kappan* 72 (December 1990): 270–271.

Cunningham, William G. *Systematic Planning for Educational Change.* Palo Alto, California: Mayfield, 1982.

de Neufville, Judith Innes. "Usable Planning Theory: An Agenda for Research and Education." In *Strategic Perspectives on Planning Practice,* ed. Barry Checkoway. Lexington, Massachusetts: D. C. Heath, 1986.

Digman, Lester A. *Strategic Management: Concepts, Decisions, Cases.* Piano, Texas: Business Publications, 1986.

Dror, Yehezkel. "Planning as a Mode of Policy-Reasoning." In *Abstract Thoughts: Concrete Solutions Essays in Honor of Peter Nash*, ed. Leonard Guelke. Department of Geography Publications, Series no. 29. Waterloo: University of Waterloo, 1987.

DuBois, Edward N. *Essential Statistical Methods for Business*. New York: McGraw-Hill, 1979.

DuBois, Philip H. *A History of Psychological Testing*. Boston: Allyn and Bacon, 1970.

Eddy, William B. *The Manager and the Working Group*. New York: Praeger Press, 1985.

Enzer, Selwin. "New Directions in Futures Methodology." In *Applying Methods and Techniques of Futures Research*, ed. James L. Morrison, William L. Renfro, and Wayne I. Boucher. San Francisco: Jossey-Bass, 1983.

Eversley, David Edward Charles, and Mary Moody. *The Growth of Planning Research Since the Early 1960s*. London: Social Science Research Council, 1976.

Ewing, David W. *The Human Side of Planning*. London: Macmillan, 1969.

Faludi, Andreas. *Planning Theory*. Oxford: Pergamon Press, 1973.

Fowler, Floyd J., Jr. *Survey Research Methods*, rev. ed. Newbury Park, California: Sage, 1988.

Fox, William M. *Effective Group Problem Solving*. San Francisco: Jossey-Bass, 1987.

Glasser, William. "The Quality School," *Kappan* 71 (February 1990): 426–433.

Gleick, James. *CHAOS: Making a New Science*. New York: Penguin Books, 1987.

Gluck, F. W. "A Fresh Look at Strategic Management," *Journal of Business Strategy* 6 (Fall 1985): 4–19.

Goodman, Paul S., and Associates. *Designing Effective Work Groups*. San Francisco: Jossey-Bass, 1986.

Gray, Daniel H. "Uses and Misuses of Strategic Planning," *Harvard Business Review* 64 (January–February 1986): p. 89.

Hall, Gene E., and Shirley M. Hord. *Change in Schools: Facilitating the Process*. Albany, New York: State University of New York Press, 1984.

Hall, Peter. *Great Planning Disasters*. London: Weidenfeld and Nicolson, 1980.

Hammond, R. "Context Evaluation of Instruction in Local School Districts," *Educational Technologies* 9, no. 1 (1969): 13–18.

Hansen, Merrell J. "Site-Based Management and Quality Circles: A Natural Combination," *NASSP Bulletin* 74 (October 1990): 100–103.

Havelock, Ronald G., and Alan Guskin. *Planning for Innovation Through the Dissemination and Utilization of Knowledge*. Ann Arbor, Michigan: Center for Research on the Utilization of Scientific Knowledge, University of Michigan, 1973.

Hawking, Stephen W. *A Brief History of Time*. New York: Bantam Books, 1988.

Hayes, R. H. "Strategic Planning—Forward in Reverse?" *Harvard Business Review* 63 (November–December 1985): 111–119.

Helmer, Olaf. *Looking Forward: A Guide to Futures Research*. Beverly Hills, California: Sage, 1983.

Herman, Jerry J. "A Decision-Making Model: Site-Based Communications/Governance Committees," *NASSP Bulletin* 73 (December 1989): 57–62.

———. *Work and Nature of Man*. New York: Wiley, 1966.

Herzberg, Frederick. *Social Technology*. New York: Basic Books, 1966.

Hickman, Craig R., and Silva A. Michael. *Creating Excellence: Managing Corporate*

Culture, Strategy, and Change in the New Age. New York: New American Library, 1984.

Huddel, Eugene. "All that Glitters Isn't Gold—Four Steps to School Improvement," *NASSP Bulletin* 71 (May 1987): 80–86.

Hughes, Barry B. *World Futures: A Critical Analysis of Alternatives.* Baltimore, Maryland: Johns Hopkins University Press, 1985.

Jemison, D. B. "The Contributions of Administrative Behavior to Strategic Management," *Academy of Management Review* 6 (1981): 633–642.

Jones, Thomas E. *Options for the Future.* New York: Praeger, 1980.

Joseph, E. C. "An Introduction to Studying the Future." In *Futurism in Education: Methodologies,* ed. P. Hencley and J. R. Yates. Berkeley, California: ETC, 1974.

Katz, Elihu, Martin L. Levin, and Herbert Hamilton. "Traditions of Research on the Diffusion of Innovation," *American Sociological Review* 28 (April 1963): 237–253.

Kaufman, Roger A. *Educational System Planning.* Englewood Cliffs, New Jersey: Prentice-Hall, 1972.

Kazmier, Leonard J. *Basic Strategies for Business and Economics.* New York: McGraw-Hill, 1979.

Kelly, N. H., and R. N. Shaw. "Strategic Planning by Academic Institutions: Following the Corporate Path?" *Higher Education* 16 (1987): 332.

Lane, I. M. "Making the Goals of Acceptance and Quality Explicit: Effects on Group Decisions," *Small Group Behavior* 13, no. 4 (1982): 542–554.

Lauenstein, M. C. "The Failure of Strategic Planning," *Journal of Business Strategy* 6 (Spring 1986): 75–80.

Lieberman, Myron. "Why Reform Was 'Dead on Arrival'," *Education Week* 5 (January 29, 1986): 20–22.

Lionberger, Herbert F. *Adoption of New Ideas and Practices: A Summary of the Research Dealing with the Acceptance of Technological Change in Agriculture with Implications for Action in Facilitating Social Change.* Ames, Iowa: Iowa State University Press, 1960.

Livingston, J. Sterling. "Pygmalion in Management," *Harvard Business Review* 47 (July–August, 1969), 81–89.

McClanahan, Randy R. "The Development, Utilization, and Analysis of a Normative Futures Research Method in a K-12 Educational Facilities Survey." Ph.D. diss., University of Nebraska-Lincoln, 1988.

McCune, Shirley D. *Guide to Strategic Planning for Educators.* Alexandria, Virginia: Association for Supervision and Curriculum Development, 1986.

Mager, Robert F. *Preparing Instructional Objectives,* 2nd ed. Belmont, California: Fearon, 1975.

Miles, Ian. "The Developemnt of Forecasting: Towards a History of the Future." In *The Uses and Abuses of Forecasting,* ed. Tom Whiston. New York: Holmes and Meier, 1979.

Mintzberg, H. "Patterns in Strategy Formation," *Management Science* 24 (1978): 934–948.

Moore, C. M. *Group Techniques for Idea Building.* Newbury Park, California: Sage, 1987.

Moore, J. W., and L. F. Langknecht. "Academic Planning in a Political System," *Planning for Higher Education* 14, no. 1 (1986): 1.

Morrison, James L., William L. Renfro, and Wayne I. Boucheri, eds. *Applying Methods and Techniques of Futures Research: New Directions for Institutional Research.* San Francisco: Jossey-Bass, 1983.

Mort, Paul R. "Educational Adaptability," *School Executive* 69 (November 1951), pp. 46–47.

Naisbitt, John. *Megatrends: Ten New Directions Transforming Our Lives.* New York: Warner Books, 1982.

Naisbitt, John, and Patricia Aburdene. *Megatrends 2000: Ten Directions for the 1990s.* New York: Morrow, 1990.

The National Commission on Excellence. *A Nation at Risk.* Cambridge, Massachusetts: USA Research, 1984.

Nunnery, Michael Y., and Ralph B. Kimbrough. *Politics, Power, Polls, and School Elections.* Berkeley, California: McCutchan, 1971.

Olsen, John B., and Douglas C. Eadie. *The Game Plan, Governance with Foresight.* Washington, D. C.: Council of State Planning Agencies, 1982.

Porter, Lyman. "Job Attitudes in Management: Perceived Need Deficiencies in Need Fulfillment as a Function of Job Level," *Journal of Applied Psychology* 47 (December 1963): 386–390.

Press, S. J. "Qualitative Controlled Feedback for Forming Group Judgments and Making Decisions," *Journal of the American Statistical Association* 73, no. 363 (1978): 526–535.

———. *Bayesian Inference in Group Judgments and Decision-Making Using Qualitative Controlled Feedback.* Technical Report #47. Riverside, California: University of California, 1979.

Price, K. H. "Problem Solving Strategies: A Comparison by Problem Solving Phases," *Group and Organization Studies* 10, no. 3 (1985): 289–299.

The Prophesies of Nostradamus. New York: Avenue Books, 1980.

Rogers, Everett M. *Diffusion of Innovations.* New York: Free Press of Glencoe, 1962.

Rogers, Everett, M., and Floyd Shoemaker. *Communication of Innovation.* New York: Free Press, 1971.

Rogers, Everett M., and George M. Beal. "The Importance of Personal Influence in the Adoption of Technological Change," *Social Forces* 36 (May 1958): 328–333.

Rosenholtz, Susan J. "Political Myths About Education Reform: Lessons from Research on Teaching," *Kappan* 66 (January 1985): 347–352.

Ross, Donald H. *Administration of Adaptability: A Sourcebook Drawing Together the Results of More than 150 Individual Studies Related to the Question of Why and How Schools Improve.* New York: Metropolitan School Study Council, 1958.

Rue, Leslie W., and P. G. Holland. *Strategic Management: Concepts and Experiences.* New York: McGraw-Hill, 1989.

Ryan, Bryce, and Neal Gross. "The Diffusion of Hybrid Seed Corn in Two Iowa Communities," *Rural Sociology* 8 (March 1943): 15–24.

Sackman, Harold. *Delphi Critique: Expert Opinion, Forecasting, and Group Process.* Lexington, Massachusetts: D. C. Heath, 1975.

Sarason, Seymour B. *The Predictable Failure of Educational Reform.* San Francisco: Jossey-Bass, 1990.

Sergiovanni, Thomas J., and Fred D. Carver. *The New School Executive.* New York: Dodd, Mead, 1974.

Shanker, Albert. "The End of the Traditional Model of Schooling—and a Proposal for Using Incentives to Restructure Our Public Schools," *Kappan* 71 (January 1990): 345–357.

Sports Illustrated, April 2, 1984.

Staff Development Strategic Plan. Omaha: Westside Community Schools, May 1989.

Stevens, Dorothy J. "Trend Analysis." University of Nebraska, Lincoln, Nebraska, 1988.

Stinnett, Nick, and John DeFrain. *Secrets of Strong Families*. Boston: Little, Brown, 1985.

Stufflebeam, Daniel L. "The CIPP Model for Program Evaluation." In *Evaluation Models*, ed. George F. Madaus, Michael S. Scrivens, and Daniel L. Stufflebeam. Boston: Kluwer-Nijhoff, 1983.

———, and William J. Webster. "An Analysis of Alternative Approaches to Evaluation." In *Evaluation Models*, ed. George F. Madaus, Michael S. Scrivens, and Daniel L. Stufflebeam. Boston: Kluwer-Nijhoff, 1983.

Sybouts, Ward. "Consultation Services Used In Schools." Univesity of Nebraska, Lincoln, Nebraska, 1986.

———, and Dorothy J. Stevens. *Technology in Education: The Past, Present and Future*. Tempe, Arizona: University Council on Educational Administration, 1990.

Tavernier, G. "Shortcomings of Strategic Planning," *International Management* 31, no. 9 (September 1976): 45–47.

Timar, Thomas. "The Politics of School Restructuring," *Kappan* 71 (December 1989): 264–269.

Toffler, Alvin. *Future Shock*. New York: Random House, 1970.

———. *The Third Wave*. New York: Morrow, 1980.

———. *Powershift: Knowledge, Wealth and Violence at the Edge of the 21st Century*. New York: Bantam Books, 1990.

Trade, Gabriel. *The Laws of Imitation*. New York: Holt, Rinehart, and Winston, 1903.

Van de Ven, Andrew H. *Group Decision Making and Effectiveness*. Kent, Ohio: Kent State University Press, 1974.

Van Gundy, Arthur B. *Techniques of Structured Problem Solving*, 2nd ed. New York: Van Nostrand Reinhold, 1988.

Walker, Terrance L., and Judith E. Vogt. "The Social Administrator as Change Agent: Skills for the Future," *NASSP Bulletin* 72 (November 1987): 44–48.

Waterman, Robert H., Jr. *The Renewal Factor*. New York: Bantam Books, 1987.

Wilkening, Eugene. *Acceptance of Improved Farm Practices in Three Coastal Plain Counties*. Technical Bulletin 98. Raleigh, North Carolina: North Carolina Agricultural Experiment Station, May 1952.

Wolf, Richard M. *Evaluation in Education*. New York: Praeger, 1984.

Worthen, Blaine R., and James R. Sanders. *Educational Evaluation: Theory and Practice*. Worthington, Ohio: Charles A. Jones, 1973.

Yetton, Phillip, and Preston C. Botber. "The Relationships Among Group Size, Member Ability, Social Decision Scheme, and Performance," *Organization Behavior and Human Performance* 32, no. 2 (1983): 145–149.

Yip, George S. "Who Needs Strategic Planning?" *Journal of Business Strategy* 6 (Fall 1985): 30.

Index

About the Author

WARD SYBOUTS is the Director of the Bureau of Educational Research, Service, and Policy at the University of Nebraska at Lincoln. He is the author of *The Management of School Activities* (Greenwood Press, 1984). He was a public school teacher and administrator for 13 years and has published in several major professional journals.